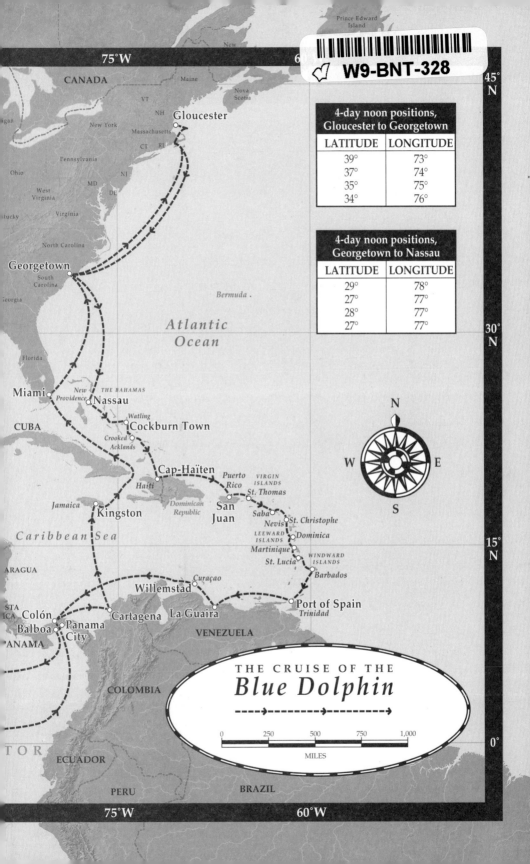

4-day noon positions, Gloucester to Georgetown	
LATITUDE	LONGITUDE
39°	73°
37°	74°
35°	75°
34°	76°

4-day noon positions, Georgetown to Nassau	
LATITUDE	LONGITUDE
29°	78°
27°	77°
28°	77°
27°	77°

THE CRUISE OF THE
Blue Dolphin

0   250   500   750   1,000
MILES

The Cruise
of the *Blue Dolphin*

The Cruise
of the *Blue Dolphin*

A Family's Adventure at Sea

NINA CHANDLER MURRAY

THE LYONS PRESS

Guilford, Connecticut
An imprint of The Globe Pequot Press

The Lyons Press is an imprint of The Globe Pequot Press.

ISBN 1-58574-695-9

Printed in the United States of America

1 3 5 7 9 10 8 6 4 2

Library of Congress Cataloging in Publication Data is available on file.

For My Family

Contents

Acknowledgments

I HAVE RETURNED many times to my journal that recorded my daily life on board the *Blue Dolphin* on her voyage in 1933 and have usually been inspired to write up the experience. My first try was for an assignment in an English class my senior year in high school; and since then, I've made abortive attempts to round out the document, relying not only on my journal but also on the correspondence that took place between our family aboard ship and those at home, the arrangements that my father made with Amory Coolidge on chartering the *Blue Dolphin*, manifests, and a blueprint of the interior. I have also referred to the daily log of the *Blue Dolphin,* the journal of the late Ted Wyman, our mess boy for the trip, my mother's pastel drawings, and our photographs. All through these years, writing and rewriting this adventure, I have had assistance from too many people to list here.

This latest attempt comes late in my life and with a lot of help. My first thanks go to my brothers and sisters, Alfred and Will Chandler, Quita Parrish, and Sophie Consagra. They not only came up with memories that I knew nothing about but were also quick to correct any misinterpretations that I might have made. My five children, Caroline Janover, Sandy Davis, Ann Kelso MacLaughlin, Quita Palmer, and Maude Fish and my twelve grandchildren have tolerated my absorption in this task and have been constant reminders to me of the excitement and perils of growing up.

David Michaelis and Frank Sulloway were generous in taking time to carefully read the manuscript and make corrections and suggestions. I am particularly grateful to Frank for his splendid collection of photographs of the Galapagos that he so generously shared with me. Carolyn and Roger Horchow are to be commended for their enthusiastic support and Kerith Gardner for her long-term interest in the fate of a thirteen-year-old girl out to explore the world. Martha Wilson and Schuyler Kuhl kept me sane as they made repeated rescues of the manuscript from computer glitches. Bill Goodman, as editor and agent, has generously shared with me his wide range of literary experience and continually demonstrates his delicate tact. Lisa Purcell has been an enthusiastic, efficient supporter and a kind editor throughout.

It is to Tom Congdon that I am most indebted. He agreed to help edit this manuscript and did so with élan, firmness, sympathy, and always with an enlightened sense of humor. The deep pleasure I have in writing was ensured and increased by Tom's support and his vast knowledge of the English language.

"The great flood-gates of the wonder world swung open."
—Herman Melville, *Moby Dick*

1

Rain

MY FATHER WAS forty-one, my mother forty. They were having troubles. But then all America was having troubles. It was 1933 and the country was in the middle of the Great Depression. Bellanca Aircraft Company of Wilmington, Delaware, in tune with the times, fired Pa (downsizing was a euphemism yet to be invented), so he no longer flew around the country in his single-engine propeller plane acting as Bellanca's corporate secretary, treasurer, and vice-president in charge of sales and services. For a while he tried to run a bus company, but that failed, so he had to settle for the job of taking care of his mother-in-law's ample finances. After dealing with Undersecretaries of War in Washington, he found it hard to explain money matters to my grandmother and finally resorted to drawing pictures for her. One day he showed me a dramatic example from the series he called "Nana in Wonderland." It was a chart attempting to explain taxes, with one side entitled "Now" and the other side headed "After." Each character—Nana, the heirs, the charities, and the IRS—was represented by a stick figure. Nana was wearing a skirt, the IRS a top hat.

And then there was Mother's problem. She was growing suspicious of the amount of time Pa was spending in New York looking for work. Trapped at home with five children and her often-imperious mother, she did what she always did in untoward circumstances: built conjecture upon conjecture until she had The Truth. One morning she came into my room, where I was having an asthma attack, threw herself on my bed and burst into tears, declaring that Pa was seeing another woman. I was only thirteen and was more interested in breathing than figuring out why another woman would make my mother cry, but I was curious. I had never seen my mother cry before.

These troubles, I must admit, didn't bother me. I was preoccupied with the joys of ending school in June and excitedly anticipating our annual summer vacation on Nantucket Island. These three summer months were the highlight of our year. Nantucket had become our real home. The rest of the year we lived in our grandmother's house, not one of our own. In Nantucket, not only were we alone in our own house, but my older brother Al and I also had the extra safety of a gang, membership tightly controlled, and the pleasure of spending our days exploring the scarcely inhabited small island. Nantucket is thirty miles out into the Atlantic off the southern coast of Cape Cod with moors like Scotland and endless miles of unbroken white beach. We swam daily in its surf and sailed and raced in its long, enclosed harbor. Just getting to Nantucket was an adventure in itself, requiring an overnight voyage on a steamer that ran from New York to Fall River and then a jog over to New Bedford. It ended in a five-hour boat ride, docking for passengers, cars, and horses at Woods Hole and Martha's Vineyard, sailing out past the bright red, anchored lightship with the enormous white letters CROSS RIP on its side, and tossing newspapers to its crew, before making its way to Nantucket over the high seas, no land in sight.

On coming into Nantucket this particular summer, we set to immediately, under Pa's supervision, preparing our Rainbow Beetle Cat sailboats for racing. Ma walked out of the house every morning with her easel and paint box and came back smiling. As a result of all this activity, the tension between Ma and Pa seemed to lessen. But then on the first day of July it began to rain and went on raining for twenty-three of the next thirty-one days. Squall followed squall, interspersed with thick fog and occasional thunderstorms that made sparks spit from the electric outlets.

The children grew unruly, and Ma and Pa began having cross exchanges again.

Once on the island, Pa no longer made his controversial trips to New York but stayed close by. My father, in his prime, was a tall, clean-cheeked Santa Claus of a man: jolly, wobbly of flesh, with thick curly brown hair and a buoyant spirit. He laughed a lot. His laugh was almost a tic. He had a passion for story telling and we children knew his stock of tales and could recite them almost verbatim. He was also given to quoting. "Now remember John Locke," he would pop at us. "John Locke said, 'A man's intelligence is limited by his experience.'" We all certainly knew what he would say as we left the house. "God created this world for us to enjoy," he would shout. "Don't let the Old Boy down!"

On these rainy days, Mother, as usual, did not pay us much attention, so Pa tried to divert us from mischief with geography lessons. In the living room there was a grand world globe, three feet high, which stood firmly on three clawed feet. He called us to it and showed us the routes of discovery taken by Magellan and Columbus. He traced the long-lined flight routes of his pilot friends and aviation pioneers, Wesley Smith and Burt Balchen, who had autographed their paths on our globe; Balchen accompanied Admiral Bryd to the Arctic. We five children, as well as our visiting cousins and friends, stretched out on the floor, leaning on our elbows, listening, watching the green and blue rectangles of the map revolve slowly, hypnotically. We were used to this form of family diversion. We had grown up with it.

Ever since I could remember, Pa had lulled us rabble into a peaceable mob with imaginary wanderings and dreams of other worlds. Whether we were piled up in our Model A Ford sedan at the Rosemont station outside of Philadelphia, waiting for the Paoli Local to bring Mother back from her classes at the Academy of Fine Arts, or riding in the Willys-Knight touring car with the sleeve-valve motor, making a marathon drive to our grandmother's rice plantation in South Carolina, or just sitting through a family meal, Pa's stories and lectures would go on and on. He supplemented this often-repetitive diet with nightly readings of novels. He loved the British—Scott, Stevenson, Kipling.

On one of these wet Nantucket mornings, Pa and Ma were having a particularly heated argument. Pa had started it.

"Carol, you're wasting time and money having all our meat and eggs and vegetables—the whole pile—sent up here from Wilmington. Most of the stuff doesn't travel well. Look at all the eggs—broken on arrival. What a mess. They stink. Don't you think it would be more sensible to buy our food here? The local people, you know, need our money in this depression very much. We really should support them, don't you think?"

"Certainly not," she snapped back. "Why on earth do we run a farm if we can't eat its produce? Just let it rot? Don't be ridiculous."

This spat soon built up enough atmospheric pressure to propel Mother out of the living room, where the family was gathered, to her desk in the hall. We could hear her muttering angrily over her lists, of which there were many. Yet, we five children weren't paying much attention to this squabble. We had long since accepted that this was just the way parents behaved, nothing unusual, although lately the tension was beginning to make me uncomfortable. Pa sank into his big chair, which was covered with a chintz print of fox hunters in pinks, and stared at his favorite 1815 map of the United States hanging over the sofa. He grunted now and then to let us know that he still had a few remarks he could be letting off at Ma but was restraining himself.

The three of us older children, all the while, had been helping Willy, age nine, prepare his weekly explosion in the fireplace. Mother had started this ritual after finding Will on several occasions setting off firecrackers in the closet in the attic of our old wooden house. She was hoping for a safer, supervised setting for his incendiary bent. First we built a tall castle in the back of the fireplace with old Lincoln Logs, regular firewood, carved shingles, and sticks. Then Quita, age eleven, and I cut out photographs of brides and debutantes from Sunday's brown *New York Times* rotogravure society section and pasted their simpering faces in the castle windows. Willy, disemboweling firecrackers for their gunpowder, worked on his hands and knees. He planted his piled powder under the castle and laid a long fuse out over the brick hearth. Sophie, the stocky baby of the family, only six, sat on the sofa playing with her china-animal family.

Brother Alfred, almost a lordly fifteen, sat cross-legged by the hearth watching us. He was referred to by our parents as "the growing boy" and treated preferentially. Just that morning, we younger children had come down early for breakfast and asked for scrambled eggs. "No eggs left this morning," we were told. "Sorry." Yet Al, who had slept late, came to the breakfast table, ordered eggs, and got them. This, as always, annoyed Quita, Willy, and me, but we knew complaints would not be registered and said nothing. Now Al wasn't helping build the castle, just carping in his newfound low voice. "Nina, two of those queens just fell in the moat. Why don't you make them stick? Do a good job while you're at it."

I turned around and slapped him across the cheek. Pa, witnessing this aberration, stood abruptly. He hated any kind of violence or pain. He certainly had never touched even a finger to us in rebuke. At first he said nothing but paced the small room, his heavy frame swaying as he side-stepped us. I waited, stunned by my own act, ready for punishment. I could not remember ever hitting anyone before.

At last Pa sputtered, "So . . . This is . . . Now, do you realize . . . ?" He did not seem to be directing his shifting, unassembled thoughts to any of us in particular. "Are you aware . . . ?"

I was only aware of Father Zeus ready to release his lightning from a mountaintop to strike me dead. At last his thoughts coalesced. "This is the last year in our family life that we can all be together for a trip, one unit, off to sail the seas and seriously explore the world," he announced to his silent children. "Don't you see? The year after next, Alfred, you'll be in Exeter, the fates willing, and you, Nina, you will be going off to boarding school too." His eyes brightened as the glorious magnitude of the new project took hold of his imagination. "So! We must make plans immediately. You'll all go to school, of course. My school. I'll teach you, and it's about time you were taught something. That progressive school you kids go to gives me a pain. I'm sick and tired of hearing how you've learned to put on your galoshes to music. Nina, you don't even know your multiplication tables. What's nine times seven?"

I stared and couldn't answer. Nine and seven were sharp and lonely numbers. They didn't go together. They certainly shouldn't multiply.

"You see? So. How about a family trip? Where? Any ideas?"

Willy, at the hearth, lit the fuse. The castle went up in a fiery explosion. The pretty young ladies went on smiling through the flames and then crumpled. Sparks flew out on the Turkish carpet. We cheered and gathered again around the globe.

In short order we had agreed, except for Ma, who still sat at her desk engrossed with her lists, that we must make plans and do so immediately. We would go by boat, of course, our own boat, a sailboat. Motorboats were anathema to us. They made big waves that ruined our sailboat racing speed; and besides, they smelled. A cruise ship never occurred to us. I am sure we had never even heard of travel agents. All five children spoke for the country they wanted to visit.

"Dearest," Pa called out pleasantly to Ma, "come and hear what we've dreamed up for our family."

He had characteristically forgotten how mad he was at her. She came into the room slowly and sat by Sophie and smiled the artificial smile she'd practiced on so many social occasions. "Now what?" she said softly. It was clear she wasn't paying attention to the rippling babble of the swift flowing family brook.

Eyeing the way ahead, Pa caught sight of a formidable dam blocking the stream. These were depressed times after all. We didn't have money for such grandiose travel plans, but Pa was a businessman and now an official financial guide for my grandmother, and he prided himself on directing resources. "Ahhh . . . NNN . . . D . . . ahhh," he growled. We all knew what he was doing: holding onto the floor, preventing interruptions while he marshaled his thoughts for a conclusion. Finally it emerged. "Now is the time to go see Nana."

Nana was my mother's mother, Lena Ramsay. Just under five feet tall, white-haired, and with sad dark-brown eyes, she was the family matriarch. She had grown up just after the Civil War, with seven sisters and one brother in a modest townhouse on a quiet, tree-lined street in Wilmington, Delaware. The Misses Hebb had taught her a well-formed handwriting and how to be a Victorian lady knowledgeable in conversation and literature. At nineteen, she married a young impoverished engineer who had been courting her elder sister, but who surrendered completely to the mild manner of the younger, prettier girl. He and Nana eloped, causing immense consternation in both families. When they appeared in Wilmington to announce their surprise, Nana's irate mother pushed the new bride up to the attic room to meditate on her rash action and forced her to stay there for a few days as penance. She sent Will, the groom, off to his family where he was berated for marrying beneath his fine Virginian social status and not following his long list of accomplished ancestors in a military career, reminding him he'd had the distinction of being born in the Presidio in San Francisco. Once that storm was over and the married couple reunited, young Will Ramsay rose rapidly in the DuPont Company and was soon comfortably settled at the executive level. He moved his family out to Guyencourt, seven miles from the city and called his new estate Dalhousie after his ancestors' Scottish castle. When he died of pneumonia at the age of fifty-one, he was acting chief engineer, director, and vice-president of the DuPont Company. His death left Nana with five children, large real-estate holdings, and a fortune.

New wealth did not change Nana. She remained a humble, almost ascetic person. To outsiders, this quiet lady with fresh pink coloring and girlish skin, dressed in tweed skirts, cotton blouses, and fusty cardigans in winter and green seersucker dresses in summer, seemed a recluse. She seldom went out and rarely entertained. Occasionally ladies from the neighboring estates came for tea, or young musicians and artists who had known Nana's largesse dropped in to play the piano or show her their sketches.

Nana retained deep pride in her forebears. She was happy to point out that the Canbys, her Quaker family, had arrived and settled in Wilmington long before the duPonts came over from France. The Canbys had set up their flourmills on the banks of the Brandywine, and it was only later that the gunpowder factories of the duPonts were built alongside them. She made us feel the duPonts were just a little bit nouveau—though powerful, of course, being so rich. She would never, during her lifetime, sell any of her DuPont Company stock because of her loyalty to her husband and his company. They were the only stocks she owned. The idea of moving to a balanced portfolio was out of the question. She never allowed such a deviation when it was periodically proposed.

Nana's bedroom, on the corner of the second floor of her large house, was small, the furniture simple. No curtains or shades blocked her view. She could lie in her narrow Napoleonic sleigh bed and spot birds she had named for dead friends. She called the male cardinal "Will," certain her husband's spirit inhabited this flamboyant bird. She loved gazing through the great trees of the grove, down the sweep of the lawn to the pond.

Nana began her day doing up her hair. She bent at the waist and brushed the silvery curtain before her face one hundred strokes, then pinned it up in a bun on the top of her head with tiny white wire hairpins. Finally, she tied around her head a green ribbon taken from the wrappings of her new Wamsutta supercale sheets. Before breakfast, she sat at her desk by the window in her bedroom and cut up envelopes and invitations from yesterday's mail to use for lists and reminder notes. When the day began in earnest, she stepped from this austere room into another world where she worked in a naive and instinctive fashion as the queen, for Nana had another self that lived along with the shy ascetic. This was the autocratic, regal self that could emerge suddenly with startling strength. Before our family moved in to live with Nana in 1930, I remember visiting her alone at Dalhousie. I left our nearby family farmhouse—jumbled and confused, with the funny papers on the floor, block castles built in bedrooms, and makeshift tents over a bed or two, a noisy, child-filled, child-dominated household—and walked into the cool, silent serenity of Dalhousie.

Dalhousie had three floors and twenty-six rooms. Its oldest room, the den, was the original log cabin. We held the deed for it from William Penn. Generation after generation had added to this log cabin until, at the turn of the century, my grandfather transformed what had been a big farmhouse into a mansion. Tillie, the maid, met me at the door and led me to Nana's bedroom. Nana was entertaining an enigmatic illness that kept her company throughout her life. That day she wore an uncharacteristic floor-length gold-brocade dressing gown with collar and cuffs of breath-soft white fur. My instinct was to fall on my knees and wait for her to touch my shoulder with a wand, for fairy godmothers and all-powerful grandmothers were one and the same in my mind.

Nana's orienting passion was caring for her ever-growing family. She spoiled us with her worldly goods and armed us with her old-fashioned wisdom.

We deserted our places around the globe that rainy day in Nantucket and pulled on our slickers, Mother helping us reluctantly. Pa was right; now was the time to go see Nana. We climbed into our canvas-covered touring car and drove out to Wauwinet, the little village at the end of the harbor, past the sand road to the roller-coaster hill that led to Altar Rock, past the wet dark-green tops of the Hidden Forest, to the house in the pine woods that Nana had rented for the summer. We found her there, in that old mildew-smelling house, reading aloud, spotlighted by a standing lamp, the only brightness in the sparsely furnished, dark room with its bare wooden walls. Five of our first cousins lay about her on the rugless floor, listening.

She was not amused by our boisterous arrival. She pursed her lips and frowned, not looking at us and concentrated on her interrupted story. Pa began.

"Nana, we have all been studying how our lives should go for the next year or two, and we want to try an experiment. We're really excited, and as you know, Emerson said, 'Nothing great was ever achieved without enthusiasm.' Now here's what we have thought of so far." Al and I chimed in with our own particular visions: Al would really learn geography, and I would keep a journal and write a book. Quita, a stutterer, only smiled her winsome smile. Willy had already lost track of the trip idea and was down on his hands and knees pushing a toy truck back and forth. Sophie held onto Ma's hand and scrutinized her competitive first cousins as if they would strike her if she didn't watch out. Slowly Nana's face relaxed and she turned to look steadily at Pa. Her major decisions were never made with studied logic. She inspected us, catching our enthusiasm, stood up, clapped her hands, and said, "Of course this is the year to go on a trip, but I'm sure you can't go unless I help pay for it, and if I pay, I'll certainly want to come too. So why not? We'll save on all those tuitions we pay for school. We'll have to keep Dalhousie and the plantation running, but we certainly will save some there. Sure. Let's go! I'll pay half. When do we leave?"

Mother looked genuinely startled.

2

Leads to the *Blue Dolphin*

DURING THE FOLLOWING weeks snow could have fallen on the old gray-shingled house on Mill Street, and we would not have noticed. Weather no longer had a hold on us. We were already on the high seas, our dreams rapidly becoming a reality. Pa wrote to ships' brokers who answered him by mailing packages of their listings. The living room floor was covered in rising piles of blueprints with specifications for sloops, schooners, brigantines, yawls, and ketches clipped onto them. The sofa and tables held atlases, *National Geographics*, logs, and maps. The globe, central to our planning, stayed put on its clawed feet in the middle of the living room floor. Pa went on rapid-fire missions to New York, Long Island, Boston, and Gloucester, to consult shipyards, ship chandlers, and sailing friends.

"Ship brokers never believe a word you tell them," Pa said one evening, passing plates as he sat at the end of the long dining room table. "They do everything they can to discourage you from chartering the boat you want. I tell them my financial limits and they all come back with propositions that are double my sums. I guess it's a form of a compliment, but it certainly annoys me."

"Ralf," said Ma, her voice cold with disdain, "you haven't the slightest notion how to bargain. That's a routine opening for settling any price. Did you go on to haggle?"

I felt sorry for Pa. Ma always haggled, even with the salesgirls in Wanamaker's department store. I'd blush with shame and move quickly to another counter. I was sure Pa knew more about boat business than Ma, and she should not comment, I felt, but keep carving the stringy old hens sent up from our farm.

Pa ignored her. "I think we have a captain. We've had lots of applications for the job, nearly all of them Scandinavians with expensive ideas on how to run a ship. Well, this man's an American, Seldon Boutilier." He paused and stared at my mother, his silence pulling us closer to his coming words. "He's a thrifty New Englander, Carol. He'll keep our budget. Speaking of budgets, I'm beginning to realize this is probably the only year we could ever possibly afford such a trip. In this depression, you see, we can charter a ship dirt cheap, and sailors need work desperately. We'll be helping them a lot." Pa was always making sure we were helping people.

I listened with fascination to Pa's daily updates on our plans and slipped easily into my old familiar way of thinking. Studying the blueprints and maps, I began to shape the fantastic life that lay ahead of me. A life different from the too-often invalid life I knew. Since early childhood, I suffered from chronic and terrifyingly acute attacks of asthma, often logging nine months of a year in bed. If I lay down, I couldn't breathe. If I laughed, I couldn't breathe, and I certainly couldn't breathe if I moved rapidly. Unable to lie flat, I pulled a pillow on my lap and slept bent over it, permanently warping my spine. When I was seriously ill and the emergency shots of adrenaline from Doctor Handy didn't work, Ma would come in at night and offer me a stiff, steaming hot toddy of home-brewed corn liquor that Pa bought from moonshiners in the backwoods of South Carolina. Then, with great relief and comfort, I'd pass out. A less palatable cure, invented by Ma and Nana, consisted of swallowing a tablespoon of Vaseline each morning before breakfast. I squeaked so much on breathing, they reasoned that my pipes needed oiling, but the Vaseline didn't go near my breathing tube, and it never melted. I often felt I was likelier to die gagging on that great foul-tasting egg than from my familiar asthma—and I preferred death by asthma. These long spells in bed left me lots of time for reading and spinning elaborate adventures; and now, after a week or two of Pa's planning our trip, my chest was tight again, this time not from dust mites but from excitement.

To help shape my fantasies, I returned to seafaring books borrowed from the Athenaeum, Nantucket's stately library, and realized quickly that I faced a problem: Thirteen-year-old girls never featured in these books. Once again, I saw, I would either be a girl playing a boy's role or I would have to invent myself as a girl adventurer. I preferred known roles, so I practiced being Jim Hawkins in a sequel to *Treasure Island* and reread Kipling's *Captains Courageous* for pointers. That was just for starters. It was not until much later in our adventure that I would begin to find my true self.

Mother, on the other hand, began consulting doctors about taking her brood on this wild enterprise. They laid out in frightening detail the serious risks of tropical diseases and warned her of the great dangers for young children on a small vessel on the high seas. The doctors said the trip would be especially hard on me. I might not survive since I could easily be devastated by molds that grew in dampness, in addition to all my other allergies, and boats were nothing if not damp.

Fortunately, Mother did not put too much stock in doctors. She had invested a lot of time and money in special New York consultants to help me. They had prescribed years of inoculations, but it hadn't done much for me. "A change of air"—this had always been Mother's solution for stubborn health problems. She and Pa had been planning to send me to live in Colorado, but the cruise was the treatment plan she now adopted. The doctors resigned themselves to her stubbornness.

In one matter, Ma and Pa did accede to the dire warnings of authorities and friends. They decided that Sophie, age six, would be in mortal danger on a small ship sailing the high seas. She would remain at the plantation with mother's sister and her husband, Mary Morris and Bill Phelps.

Childless, they were already our auxiliary parents. They lived over the hill from our place in their old stone house, surrounded by fine art and precious antiques, tastefully arranged. They enriched our existence by adding the glamour that was absent in our daily life. They let Quita and me come to their cocktail parties, where we ogled the fancy dresses, watched the guests get drunk, and envied the women's makeup. (Ma and Nana would never allow any foreign substance to sully their or our fresh facial skin, not even soap.) Bill Phelps and Mary Morris also taught me table manners and the benefit of cold showers on awakening (in spite of the fact that I wasn't being challenged by hangovers) and encouraged me to read Evelyn Waugh and *Vogue* magazine. Uncle Willy's humor was sardonic and off-color. He let me inspect Pete Hurd's pornographic sketches of witches and read me salacious limericks written by his friend, the poet Conrad Aiken (who often handed on the equally lecherous limericks that T. S. Eliot was sending him).

Leaving Sophie to live with our aunt and uncle for her own protection, while her family sailed forth on their great adventure, was the one serious error of the whole scheme. Sophie never forgave us for deserting her. Suddenly an only child, she hated her loneliness, and was bewildered by the irrational and ambiguous behavior of her alcoholic caretakers. Uncle Willy overwhelmed her with his teasing, and Aunt Mary Morris's endless chatter bored her. She found no solace in the drunken house parties.

I had long since learned that my mother could be calm in the face of any great change in her life, but what she now faced was monumental. In a matter of a few weeks, she had to close our summer and winter houses, make arrangements for the servants in our absence, and buy us all new wardrobes. In addition, she had to take on the new and unfamiliar responsibilities of running a schooner. "That woman in New York," the one Pa had been seeing who made Ma cry, seemed to be motivating Ma to manifest her excellent managerial abilities. She was showing off to Pa, and I think she was counting on his loyalty in return.

One of the more formidable tasks Pa assigned her was to travel to Boston to visit the S. S. Pierce store and, in one day, order provisions for fifteen people for five months. That night she came home triumphant, having bought two tons of food, including several cases of canned butter, thirty pounds of coffee for the family (at $.35 a pound), thirty pounds of coffee for the crew (at $.19 a pound), one hundred pounds of sugar, ten pounds of shredded codfish, a gallon of molasses, thirty-eight pounds of roast beef and sirloin steak (at $4.25 a pound), and two kegs of kippered herring. That much kippered herring sounded alarming to me. Was the crew supposed to eat all those kippers? I knew Pa would, but his southern children were going to object.

Eugene Speicher, a popular portraitist of the day, painted my mother when she was twenty-three, the year before she married Pa. I used to practice my piano lessons beneath the portrait in Dalhousie's big sunny living room. I trilled through the obligatory Czerny exercises, glancing at Mother from time to time, awed by her beauty and her penetrating gaze. Her fine dark-brown hair was swept over her forehead and then pulled back up in a thick bun on the top of her head. Her cheek bones were high, her chin narrow, and her nose, described by Pa as "Roman," was thin and arched. Her neck was long and gently curved. For her sitting she had chosen a misty dark-blue voile dress with a double white collar that spread out in soft folds over her shoulders. Beside her on the table stood a bowl of orange and red zinnias: like Mother, straightforward, simple, sturdy, and colorful. The artist had caught the secret of Mother. She sat as respectable as any young woman could be, her hands quiet in her lap, but one of her double-jointed thumbs was thrust up and backward, impertinent, making sport of the business of "sitting." She looked as if she were hitchhiking and eager for a lift.

Ma, like her mother, had been pulled into adulthood by the Misses Hebb. After graduating, she had set off for the socially required grand tour of Europe with chaperone in tow. On her return, exhibiting her lifelong penchant for the unorthodox, she announced her plan: She would be a painter. Leaving Wilmington, she attended the Art Students' League in New York, working with John Sloan, George Bellows, and later, George Grosz; and that spring she moved to Woodstock, New York, to attend the League Summer School. In 1916, she came back home to be her sister's maid of honor. At the wedding, she met Pa, who had come as an usher for the groom. A year later, on December 5, 1917, Ma and Pa were married before the blue-twill-cushioned bay windows in the living room at Dalhousie. On the following Christmas Day, Pa sailed to France to fight the Great War To End All Wars as a member of the Twenty-First United States Engineers.

Pa's entire war experience was spent at the front, at St. Mihiel and the Argonne. He relished his war years and loved to tell funny stories about his adventures, chortling between anecdotes. I objected. Having read novels about the war and seen the awful pictures of the agonies and death scenes in the trenches, I felt it was his moral duty to agonize. I would go limp with embarrassment when he laughed while he was reciting his stories. I chided him but he would patiently explain to me that war was hell and there was no sense in letting it drive you crazy if you could help it. He managed to make war a cosmic joke and laughed at it, extolling the great and lasting friendships he made on the front lines, reuniting with his buddies every year until they all died off. I'd sulk when he'd tell his merry stories, over and over again, but at the end of his life, I was surprised to discover that Pa had been responsible for constructing railroad lines for 1,183 locomotives and 21,900 freight cars imported from the United States and had received a medal for bravery for rescuing several of his troops who were smothered under mud during a heavy bombardment. Pa's nineteenth-century rational optimism allowed him to see the world as getting better and better all the time; he made even the most ghastly horrors seem cheery, a normal part of the onward-and-upward-forever thrust of civilization.

When Pa was on the front lines fighting the War To End All Wars, he filled the endless days of bombing, shelling, and mud with pedagogy. He found an old freight car and turned it into a school. From the depths of a discarded decrepit armchair he'd salvaged, he held classes for privates, non-coms, and officers. Two illiterates in his company wanted to learn to read. Several noncoms requested a class in algebra and geometry. His favorite class, however, was a group of railway engineers and firemen from New Mexico who sat enthralled as he told them the history of the towns they had marched through and the exploits of Clovis, Charles Martel, Charlemagne, and Francis I. He loved to teach.

My brother Alfred was born at Dalhousie while Pa was in France. After the war, his former employer, the Baldwin Locomotive Works of Philadelphia, assigned Pa to the South American desk in Buenos Aires, where he would sell their locomotives and help build up railroad systems in Argentina and Chile. Three months pregnant with me, Ma sailed with Pa and Alfred for South America on the *Vestris*. When the coal it carried caught on fire the ship was forced to be abandoned at sea. She was listing dangerously when passengers and crew crawled down ladders into lifeboats. Of all the mothers on board, however, ours was the only one to think ahead; she carried off Alfie's potty-chair and the sterno stove used to heat his food. When the lifeboats landed at St. Lucia in the West Indies, and the women and children were put in police barracks to await rescue, Mother was the women's heroine, for only she could provide plumbing and cooking equipment for all the children.

Ma and Pa lived for four years in Buenos Aires, where Quita and I were born. When Ma found she was pregnant with Willy, however, she announced that she wanted to go home; so, Pa brought us back home, left the Baldwin Locomotive Works, and settled us into our new house in Radnor, Pennsylvania. During this period, Pa moved from trains to planes and helped form the Bellanca Aircraft Corporation. He also started Island Airlines, one of the first commercial flights to and from Nantucket. He used pontoons on his single-motor Bellanca propeller plane and terrified the parents of young racing sailors as he flew in and out of the harbor, whirring over their precious children.

The depression ended all that however, and now Pa's newest preoccupation was to be our teacher. His immediate problem was how to explain to school authorities that he could educate his children on a ship. Taking children out of school for lengthy spells did not bother authorities in those days as much as it does now. Losing five tuitions for a whole school year during a major depression did. The usual arguments were forcefully presented to Ma and Pa: The children would fall far behind in their work and would probably have a hard time getting into college. They would have to repeat grades; they would lose the benefit of friendships of their peers and would miss organized sports; they would not learn appropriate social skills, etc. etc. Pa came home one morning after a meeting with the school officials and said to us, "Mark Twain sure had it right: 'In the first place, God created idiots. That was for practice. Then he made school boards.' Don't worry. You kids will be educated, no matter what those teachers say."

My father was serenely confident that he could teach us as well as he'd taught his troops. He'd had a public school education in Brookline, Massachusetts, before he went to Harvard, where he learned a lot by rule and rote. He was partial to the classics, both Greek and Latin. He never showed any sympathy for our teachers trained in modern progressive methods that let pupils unfold from within, supposedly developing individual talents that ensured happiness and healthy self-esteem.

Mother didn't give much thought to our education. She felt her daughters wouldn't need much—just enough to choose a good husband who would make a good father. They certainly wouldn't need college since that would only reduce their eligibility. Bright young men, she proclaimed, didn't want competitive bright young women as wives. "College girls," said Ma with derision, "are 'bluestockings.'" She made them sound as if they had a communicable disease, but bluestockings seemed rather chic to me, although I had trouble visualizing them. No matter, I got the drift. She liked our progressive schools because the boys in our class would grow up to be the most eligible in town and their female classmates would be right there to snag them. Yes, her daughters could be smart, but socially smart, not brainy smart. Assuming her sons would manage no matter where they went, she had tremendous confidence in all her children's abilities.

Reluctantly, the school authorities supplied us with curricula and books, supplemented by materials from the home-schooling experts, the Calvert School in Baltimore. It never seemed to occur to anyone that Pa was outdoing the progressive John Dewey in making us "learn by doing."

Pa wanted to maintain a strong friendship with a fellow fired Bellanca executive. He and his friend were planning to go into business together, so Pa, to keep the connection alive, sensibly asked the friend if his son would like to sail with us. This added another lush border to my already luxuriant romantic garden of a mind. At thirteen, I had read a lot of novels. That summer I was just beginning the novel *Anthony Adverse* and was intrigued by it, a life history told from birth to death, with all the adventures and love affairs in between. I had already decided I would keep a journal of my voyage, my adventure. To find that my companion on this trip would be a sixteen-year-old male, dark and Hollywood-handsome, made me curl in on myself in joy. When would this novel ever begin? How would my hero, John Hurlburd, link up with the heroine, me? Who would work out the plot—God? Fate? Ma or Pa? Ma *and* Pa? Me?

Pa chose our ship, a schooner, the *Blue Dolphin* out of Gloucester, Massachusetts. We would charter her from her owner, Amory Coolidge of Boston. He showed us a huge blueprint of what would be our new home. We studied the plans and the photographs when they came in, and I was pleased by the gorgeous long curving bow and the handsome white super-structure.

"That's one beauty of a schooner," said Pa. "Remember when I told you about the *Blue Nose* and the *Gertrude Thebaud*, those two famous Gloucester fishing boats that raced against each other in 1930? Well, the *Blue Dolphin* is a replica of those two. Like them, she was built at Shelbourne, Nova Scotia, but she's different. You see here? She's marconirigged on the mainmast but gaff-rigged on the foremast. The real Gloucester fishermen are gaff-rigged on both masts. Those spreaders do seem sort of stubby, but there's probably a good engineering reason for that. Makes her more seaworthy, maybe. Look at the beamy black hull. That will make it roomier below, of course, but her interior is a yacht's interior, not an empty hull for fish."

By September, miraculously, we were ready to go. Dividing our forces, Pa, Al, and John went to Gloucester to help with the final outfitting and the storing of Mother's S. S. Pierce tonnage of food. The *Blue Dolphin* was tied up next to the aptly named Gorton Pew Cod Fish Factory, and the cod gave our ship a distinctive Gloucester fisherman aroma as the voyage began. The men were to sail down around stormy Cape Hatteras to save the women the rough shakedown passage. The women would then join the *Blue Dolphin* at the plantation in South Carolina. Nana, Mother, Quita, and I—along with little Willy—returned to Wilmington to close up the house and pack. Willy, who sulked on being separated from his fellow males because of his age, kept insisting he was older, which was true. He had just turned ten.

And then, suddenly, Mother collapsed. She simply could not get out of bed. Pa learned of this when he made his nightly after-five telephone call home from Gloucester. He had to wait for the rates to go down at five to avoid Ma's scolding, and then, by Ma's fiat, he had only three minutes to talk. That was all he needed to learn the dire news. He rushed to Boston and caught the *Quaker*, the night train to Washington, via Wilmington, calling Captain Boutilier from the station in Boston and ordering all work on the *Blue Dolphin* and preparations for the trip stopped until he found out what was wrong with Ma. The doctor finally proclaimed that Mother was not sick with any kind of dire illness, just exhausted. Good, said Pa, she's about to have an extended rest. Mother knew better.

Pa was verging on exhaustion himself. He told Ma he thought the ship would never be able to sail on time with all the problems that came up: getting the sails rigged and the stores stored, especially stowing two tons of food in lockers behind long seats along the saloon walls and under floorboards. He reported that there was hardly room to move about in all the chaos. At last, however, Pa, the boys, and the crew were off, not on a morning departure as planned, but sailing a few minutes after midnight.

The *Blue Dolphin* arrived at Winyah Bay, downriver from Georgetown, South Carolina, and anchored off our Cat Island, ending a stormy seven-day sail. Once the crew had recovered and last-minute provisioning accomplished, the overseer of the plantation drove Al, John, Quita, and me down the rutted, sandy roads from the plantation house to the dunes that bordered the bay. Mother, Nana, and Willy followed us. Al and John, now sophisticated seasoned sailors, coolly sang "Good-bye Again," but Quita and I stayed silent and tense in the oppressively hot afternoon.

The dazzling light made the white sand dunes and green palmettos shimmer. Out on the bay, the ship stood alone, her sails furled. Flapping lazily from the stern, reminiscent of lions and faraway colonies, flew the red Canadian flag.

"The nickname for that flag is 'Blood and Guts'," said the knowledgeable Alfred. "We fly under Canadian colors. It saves taxes."

From the foremast flew the familiar pennant of the Nantucket Yacht Club—supplied by Pa—navy blue with a white star. On the mainmast flew the Chandler house flag. Dreamed up by Pa specially for this occasion, the swallow-tailed pennant was divided into horizontal bands like the Argentine flag—pale blue represented the River Plate, a nod to Argentina, a place that had been truly happy and rewarding for both Ma and Pa, where two of their daughters had been born, and where Pa had led a successful career. He always welcomed questions about the flag because it let him tell again of his happiness there with Ma. He said the white in the flag stood for purity of the soul, a tip of the hat to his beloved Emerson.

We stood momentarily at the top of the dunes absorbing the symbols and then ran down the slopes to the dock, singing "Hail to the Nantucket Yacht Club," the only rallying song we knew. We forgot about the little cactuses in the sand and arrived leaning over to pull them from our socks, flushed and undignified, in contrast to our father, who awaited us on the dock.

Pa wasn't much for dressing up. In Nantucket his rumpled, ragged pale-blue cotton jacket, white shirt without tie, tan duck pants, and battered blue cotton hat, brim down, were his uniform. Our friends called him "Pooh Bah," behind his back of course. But here he stood transformed, an admiral, surely, with a white yachting cap with blue visor, a navy blue flannel jacket with the Nantucket Yacht Club button in the lapel, a buttoned-down collar on his white shirt, a striped tie, and white pants.

"All aboard!" he commanded sternly.

"Yes, sir!" we replied in quiet obedience for once and jumped into the launch. It was clear that life with father would now be dramatically different.

The crew stood by as we climbed up the ladder to the deck, silent, watching us carefully. Mother held back, eyeing the men. Pleasing Pa had paled as motivation now that the magnitude of the adventure was upon her. Her expression was of bewilderment. Mother had always had the help of submissive house servants, but now she was realizing that she would have to deal with strong independent New England men: a captain, a first mate, a chief engineer, a cook, two seamen, and a mess boy.

Just watching Ma made me uncomfortable, and I felt shy under the gaze of the crew, so I grabbed Quita's arm and pulled her belowdecks to study our new home. I had memorized the layout of the *Blue Dolphin* from the blueprints, but I needed an architectural fix. We came down the center companionway into the corridor leading to the saloon, which filled the whole ship's center. When I'd seen the term "saloon," on the blueprints, I'd visualized something Western, with glittering swivel chairs, perhaps, and a small bar in the corner. This room, I now noted with disappointment, resembled a Victorian parlor, dismal after the glare of the bay outside. It smelled stuffy. The walls were paneled in dark mahogany and lined with bookshelves. The built-in couches, covered with stiff, cracking brown leather, would be converted at night into Al's and John's bunks. I had not been prepared for décor this formal.

On the wall amidships—dividing the engine room and crew's quarters from the family quarters—stood a black Franklin stove with an open hearth. It smelled of stove polish and didn't seem to fit with a voyage to the tropics. On the starboard side, the space was filled with a square table on gimbals. In port, when the table was pinned in place, it stood stationary; but once we were at sea, with pins out, it remained horizontal and level no matter how much the ship heeled. Later, when we were underway, the ship well over on her side, I'd come to marvel at the miracle of serenely secure table settings on what seemed to be a table angled at ninety degrees.

I turned to leave the saloon and was startled to come face to face with an actual shrunken human head, a wizened, pickled former Ecuadorian Indian of middle age. "Gleeps!" I exclaimed, bringing Quita to my side. The unsmiling, swarthy savage hung at eye level on the brown mahogany wall and stared at us with piercing black eyes. I backed away, grabbing Quita's hand, squinting at the large pores and the straggling blue-black hair. "Let's get out of here!" I said, and we hustled into the corridor.

Just to the stern of the saloon on the starboard side, we found our stateroom. The central companionway, or stairway to the deck, ran up by our door. Good, I thought, ever alert to the terrible threats to my life and limbs, we'll have easy access topsides in case of sinking. A wide lower bunk and narrow upper bunk lay along the hull of the ship. A hatch above the tall bureau let in sun, air, salt spray, green sea, and rain. The tiny closet at the foot of the bunks had a curtain instead of a door. The curtain, like the dining table, hung plumb when the boat listed; it would appear in my half-sleep as a spooky swinging ectoplasm.

Across the corridor was a double stateroom, much like Quita's and mine, which was to have been for Ma and Pa. I had overheard them in a heated discussion on which of them would sleep in the upper berth. They could not agree. Willy was assigned the upper berth and Ma took over the single stateroom across the passageway from Pa with its wedge-shaped wooden bench between her bunk, the corridor wall, and her bureau.

Next to Pa's stateroom was a tiny closet of a room, no longer called a bathroom, but the nautical term, "the head." A small transom over the door let in the only light. The bathtub immediately caught my fancy. It was about four feet long, and rested on a high ledge. To get into it, you climbed a little flight of stairs. When you pulled out the plug, you let in the ocean and filled the tub. The effect was dramatic, particularly at night when the water was phosphorescent. To let the water out, you pulled another plug and the water drained off into the bilge where the pumps took care of it.

At the beginning of the trip, Pa realized we would need extra water for the longer segments of our voyage, so he bought oak barrels from his moonshining friends. We used water from them for washing in the basin. Unfortunately, he had failed to rinse the barrels out, so the water flowed from the spigot a pale corn-liquor brown, adding a sweet smell to the already dense atmosphere of the room. I objected to the taste when I brushed my teeth and was embarrassed when we went ashore, freshly washed, for I was sure I was stinking like a drunken sailor.

This little room reeked of dampness, for the "running water," except for the basin, was salt and made the room sticky and stale. "P-p-p-ew," said Quita and pulled me down the corridor, past the oilskin locker, to the chart room—an open space dedicated to navigation. Above a wide table were shelves for sextants, charts, and the chronometer. The after companionway ran up to the deck beside the chart table.

Nana, in one of her entitled moods, had decided she, not Ma and Pa, would live in the master cabin. Her door was opposite the chart room, her cabin spread out toward the stern, spanning almost the width of the ship. Nana would sleep in a wide berth on the starboard side with a long cushion-covered berth opposite her on the port side. She also had a large closet and a head of her own. Her cabin had lots of light because of the double transom hatch in the cabin ceiling. I liked this cabin the best. It was spacious, sunny, and cheerful, but I wondered why Nana didn't help Ma and Pa when they were arguing about who would sleep in the upper berth by offering them a proper room of their own? She would have fit nicely into the single cabin.

The noise of the anchor chain coming up through the hawsepipe brought us quickly to desk. The time was 3:30 P.M.; the day, October 30; the year, 1933. Our adventure had begun.

3

Initiation Rites:
The Hurricane

W E LEFT THE bay in a flat calm under power. At the start, Al and John made me feel an outsider. They pushed Quita, Willy, and me toward the stern, so they could be free of us and demonstrate their strength as they helped Sims and Smitty raise the sails, hauling all together on the halyards. This was a familiar feeling, being an outsider.

I was born in a foreign country; therefore, I reasoned, I was fated to be an outsider. And my mother and father didn't exactly match other mothers and fathers either, which further removed me from the aspired inner circle. Mother, the artist, never spent time at bridge parties or ladies' lunches, and Pa flew airplanes around the country, which was most unusual then. No one we knew did that sort of thing. While our classmates celebrated Christmas with parties and Christmas trees and lights, we were far away on our isolated island in South Carolina with a father who would have nothing to do at all with what he called the Papist and commercial celebration of Christ's birth. He wouldn't even give us Christmas presents.

Because of these realities, I had long since learned to try to gain the attention of my schoolmates' cliques by practicing eye-catching derring-do before them. Once, when I was playing soccer, in my usual non-athletic position of goalie, I pretended I was about to faint and staggered towards the most attractive boy on the field, inviting rescue. My act was so convincing that the principal of our school rushed out on the field, lifted me in his arms, and carried me to the Health Office where I regained strength with alacrity. And I would be the first to break strict rules to gain status when I was tagging along with Al's gang. We played in the great barn by our house where a manure can traveled on a track, past the rear of the cows, through the barn and out over the manure pile towards the bull pen. Although we were forbidden to do so, we turned the can upside down and climbed up on it for the ride, taking turns pushing it faster and faster out over the manure pit and the bellowing bull, bellowing because we'd peppered him with BB gun shot. I always wanted to be a leader among men and leapt on the upside-down manure can first, facing the greatest danger.

So it wasn't anything new to feel the outsider, but I was at a loss in this new setting to know how to find my way to insider status. What could I show off? Mother had already told Quita and me that we were not allowed to climb the ratlines, the rope ladders up to the spreaders on the masts, even though Al and John could race up and down them whenever they wanted to. She never explained her reasoning on this dictum, but it certainly limited my range and angered me, too. Al was not that much older than I, and I was just as agile as he and had sailed in small boats as much as he had, so the danger factor couldn't be the reason. I suspected that it was because girls weren't supposed to display their bottoms even if they were wearing long pants. Did she think the crew would be stimulated? I couldn't see why. And I wished she would stop referring all the time to Quita and me as "the little girls." How could we be arousing any kind of prurient interest if we were just little girls? I gave up trying to understand my mother and managed a twinge of satisfaction when I noted that John and Al looked puny compared to the hefty crew hauling on ropes. Those boys weren't all that great.

The clatter of getting under way, the racket of slatting sails as we hit the roll of the sea, the shouting of the crew made me huddle against the wheelhouse and keep my mouth shut for once until I heard the call for supper.

That first night out, we were to celebrate Quita's twelfth birthday. Charlie Hatcher, our elongated, hollow-cheeked cook, had been alerted and had prepared his version of a birthday party. Supper began unpropitiously—S. S. Pierce's canned beans and pork with canned brown bread. Mother, surveying the brownness of it all, sent her left eyebrow rising dangerously high, a warning sign we all knew meant trouble ahead. She was not only an artist who enjoyed luscious colors but was an "eat-your-greens" type of mother too. For the time being, however, she graciously refrained from making any comment on the brownness and tinniness of this meal. Our dessert, an inspired Charlie creation, was a tall chocolate, many-layered cake with caramel icing on the outside and strawberry jam between the layers. Thirteen candles circled the cake, one for each year and one to grow on. Whatever we were thinking, we bellowed out the obligatory "Happy Birthday To You" and then went on deck to watch the lopsided moon rise over the quiet ocean.

That night in my upper bunk I tucked my rag doll, Sophie, under the covers beside me. Though their names were the same, this doll was not to be confused with my sister Sophie. My doll had been my constant companion since my third birthday. Sister Sophie had not come into my life until I was seven. My doll Sophie was flat and made of worn gray cloth, and she had a painted face with large faded blue eyes and a rosebud mouth. Three painted brown curls came down her forehead out from under her white cap. Her legs were bowed, but that went unnoticed because she still wore her original nightgown and slip, both long, flowing, yellowing lawn with fringes of lace at hem and neck. She was the only plaything I was allowed to bring, since we were each allotted so little storage space. I was pleased to have my old friend with me as I fell asleep listening to the water gurgling past my ear. I needed this link to my childhood as I sailed into the unknown.

Ted, the mess boy, strode through the ship the next morning with his wakening call. Crossing the saloon, he boomed out at the boys,

Up, lad: Thews that lie and cumbered
Sunlit palates never thrive;
Morns abed and daylight slumber
Were not meant for man alive.

Clay lies still, but blood's a rover;
Breath's a ware that will not keep.
Up, lad: When the journey's over
There'll be time enough to sleep.

To this day, sixty-nine years later, Al can recite these last two verses of A. E. Houseman's poem, *Reveille*, word for word. After all, he heard it every single morning for the length of our voyage. He should remember it. So can his children, for he used this waking call on them, too, as they were growing up.

Coming along the corridor, Ted called, "Rise and shine!" when he passed our cabin door and marched on to Nana with a kettle of hot water. Such a pleasant way to be awakened, I thought, pulling the blanket modestly under my chin as Ted went by the open door.

Ted Wyman was Pa's particular pet. He was twenty-nine and sandy-haired, his pale skin amply covered with freckles. He had a long pointed nose and chin and was very thin. His body presented many sharp angles, a geometry problem waiting to be solved. He had finished two years of engineering college, had a marine engineer's license, and had already been to sea. He'd spent two years on a square-rigged ship, the U.S.S. *Nantucket* of the Massachusetts Nautical School. Then he made three voyages on a steamship to Buenos Aires and a voyage to San Francisco, where he worked on hydrography with the Coast and Geodetic Survey. Because of the Depression, the only job he could get that summer was working on the dock catching hawsers for the ships of the Nantucket Steamship Authority. When he heard of Pa's wild idea of taking his family to sea, he called Pa and begged him for a job. He had already been told that he would be laid off by the Authority in the fall and longed for yet another adventure at sea. He knew a mess boy was not essential for our crew, so to persuade Pa, he said he would take no pay. Following an extended meeting with him, Pa, liking him so much, signed him on. A consummate peacemaker, the man most tolerant of boisterous children, Ted quickly became our favorite crewmember.

As I lay in my bunk I tried to sort out all the new noises of a sailing ship under way, the water slapping the wood right next to my ear, the strained sound of masts resisting sail pressure, the crackle of sails suddenly gone limp, the creaking of the hull, I tried to visualize what I had left behind. I thought briefly, with disdain, of my friends at home in their Best & Co. dresses. I could see them going to regular old school, classes by the hour, lines at the cafeteria. And here I was, surrounded by men, heading into the yonder for real. I let out a soft whistle, astounded by my luck.

The next morning, I crawled awkwardly down from the upper bunk and sat on the wooden rail that held Quita's mattress in place. We continued our argument, *sotto voce,* on how long I could have the upper bunk before she could have her turn. Bumping into each other in the narrow space between bunks and bureau, we dressed. I pulled on a pair of heavy white cotton bell-bottomed trousers with red buttons across the front, Navy style, and red stripes down the side. I tore off the price tag and the paper labels reading, "Atlantic Clothing Company, 328 Atlantic Avenue (Near Rowe's Wharf) Boston, Massachusetts, Crew Outfitters and Yacht Uniforms." Well, which was I, I wondered, crew or yacht? These pants, a couple of jerseys, our sou'westers, long oilskins, gob hats, and khaki shorts were our seagoing wardrobe. Hanging in our narrow closet, swinging with our ghost curtain, were two twin plaid gingham dresses for Quita and me to wear ashore.

Trying to affect nonchalance, I slowly climbed up the companionway to the deck. The wind had come up at three A.M., and now we were scudding right along under mainsail, foresail, and two jibs. I found Willy in the fisherman's pulpit on the end of the bowsprit, gazing at a school of porpoises leaping and darting before us.

Breakfast was a novel adventure: whole oranges, oatmeal with molasses, hot cocoa, those kippered herrings, and fresh baked bread. I finished it all, went topsides, made it to the leeward rail, and lost it all. Quita followed me, did the same, and went back to her bunk. In short order, Mother, Nana, and Willy succumbed to seasickness and retired to their bunks. I elected to remain in the cool, fresh air. The thought of facing that shrunken head and breathing the dead leather smell of the saloon kept me propped up against pillows by the wheelhouse close to the seaman steering the ship. My new hoped-for personality, the debonair sailor-boy-girl, went overboard with my breakfast. Ted saw my distress and went below to fetch his favorite seasickness cure. "Don't worry, Nina, it's no disgrace to be seasick," he said as he presented his offering, "I lost my first meal, too, after we left Gloucester. Your sea legs will come quickly. Best cure is just to keep on working and eating. Here try this." He presented me with dried, uncooked salted cod to suck with hard pilot biscuits for a chaser.

As I sat there, shivering from cold and nausea, the cod in my mouth, I shifted from excitement to feeling sorry for myself. The cod tasted awful beyond the awfulness of vomit. Was that the cure then, being worse off than seasick, never mind better? Was this the way I became an insider? Must I go through awfulness to find myself? Certainly that was what happened in a lot of the novels I read. I'd better prepare myself. Undoubtedly there would be worse to come.

Then came a revelation. Staring spellbound at the sea, like Willy watching the porpoises, I was aware for the first time in my life of a magnificence. Before me, beneath me, behind me was a terrifying, powerful living force, the sea. The abrupt arrival of this new and unfamiliar sea was so frightening, I felt the need to make it manageable: This is a giant, I thought. I know giants. There are ways to deal with giants, but the force of the sea?

"Hey!" called Al from the bow, "look at the cute little birdies!" A flight of tiny irradiate blue creatures with white breasts streaked across the bow. Two fell flopping on the deck, gasping, and Al held them up. They were flying fish.

"Look there," called out Nana, who had come up for air, pointing beyond the stern, "over there. Mother Carey's chickens." Nana, the family authority on birds and beasts, went on. "See that sooty black-backed bird. Look! Did you catch the black stripe running down his white belly? That's St. Paul's bird. He walks on water." Her voice dropped. "An omen. Mother Carey's chickens come before a storm." She sniffed the wind and went back to her cabin.

Captain ordered an extra sail set, the fisherman's staysail, a wide skirtlike piece of canvas that hung high aloft between the two masts, but its halyard broke and the huge sheet of canvas fell to the deck, slapping in the wind, lashing at the struggling crew. Part of the sail went into the sea, dragging the boat over to leeward. Al and John joined the battle with the sail, helping the crew haul it in. They taunted me. Although I simply wasn't up to helping, they made it sound as if I just wanted to loll around while the men did the serious work.

By the next morning, my giant had changed. His sparkling blue waves were gone, and now he came on sullen, stony gray, rising in long swells. The sun had disappeared. Squalls of hard rain and wind attacked us. I was more aware than ever of the sea's great, crushing weight pressing against us, wave after increasing wave. The wind shifted from the northeast to easterly as the storm engulfed us. Al and John, unfazed by the increasingly bad weather, invented a game. When the ship heeled over in the rising wind, they crouched on the windward, or high side, of the deck and slid down its wet slope until they reached the scuppers and leeward rail, already running close to the sea. There they reached out to try to grab the floating masses of Sargasso seaweed. As they passed my reclining form, they went on jeering at my seasickness. Then Al, having reached the leeward rail once again, leaned over to make his catch of seaweed, felt the wind take his gob hat off his head, saw it sail off to sea, and made an instinctive leap to catch it, losing his balance in the process. John grabbed him just before he went overboard.

"There!" I shouted with some satisfaction. "Serves you right. You were showing off," wishing, of course, that I had the strength to do the same. We were quiet then, on guard, knowing how close we all were to life-threatening danger. We watched the rising seas and waited. An ominous pall hung over the deck.

That night the boat pitched and jerked us about, and I had little restful sleep. In the morning, on our second day out, the wind reached full gale force, blowing over sixty miles an hour. Waves rose in walls of water, blue-black with intense green tops that the wind tore away in boiling white foam. Spray soaked anyone on deck. A filmy spume coated our hair and clothes. The captain ordered us hove to on the starboard tack.

Quita and I held onto each other on deck trying to keep our balance. "This is like swimming in the surf in Nantucket," I cried out to her. "We're okay unless a seventh wave comes along." I was remembering how we'd shout warnings at each other when the seventh wave loomed over us, the wave that came out of synchrony with the others, caught us and ground us against the hard pebbles. We seemed to be building up to several seventh waves now.

"Ah-ah-ah-I'm going back to my bunk." Quita forced the words out, her teeth chattering. "I'm s-s-sick."

"I'm not going down there," I told her. "It's too wet. The water comes in the hatches even when they're closed. And that dumb porthole right above my mattress leaks. It's too stuffy down there. And besides, it smells. You like that smell? Nope, I'm going to stay up here and get good, clean water washed over me. Doesn't it scare you down there? Wow!" I exploded, "Look at that wave there! Doesn't that scare you?"

"N-n-no. It's just like s-s-sailing our Rainbows at Nantucket. There, when the wind b-b-lows higher, you h-heel over more and b-b-bigger waves come over the b-bow and s-s-soak you. Now we're in a b-b-bigger b-b-boat, s-s-o you get huger waves and get even wetter." With this serene logic, she descended the stairs.

Then I started shivering too, I finally admitted to myself I'd prefer being sick below. I joined Al and John who were just returning to the saloon after a visit forward to the galley where they had solicited cookies from Charlie and had had a talk on the hazards of cooking on high seas. Charlie, they reported, had spread burlap bags on the galley floor to give his tattered blue carpet slippers greater traction. And they said Mr. Doyle, the first mate, had lost his balance and rolled over the galley table knocking it loose from its fastenings.

Al, John, and I were alone in the saloon. Nana and Mother had long since elected to stay in their cabins; Pa and Willy were hanging on to each other on deck. I slouched down in the big stuffed chair and listened to Al who was talking with the excitement that came over him whenever he discovered a new idea, pushing his words against each other until they flowed together without periods or pauses.

"Do you realize how that storm trisail, the stuns'l, works? I've just figured it out. Watch how the wind hits it," gesturing to clarify his point, "and then you can see how wind, sail, and sea work together. It's amazing! The sail and the wind are in balance and keep the boat more or less stationary in the sea."

John nodded, assimilating Al's physics lesson. I was just beginning to sense how sweet John's patience was. Al rushed on, "And the boat never luffs out of control. If we ever luffed, if we ever lost the wind out of our sails, even for a minute, we'd be slapped down and all hands lost. Sims says you have to maintain steerageway or you go down."

John made no comment. He turned to me and offered a piece of his cookie. I dared to try it. His kindness gave me confidence enough to contribute to our new pool of knowledge of the sea. "Ted says the waves are thirty feet high now. Isn't that taller than a two-story house? Boy! Do I believe him. And Captain says to look out for the seventy-foot wave because it'll be coming along. That must be our good old seventh wave." I didn't seem to impress either of the boys, even though I was reporting earnestly and accurately.

At that moment Ted came into the cabin with Willy by his side. "Now, there are certain things you must not do in a storm." Ted sat in one of the captain's chairs by the table and began enlightening us novices on how to survive gales and hurricanes. Willy sank down on the arm of my chair. "You can't let one of those monstrous waves hit your stern and swerve you broadside to an oncoming wave. That's called broaching, and that you don't want to do. And you don't want to get pitchpoled either— that's when a wave lifts your stern with such force that on the way down you somersault. No good. Of less danger, but you better pay attention, is when a green wave breaks over your stern. That means your ship poops." I socked Willy to make him suppress his laughter and pay proper attention. I could see nothing but doom in these lessons.

"Now, do you know what to do if a man gets washed overboard?" Ted went on solemnly. "You fling him a life preserver and point to him. Keep pointing to him, keep pointing, keep pointing, keep pointing so the helmsman can turn the ship to where the poor doomed lubber is thrashing away." He looked over at me, saw my fright. "Nina, cheer up. This is just practical advice."

By nightfall, our run down the slope of the huge waves was so steep that our bow plunged deep into the sea at the bottom of the trough, making each rise out of the depths more and more problematic. Now I had to worry about broaching, pitchpoling, and pooping. The ship seemed to roar in pain as tons of green water rushed to the stern. I trembled in compassionate union with every struggling plank. Belowdecks, the cabins were airless, hot, and wet. The acrid commingled smells of leather, engine oil, wet varnish, wet clothes, marlin, and stale dampness hung over us, heavy and sour. The din, both below and topsides, was unnerving. Books tumbled from the shelves in spite of racks built to hold them. China banged and rattled. Chairs turned over. The ship creaked and snapped, and the wind, I found to my surprise, really did whistle and whine, and now was shrieking in the rigging just as it did in Conrad's *Typhoon*.

"So this," said John, with a tone of deep regret, the ship rising higher and higher on each wave before its swoop downward, "*this* is sea level? What's level about it?" He leaned down and began once more picking up the toppled chairs and spilled books. "Gee," he grumbled, "how many times do I have to do this chore?"

Only the men ate supper that night. I retired when I smelled cabbage. I lay on my upper bunk and rode our ship, a sea horse, goaded to a frenzy by that awful giant, the sea. Pitching, bucking, jerking, all muscles taught, I tried to keep from being thrown to the floor and watched our gingham dresses in the closet as they stood out straight from the slanting bulkhead.

I was touched when Ted appeared at our door announcing, "O.K., girls, here's your supper. Nina, this time your cod's cooked. Try it with these pork and onions and a touch of cabbage. It'll nourish your soul."

"Please just leave it on the bureau," I said weakly, trying to be polite and holding down the urge to vomit. Ted smiled and left to be followed by Pa who seemed genuinely concerned about our state of health. He wanted to be sure we ate something and tried to fork food into our mouths. He coaxed and laughed, but neither Quita nor I wanted to even get near that supper and turned our heads to the ship's side. Pa finally gave up. He squeezed his big frame in between our bunks and bureau, and carefully tucked us in. Then he tried once more to tighten my leaking porthole. He spoke to us softly. "Now this is a bad storm for sure, but it's what every ocean traveler expects. We are being initiated to the sea. You are doing wonderfully. You are becoming real sailors, not fair-weather sailors. Soon you'll be just like the boys, up and around and helping sail the ship." He patted us each on the shoulder, kissed us a peck on the forehead, and left. I was astounded. Pa never tucked us in at home and never, never kissed us under any circumstances.

Sleep was impossible. I had to stay alert to keep from being tossed out onto the bureau. In the middle of the night, I heard the soft sound of sobbing coming through the cacophony of the creaking, groaning, slatting ship noises. It was Quita below me. I held tight to the side of the berth to keep from being thrown to the floor, and leaning over, said, "What's the matter, Quita?" After a few more sobs, she answered, "I miss S-s-Sophie. I want to go h-h-home." Then pushing on faster, she loudly declared, "I want to go home. I want to go home to Sophie." Sobs stopped her talking, but then she began again. "I'm going to d-d-d-drown and I'll never see Sophie again."

"No, no, no, Quita. We'll be all right. We'll go back to Sophie," but I lacked conviction. I slipped under the covers again and held tight to my doll as Quita cried herself to sleep.

The next day the storm increased in momentum. The Captain, working mightily to keep his balance, came into the saloon where we were all gathered. "From now on," he said, speaking firmly like the master of the ship he was, "no one can go up on deck. Only the crew on watch is allowed up there." Winds were now blowing a steady seventy miles an hour, moving to hurricane force in persistent gusts. The sea was no longer blue or gray. It was white.

Desperate for air and seeking a way out of the noisome atmosphere of the saloon and the howls of a ship straining for her life, I crawled halfway up the after companionway under the cover of the sliding wooden hatch. On deck, Captain Boutilier and Pa stood close to a scowling Smitty. To save himself from being washed overboard, Smitty had knotted a heavy rope around his waist and tied one end to the binnacle. Now I understood the phrase "lashed to the wheel." All three were only a few feet from me and gave me the comforting sense of strong men in control. Keeping their precarious balance, holding their sextants by their sides, Pa and Captain stood there, hoping the sun might break through long enough for them to get their routine morning navigational fix. They realized very quickly that they would see no sun that day and came below to the chart table. Sitting above them on my step, I listened to their conversation.

"We must be at least forty miles off course," said Captain. "But all we can do now is sail by dead reckoning."

Pa leaned over the chart.

"How far would you estimate we are off the Florida reefs?" he asked. "Should we turn on the motor and try and work our way out to sea?"

Captain dropped his voice and mumbled an answer. I couldn't hear whether or not we were about to crash on a shoal, but knew I had better prepare myself for the worst. Even if we weren't going to run aground, I understood clearly that we were lost and drifting. Captain shook his wet head wearily, the seawater dripping onto the floor from his long green slicker. "This is the worst storm I have ever been in," he started, and noting my fright, he let his voice trail off. "That is," he quickly added, "with ladies aboard."

We had managed to launch our adventure in the year of a record-breaking number of hurricanes—twenty-one in all. We were moving into one of them. I was not reassured by Captain's remark as I watched him and Pa ricochet down the passageway towards the saloon, talking together, and I was alone again on my solitary perch looking out at the roaring chaos. All I could see, past Smitty and the stern rail, was the wild ocean—no land, no other ships. We had no two-way radio, no modern pathfinders. Radar was an invention of the future. Our lives depended on pieces of wood screwed together and a crew who knew how to keep them in one coherent piece.

At that moment, a tiny bird fluttered to a landing before me on the sill of the companionway, buffeted, exhausted, its breast tremulous. It was a yellow-green warbler, perching there quietly, showing no fear of me, scrutinizing the awesome storm with black, staring eyes. For an instant, I felt the delicious warmth of love. I had an ally. Then suddenly, he blinked and with a shake of his bedraggled feathers, driven by some instinctive urgency, he flung himself back into the storm.

How could that tiny bird dare to fly off into such a maelstrom? Did its miniscule brain know the ends of adventure better than I? It was growing clear to me that I really did not understand what our adventure was all about. So far I only knew I was uprooted and lost. Landscapes with walled boundaries and road connections had given way to the boundless, ever-moving, tumultuous sea. My clothes were different, food too, and certainly the people, even though Mother had told me she liked Captain because he looked like our neighbor Victor duPont. Even time was marked off differently, chimed in every four hours for the change of watch, instead of settling into sensible morning, noon, and night. Here, birds walked on water and fish flew.

At that moment, Nana poked her head out of her cabin door. "They say we sail the wide Atlantic," she called out irascibly to no one in particular. "Not so. We sail the wild Atlantic. Anything after this is going to be tame." I nodded with marked affirmation. "I devoutly wish I were back at Dalhousie planting herbs," she concluded, backing into her cabin and closing the door.

It was becoming clear that my usual blissful, thoughtless acceptance of life's course as arranged by Ma and Pa was over. Now I really had better pay closer attention to their ideas and problems, since those ideas must alter my life radically as well as theirs. Shouldn't I have known right at the beginning that this trip could be a mistake? Maybe all those teachers and doctors and shocked friends had a point when they advised us not to launch on such an adventure. Birds might do it, but children? This thought triggered a memory of another time when I suspected one of my parents of fits of overconfidence.

Years before, after their return from South America and their brief stay outside of Philadelphia, Ma and Pa had come to an agreement that they would live in Delaware. To Pa, Delaware was a southern, therefore retrograde, state, but to Ma, it was the heart of the universe. In a concession to Pa's Massachusetts heritage, Ma agreed that summers would be spent on Nantucket where Pa's ancestral grandmother, Abiah Folger, had lived. Our parents felt obliged to give their children the feel of both North and South.

On one of Ma's first summers on the island, she decided part of her moral obligation to Pa was to teach us to sail, since sailing was part of Pa's northern past. Mother dutifully marched Alfred, Quita, and me down to the Old South Wharf at the head of the island's nearly landlocked harbor and chartered a Rainbow—a small, gaff-rigged boat with a red sail. The wind was gusting to fifteen knots, a strong wind for any experienced small craft sailor, and we were novices. Ma's small boating experience was limited to the *Vestris* lifeboat ride and to canoes on the pond at Dalhousie. But off we went, barreling down the harbor, running before the southwest wind. As we approached the sand cliff at Pocomo, four or five miles away, Ma decided it was time to go home. We had rather enjoyed our rush down harbor, but now we were stymied. Ma did not understand the principles of tacking, a laborious procedure necessary to making our way home against the wind, so we drifted with the sail flapping futilely. Eventually, when we were beginning to feel as if we'd never reach home again, a motorboat spotted us and towed us back to the wharf.

As for Pa, I already knew that he was too optimistic to be trusted, and besides, he was acting with altogether strange, new behavior, being so gentle with Quita and me, trying to feed us, tucking us in, tightening our leaking ports. Kissing us! I knew Pa thought mankind was moving onward and upward forever. Maybe he was trying to say that our survival in this storm was further proof, but I had the definite impression we might go the other way.

Since looking at the storm wasn't helping me, I crawled back down the steps of the companionway and made my way to the saloon, being thrown against the walls as I went. I sank into the big leather chair on the port side under the shrunken Indian head. Willy was playing with little cars in the middle of the floor.

"I hate this storm," he muttered.

"Me too. Why do you hate it?"

"I hate the storm because it hurt me."

Will pulled up his shirt to show me large purple bruises he'd got the night before when he'd been tossed out of his upper bunk, down onto the bureau, and bounced from there onto Pa's stomach.

"Too bad," I said, "Ted said he was washed out of his bunk, too, but with water, no dry toss like you had. The hatch over the fo'c's'le doesn't keep the water out. They're soaked all the time up for'ard."

Willy nodded his head and I curled up in the chair, staring at the shrunken Indian head. His blue-black whiskers stood out stiffly. For me, hope and love had departed with the little bird. Any sense of safety I had was gone. I'd come into an empty hollow where I felt no control or will. I caught another memory then and drifted back to a sunny fall afternoon after school. A friend had invited me to her house, and we were walking there together. On the way, she stopped at her church. She said she wanted to pray. As far as I could remember I had never been in a church before, and the concept of prayer was beyond me, but I went along with her. The mystery and grandeur of that space, the gloom pierced by the brilliant colors of the sun coming through the stained glass windows, struck me with awe, and I found I could even evoke in myself a semblance of what I thought might be prayer. As I knelt beside my friend, I grew angry with my father for depriving me of such wellsprings of joy. Why, I wondered, did he hate churches so much, and why wouldn't he let his children attend one, much less enter one?

My attention returned to the ship's saloon. It was gloomy enough, though, with no luminous stained glass window to bring me light. Suddenly, the Indian seemed to grow bigger before my eyes. There, I said to myself, there is an icon worthy of prayer. The mysterious Indian would save me. He could be as magic as any other old god around. I stood, and, with my back turned to Willy, looked the savage in the eye. I kissed my forefinger and placed it on his brown, wrinkled forehead.

"Please," I said to him silently, sure he, like the god my friend prayed to, would hear me. "Please rescue us. We need your help."

I patted down his bristly hair and prepared myself for results.

By the next morning the storm began to abate. Black squalls still came suddenly with sharp rain and bullying gusts, but the worst was clearly over. That night we were all present as we gathered for supper. Mother came lurching into the saloon carrying her gray sketchbook, which appropriately had a galleon under full sail embossed on the cover.

"I've loved this storm," she announced. We all looked surprised; she had been holed up in her cabin for three days, so we had assumed misery. "Well, you see I have had all this time to draw. It's been exciting, wonderful, really." I wasn't sure whether the storm or her drawing excited her, but I did know that, as always, she was keeping control of her world by painting it—knowing it, understanding it—in visual terms.

She went to Pa and presented her pastel drawings, smiling, looking him directly in the eye. The first drawing was a nice sketch of the *Blue Dolphin* right in the middle of the picture, all sails set, moving out of Gloucester harbor. The next pastel was after we left South Carolina; the ship had grown smaller and was now placed in a vast seascape. Then came two pastels of the storm. The first showed the *Blue Dolphin*, a tiny ship now, far in the distance climbing the great mountainous waves, looking lost and about to be overpowered. In the final depiction, Mother sketched the sea from the deck, looking through the stanchions and ratlines. The seas were background now, still mountainous, but the artist was safe in the foreground, in control, with all details exact.

"Dearest, those are beautiful!" Pa exclaimed and stood and wrapped his arms around her.

Nana staggered into the saloon, moved to her usual place at the foot of the table, and began her meal by reaching out to grasp a piece of bread. This was an athletic event, for the table kept going vertical in front of her. Quickly she gave up, as its constant swooping was making her ill, and instead wedged herself into the corner with her plate on her lap.

"Lordy, Lordy," she fussed, "I hope I'm not going to have to have buffet suppers like this three times a day."

I lagged behind when the others left the table for a look at the quieting sea and went over to the shrunken head, knelt on the chair below it and placed my hands as if in prayer. "I thank you," I told the head. "We are safe. I will reward you. I promise." His shiny black eyes stared right back at me. I thought I sensed a subtle nod. From that day on, I was the only one who dusted the savage and kept it groomed.

4

Rhythmic Routines

NOW THAT THE storm had cut us off definitively from our past, the
Blue Dolphin, a frail dark shell on a vast expanse of capricious power,
became our entire world. As one day followed another, we settled into the
rhythmic routine that seagoing imposes on its travelers. Family and crew
became a working team on this bobbing craft, and the children absorbed
the unfamiliar nautical lingo quickly, each of us taking our place in the
rigid hierarchy that governed the ship. Of greatest immediate importance
was trying to get things ship-shape. Tidiness was suddenly a life and
death matter. If ropes were not coiled perfectly, one of us, or the ship itself, could be in danger. So we all set to restoring order to our storm-
wracked vessel.

We sensed a fresh freedom. The sea no longer tied the crew down at
the wheel or kept us below. We moved easily about the ship, getting our
balance. The sea giant, however, was not letting me know much of himself. He remained inscrutable, constantly changing. His curling combers
relentlessly washed away all trace of our purposeful linear path, our foaming wake. The clouds parted just long enough to let us find our sights and
chart our position on the sea. Now we knew where we were, but the light
did not let me penetrate and comprehend the dark hidden forces underneath. I knew only the surface, and that was scary enough.

The chronometer's repeating bell chimed the hours. The watches, four hours on, four hours off, changed before the shining brass binnacle, the man at the wheel chanting the course to the new helmsman, a magical sing-song incantation, "South southeast a quarter east." Then the new helmsman repeated the phrase, calling it back. The meeting of the old and new watch continued below, the men bending over the crackling yellow charts on the flat counter at the foot of the after companionway. In the ship's log the watch going off duty recorded the position, the time, the course being steered, the direction of the wind, the barometer reading, and a comment in shorthand, cryptic sentences of the four hours just past—"Mod Esly wind heavy swell overcast with rain head reaching."

At the exchange of watches at midnight and four A.M., the tread of men on deck just a few feet above my head would wake me. I soon recognized the voice of Mr. Doyle, the first mate, and tingled with delight at the string of obscenities he spewed out. Mr. Doyle was a man in his middle age, nearsighted with thinning gray hair. He sagged in semicircles beginning with the bags under his eyes and continuing on downwards. His pink complexion deepened quickly to venous red when irascibility flooded him. The presence of women and children muted his brilliant swearing in daytime, but at night, he was superb. He would come slowly along the deck in the darkness, wiping the fog from his steel-rimmed glasses, half blind, still half asleep, unaware of the trap that lay in wait for him. To get more air into the cabins, we had inserted long metal tubelike ventilators in the portholes to catch the winds. Although Mr. Doyle knew they were there, he would forget them, catching one across his shin and striking his bone, with devastating results to his equanimity, which, in turn, greatly increased the knowledge of a thirteen-year-old girl who liked to decipher new languages. I stored away his precious words for use the next year when racing sailboats in Nantucket. We sailors were good at swearing, unlike the clean, clad-all-in-white tennis types at the Yacht Club. With Mr. Doyle's help, I would be able to outshine even the boys when things got tight rounding a mark.

Nana's feelings about these nightly changes of watch were not as warmly anticipated as mine. She liked fresh air and insisted on opening the hatch above her, the ventilated portholes, and the door of her cabin, which opened directly onto the chart room. She could not help hearing every remark, every noise, and the one noise that roiled Nana's regal spirits more than any other was the captain's catarrh. His rich cough, combined with the constant clearing of his throat, climaxing with a leeward spit, stirred up every germ theory Nana had. Nana was militant about germs. For her, germs had personality and purpose, both evil, and had to be met with a vigorous assault. If we sniffled, she was always ready to swoop down on us with a foul-smelling medicine, taken usually, as a precautionary measure, internally *and* externally.

On this first leg of the trip, when the captain came below at four A.M. to write up the log at the change of watch, he leaned over the chart table just opposite Nana's open door and coughed loudly and repeatedly. Finally, Nana could tolerate no more. She rose and strode from her cabin indignant, her cheeks flushed, her pink wool wrapper sweeping past the wet green slicker of the captain.

"Really!" she exclaimed in disgust and marched down the corridor to the cabin where Quita and I slept. "Wake up!" she commanded, shaking Quita in the lower bunk, knowing Quita was the person least likely to object. "Wake up! Perhaps you can sleep through this racket, this contamination, but I simply cannot! You go to my bunk. I will stay here."

The captain was still rooted to the spot, frozen in astonishment, when the thin little girl with the long wispy curls in a white nightgown came back, half awake, to take over the queenly quarters.

I liked the change of watch in the daytime because I had a new set of men to talk to every four hours. First, Captain would be in charge, with Smitty serving as helmsman. Mr. Doyle, heading the next watch, had Sims, a distant cousin of the captain's, as his helmsman. The captain awed me with his total power as commander of our ship. He was usually frowning in intense concentration, but he was gentle in manner and did not frighten. Mr. Doyle, however, was different. He treated us children with disdain and complained repetitively about the hazards of ocean travel with a bunch of kids on board. I stood up straighter when I faced Mr. Doyle, reflexively compensating for his sagging semicircles. The starch in his own shirt, the jaunty angle of his white cap with the blue visor signaled firmness, but that was an illusion. Inside his clothes, I just knew he drooped.

Mr. Doyle had grounds for his disdain. He was a true Gloucester fisherman. He had sailed on the *Gertrude Thebaud* during her great race with the *Bluenose* not so long ago, as had Charlie, the cook, which entitled them both to be known as authentic Gloucester fishermen, raising them high in the seamen's hierarchy. Mr. Doyle exploited his lofty position and antagonized the men working under him. Erban Smith, Smitty, had had as many years at sea as Mr. Doyle. He had sailed in all kinds of ships and had been a mate himself on a square-rigger, but Smitty was not a Gloucester fisherman, and Mr. Doyle let him know it. Friction between these two men never ceased. I wasn't used to grown men growling at each other and pondered over how to get them cheered up.

The two tough, leathery seamen, Sims and Smitty—men of indeterminate age—excited my curiosity the most. I recognized Smitty the instant we met. He seemed to have stepped out of N. C. Wyeth's terrifying illustrations of pirates in *Treasure Island*. Here he was, alive and just as scary as those pictures. Silent Smitty, carved by the sea, was square—square-faced, square-bodied—a crude block of a man. He wore a standard crew uniform, a blue middy blouse with a wide slapping collar down the back and a blue gob hat, but his mien transformed him from a regular crewmember into a robber from a Spanish galleon. His beard was thick and stubby and darkened his face. His bright blue eyes slanted upward in a sinister squint acquired from concentrating so long on sea and storms. A mirthless grin pulled up the corners of his mouth. Clearly here was a man who would make you beg for mercy. Simeon Boutilier, called Sims, was more oval than square. His hair looped over his sloping eyebrows, and he lisped through a large chip in his front tooth. He looked perpetually puckered. He was easy to talk with and not the least bit frightening.

Willy and Chief became fast friends right away. Emroy Martin, always called just "Chief," was our engineer and had sailed on the *Blue Dolphin* before. Mother was especially pleased to have him on board, not because we needed an expert to keep the sundry motors operating efficiently, but because Chief was the father of four and would know how to play with her children. Willy and Chief both loved engines, but Willy also loved Chief's bill-nosed pliers and used to sneak them away from Chief to stash them under his pillow. Chief was a big, soft man with a tiny Charlie Chaplin mustache. He looked like a pasty lump of rising dough. If you were to poke him, he'd surely collapse stickily about you, and you'd have to wait for him to rise again.

Most of the time we were driven by the sails, but sometimes—when we were caught in a dead calm or maneuvering into a tricky harbor—the captain would give the order to start the engine. Whenever Willy heard the first throb of the motor, he'd race to the engine room. Chief would give him an oil can, hold him out over the engine, and let him juice the jogging piston arms as they danced their jerky marionette ballet. If Willy ever hurt himself, and he did often, careening around the deck and skinning himself on edges and corners, Chief would lug him to the engine room where the soothing smell of oozing grease and warm oil quieted the bruised and bleating boy.

The fixed points in our daily schedule were three hearty meals, served religiously at seven, twelve and sunset. Meals had always been important in our family life. At home, we were used to ten or more seated together at every meal—our own seven and various visiting aunts and uncles and cousins, with Nana, of course, at the head of the long table. On the *Blue Dolphin*, however, Pa sat at the head of the square table, while Nana and Ma were relegated together at the foot, at least that was the way it seemed to me. It could be argued that Nana and Ma were at the head, with Pa at the foot, but Pa's in-charge demeanor definitely made him head of the whole family now, no arguing. John and Al sat in those sturdy captain chairs that tended to tip over in high seas. Quita, Willy, and I rushed to get the first seat on the built-in couch that ran along the starboard side of the ship, trying to avoid "Starvation Corner," where the food was served last from nearly empty dishes. The captain and crew, on the other hand, had their own table forward next to the galley.

After the first seasick days, we took up our regular practice of eating and talking simultaneously. Pa started us off at lunch. "Someone said, I think he was an Englishman, that there is no situation in which knowledge is more truly power than at sea. Now we have certainly learned that lesson."

"Yep," said Willy, "we learned not to poop," and gave himself to giggles.

"It's amazing to me," offered Al, "that we could sail so confidently when we didn't know where we were."

"Who said we were confident?" I queried.

John quietly suggested that dead reckoning was really a fine art and that it did keep us on track.

"Those Pre-Raphaelites, Rossetti, Burne-Jones," Mother interrupted, "they only paint women with goiters. Disgusting. So much sickness on display."

How like Ma. Her nonsequiturs were a constant source of mystery to me. I wished she would pay better attention and get into the flow of conversation. It was challenging, though, to try and figure out how her mind worked and how she made her links. How could she go so far away without anyone noticing?

On our first sunny morning after the storm, we were finally up to opening a goodbye present, a big box from Nantucket friends. It contained jams for mother, a book for Nana, a Red Cross handbook for Pa, a puzzle called "Imp" for Al, a roulette set for John, a magnetized checkerboard for me, a game called "Bottoms Up" for Quita, a colorful picture book for Willy, and a box of yarn and a crochet needle. What a luxury to contemplate: long hours of games! Even George (my name for the shrunken savage head), seemed to have an air of curiosity about him as he looked down on the new life stirring beneath him. Just the prospect of games relaxed me. With a reverent nod to George, I excused myself, crawled into my damp upper bunk and slept my first relaxed sleep of the voyage and had to be shaken awake for supper.

The next day, sitting down for a long lunch, I braced myself behind the swinging table and viewed my family with familiar swelling pride. I tended to think I had raised this brood myself, with occasional assistance from my mother. I expected each one of us to be stellar in youth and old age, so I noted with annoyance that Al was slumping again, sinking down in his chair, ready, as usual, to rest his elbows on the table. In spite of the fact that he had turned fifteen in September and should know better, there he was, about to err. It was time to remind him, yet again, that he would be deformed by bad posture and shunned in polite society for wretched table manners. Before I could shape my words, however, he did put his elbows on the table and it tipped. Glasses of milk, cups of tea, heaped platters of food, silverware, and china all started gliding gently down the slope toward Alfred's lap, but my shriek alerted him in time to stop the catastrophe. I turned toward Mother; she was laughing so hard she was weeping. She did this occasionally and was always sweeter afterward.

We reveled in the unfamiliar warmth of the sun that was making our noses peel. We tried out our newfound sea legs. We could lift our sights beyond the tiny world of our ship and search the horizon. John spotted a tanker off to port, riding the seas. It was an amazing sight. The bow of the ship would ride one wave with the stern perched on a following wave, and we could see sky under the hull in the gully between the waves. What a strain on any ship, to be suspended like that! We were thankful that our tiny speck of a craft just went up and down each wave, soaring and plummeting, frightening as that had been.

"Look there, kids, over there." Sims called us to the bow and handed us the binoculars. "Can you see that dark spot on the horizon?" None of us could see the spot. After a few tries on the part of each of us, Willy turned to Sims and said, "Are you sure you aren't seeing land with a camel walking on it," and then whispered to me, "I put a hair across his binoculars; and that camel's my pet cootie." Sims kept his silence with a smile that broadened when a schooner, all sails set, crossed our bow an hour later.

Pa emerged from below to join his children on deck. "Joseph Conrad," he pontificated, "wrote 'Landfall and departure mark the rhythmical swing of a seaman's life and of a ship's career. From land to land is the most concise definition of a ship's earthly fate.' You'll understand that, children, as we begin stopping at island after island."

On the sixth day of our journey, with combers rising behind us and rushing under us, hissing in the excitement of getting by, we sighted our first foreign shore when John, taking a sweep of the sea with the glasses, shouted in a high-pitched voice, "Land!"

The cry of "land" sent an electrical current through the ship. The boys ran up the rigging to the spreaders. The crew came from below and stood at the bow, arms crossed, legs braced against the roll, quietly watching the approaching shore. Quita, Willy, and I clambered out onto the bowsprit. And, oh, the land looked joyful! Earth was warm and ancient and kind to man. We did want to "fall" onto it again and rest from the cold calculating war with the sea. I remembered Nana's repeated directions when we gardened together at home: "Stand on the earth and let the feel of it come up through the soles of your feet." I could hardly wait.

The land hung in the distance, a pale, luminous green, shimmering over the edge of white surf. Standing above the shore—tall and severe— was Abaco Light, marking the outer fringe of the northern Bahamas. Here was man's guiding hand at last. We reached out for it gratefully. But that night, Quita had another nightmare and came wandering back from Nana's cabin. She told me, as I leaned over the edge of the berth, that she dreamed she was drowning and was more certain than ever that she would never see Sophie and the lush blue-green rolling hills of Delaware again. I tried to reassure her. Nana, in the lower berth, slept through it all.

5

First Foreign Port:
First Lessons

"WHY ARE WE flying that huge awful-looking yellow flag?" I asked Smitty who was coiling halyards by the companionway. We lay at anchor off Nassau harbor.

"We can't go ashore until we're cleared by the health officials. That flag stays up until we pass inspection," was his laconic response.

"You mean they think we're contagious, or something, carrying a dread disease?"

"Sure," said Ted as he passed by, "and we'll stay that way until a bureaucrat comes out and certifies us to be healthy in triplicate."

"What an insult!" I called after him as he went forward. "Of course we're healthy. Lordy, we've just survived a hurricane. We had to be healthy."

As I walked off to the stern to share my anger with Quita, I dreamed up a scheme to try the port doctor's patience. Quita and I would paint spots on our faces and collapse on deck, moaning, and see how he dealt with incipient plague.

Our entrance into the harbor did not go smoothly. The pilot boat rammed our port side, bending a handrail stanchion, and then our anchor caught on coral. All hands, boys included, worked at the windlass to free us up while the officious pilot tapped his foot and puffed impatiently on his cigarette.

Pa stood by the wheel. "We had a contract for a donkey engine to take care of just such problems," he grumbled. "I'm going to write that ship's broker as soon as we land and give him a piece of my mind."

Mother, standing at his side, didn't help. "Ralf, it's all your fault. You should have known right away before the ship left Gloucester that the motor wasn't there. Why didn't you pay attention? We could have got another one in Georgetown. So careless, really. I wonder what else you've 'forgotten.'"

The familiar parental bickering annoyed me, but the excitement of coming into our first foreign port quickly moved me forward and out of earshot. Straddling the bowsprit, I could see rays of light shining on the white sandy bottom forty feet below. The water was emerald green, so clean and clear, nothing like the darkness of Nantucket surf. On shore, tall palm trees pierced the heavy hot air. A proper fort, ancient and lichen-covered, stood at the entrance of the harbor, its cannon ports eyeing us suspiciously. The protected rows of pink houses behind the fort basked unafraid in the sun.

Tourist trade in the Bahamas and Caribbean was scant in 1933 compared to today. We came into a nearly empty harbor. Only one large steamer was unloading its cargo—hominy, we learned later. A few inter-coastal cargo schooners hung at anchor.

As soon as our anchor dropped, we were surrounded by a swarm of little rowboats manned by native boys in brief loincloths. They were only about eight years old and had come to dive for pennies. Up on the bowsprit, we looked down with awe at the shining bodies as they dove with great stamina to the bottom of the harbor and popped the coins we'd thrown there into their mouths for safekeeping. Nana, under her straw hat, which held to the top of her head with a big brown hairpin, tightened her hands together and addressed us firmly.

"Those boys shouldn't do that. They'll get terrible germs from those coins. You know, everyone knows, that coins are dirty, dirty, dirty. Don't you ever even think of putting coins in your mouths. Ugh! And be sure to always wash your hands after handling coins." Neither the boys in the water nor the admiring children on the ship paid any attention to her.

As we slowly motored into the harbor, looking for an anchorage, I was perfecting an image of myself as a glamorous wanderer. Quita and I were wearing our plaid gingham dresses. A band of felt flowers held back Quita's long ringlets. I kept rearranging bobby pins in my damp, frizzy hair, cut in a boyish bob, trying to settle it into a Clara Bow wave. I was practicing a new look, leaning my head back so my eyelids were half closed, to make me look sultry, yet still allowing me to see the boys diving. My mother shattered my world.

She came forward and announced to the crew and to her children that no one would go ashore until we had all our gear hung out to dry. In her most imperious voice, she confronted Chief.

"Now take your screwdriver, right away, and pry open the stuck bureau drawers. Then I want them soaped."

"Soaped?" Incredulous.

"Yes, soaped. I do that to my bureau drawers in Nantucket. It works. Rub the top of the sides of the drawers with soap. Then they'll slide in and out easily."

Flustered by Ma's tone of voice and the novelty of being ordered around by a woman, Chief dropped his screwdriver, and it rolled overboard. The captain mercifully stepped in and dressed him down for losing ship's equipment, anticipating Mother's tirade and sparing Chief a woman's scold. Then she turned her concentration on us.

"Just bring up all your clothes, all the bedding, mattresses too. Put everything out here in the sun. I want all our belongings dry on our return from shore."

What a degrading spectacle our trim ship was as she swung at anchor in her first foreign port, a floating laundry, a maritime boudoir, mattresses on the deckhouse, sheets over the boom, panties on the boom crotch, socks on the ratlines, my cotton underwear out there for all those men to see. Abandoning my sophisticated posturing, I wrinkled my nose in disgust and snarled, "Really, Mother!" She never even noticed my shame.

Ashore, I had to give up trying to be glamorous yet again; I could hardly walk. The sea giant had been dancing with me and left me out of step with the land. Houses leaned over me. Were they falling? Was this an earthquake? I clutched Quita, and Quita clutched me. Our walk down the main street, far from dignified—not even approximating grace—was a rolling stagger. I could smell a whiff of whisky from Quita and knew I smelled too, thanks to washing in the brownish water of Pa's unrinsed corn liquor casks. "Everyone'll think we're drunk," I lamented. And the questions came again: When, oh when, would I ever fit into a proper part? *Could* I ever fit into a proper part?

Ma and Pa were blessedly confident in their children and seemed blind to my bewilderment. They had always let us move about freely, sure we could take care of ourselves. At home, they did not specify deadlines for return after night parties or movies, and we didn't have to check in with them once we were home. We were only instructed in a firm voice to avoid the squeak in the stairs that would waken them. So when we landed in Nassau, it was no surprise to have them shoo us off on own adventures, while they tended to the business of grownups—passports, laundry, provisioning.

The five of us roamed off down the main street. "Coachies," black drivers with black horses, tailed us, clopping along, expectantly, persistently, dejectedly, waiting to catch our fare, urging us to "take a drive." "Take you to the Holy Rollers," they kept repeating. We waved them away for they seemed as sinister as hearses, and we had no wish to be associated with tourists, much less Holy Rollers.

Being children, we attracted children, in this port and all ports to follow, especially when grownups were tending to business and we were on our own. The young ones came from dark doorways and from behind walls, wordlessly, to touch us and at last to talk to us. They were unabashedly curious, and so were we.

A small black boy, matching Willy in height and shape, came up and stood before him. The two stared silently at each other. Then the boy, accepting Willy, gestured for the rest of us to follow him. He led us off through a maze of streets with no apparent end in mind. I made the growing crowd of kids halt, sitting down on a wall. I was startled by a scene that made me stop and think. There in the middle of the crossroad stood a tall, black policeman on a high structure under an umbrella. He wore a stiffly starched white tunic with gold epaulettes on the shoulders, black trousers with red stripes and a white pith helmet. A white pith helmet, to me, was the epitome of British imperialism, embedded in my visual memory by my favorite romantic movies—the likes of *The Charge of the Light Brigade*.

We had grown up in the culture of the Old South. At Nana's rice plantation on that coastal island off South Carolina, nothing much had changed since the Civil War as far as the routines of the rural days went. The families of household help and field workers lived on "The Street." They still spoke Gullah, a patois of African and old English. They pulled forelocks, sang strange African songs, and shuffled their feet back and forth as they danced on Christmas Eve. They'd lived generation after generation on our island, working the plantation, holding to their ways. It simply never had occurred to me that blacks functioned in other ways, and I stared at that policeman. He moved like an orchestra conductor, with precision and beauty. Everyone obeyed him. The British Empire had suddenly expanded my universe. Blacks could exercise power and authority. Blacks could, should, and would be obeyed. What a magical turnover of possibilities this was!

Back on board the *Blue Dolphin*, we read our mail from home. Mary Morris wrote that Sophie refused to go into Dalhousie without our being there. We felt the pain of our separation. She seemed so far away, back in the real old world, separated from us by the sea, the terrible dark storm, our new routines. Quita frowned as she heard the letter and put her head down, ready to cry.

Pa read us a Nassau newspaper. The stock market was still dropping in New York. The temperature in Nassau was 85 degrees, New York, 29. A short article on the back page told of Adolph Hitler leading the German election, promising peace through the Nazi Party and a policy of equality among nations. And even our party received recognition: "First Yacht of the Season Arrived Today. The British Yacht, *Blue Dolphin*, owned by Blue Dolphin, Ltd., of Nova Scotia, arrived in Nassau this morning with Mr. D. Claiudlerad and family aboard." Another lesson learned: Newspapers can be wrong.

Pa went on to read an article about Roosevelt, calling him, as usual, "Little Rosie." "That ridiculous Blue Eagle!" he exclaimed. The Blue Eagle was the symbol of Franklin Roosevelt's National Recovery Administration, the NRA. My grasp of politics was minimal, but I was caught up in the religious fervor for Roosevelt. Pa had read me enough about crusades and crusaders to make me perfectly comfortable with our vigorous new leader. Besides, every one knew that Roosevelt was paralyzed. Having been an invalid myself for so long, I thought of Roosevelt as triumphant over physical pain and handicap, and therefore able to lead his people, and me, out of the sickness of the Depression. I was beginning to discover that I liked to love men uncritically. And besides, it was fun making Pa mad.

"I like the Blue Eagle," I announced firmly. "It makes me brave. Roosevelt uses the symbol to ward off fear, and I think that's sensible."

Pa exploded. "Beware of symbols, Nina. Beware! They are too easy to devise and cheap to come by. They excite souls. They divide people, making them settle problems in a simplistic manner. You end up with goodies and baddies and life is much more complicated than that. Simpleminded reformers won't bring us peace on earth nor much good will toward men. They bring us the spirit of the Jesuits of the Inquisition and the *auto da fés*. They make ends justify the means. That type of reformer is sadistic, brutal in methods, fleecing the people of their rights. Symbols of Communism, democracy, capitalism, liberals, conservatives, Fascism, Nazism, falangists, pinks, red, etc. ad nauseam, whiz all about us like shots from six shooters in the hands of drunken cowboys in town for a Saturday night. Blue Eagle, indeed! It's our beautiful national bird being strangled by the red tape of bureaucracy. Its blood's stopped running. You'd go blue too if . . ."

I had turned away. I could only last a few sentences into Pa's tirades. My rudeness toward him didn't bother me. No matter how much I disagreed with him, I was sure he would never banish me, and, anyway, we always had so much left to resolve. Mother wasn't interested in politics so, as I grew older, I was becoming his favorite interlocutor. At least I would argue with him even if I didn't know much about the players in the political game, giving him a chance to tell anyone in striking distance his pet theories. Anyway, I had heard most of that speech before and was distracted by watching Mother cut Quita's hair. She was snipping off her long ringlets, worried that they would make Quita too hot. The resulting boyish bob, transformed her from a demure, fragile, gentle girl to a sunburned tomboy with a white neck.

Having practiced my preference for being oppositional, I let myself slip back into my perpetual problem of making myself up. The Nassau newspaper had declared us a yacht, but I did not want to be the yachting type. I was becoming a sailor pure and simple, a young female sailor. The newspaper notice might make its readers think of us as frivolous rich people on a vacationing yacht, but we were not. The storm, I believed, had initiated us to the real sea, not the social sea. As Pa had predicted when comforting Quita and me, seasick in our berths during the storm, we would not be fair-weather sailors at all, but seasoned explorers sailing out to learn about the world.

At this, our first port, we set precedent for the next three months of island hopping down the Antilles. We were about to start on the equivalent of the Grand Tour of Europe. The colonial cultures of each island had remained intact, as yet unspoiled by rows of hotels, motels, condominiums, and Americanized mobs. We would go from England to Spain, to France, to Denmark, to Holland, learning the various histories and cultures of Europe, led by our teacher and guide, Pa.

We spent three days in Nassau, with Pa giving us lessons on the British Empire and the natural history of the tropics. We gazed at a stunning array of fishes from a glass-bottomed boat; we hired an old Packard touring car to drive out into the country (which wouldn't go over twenty-five miles an hour and its mudguard grated against the wheel when we turned corners), and we explored dark caves once occupied by the pirate Blue Beard. I walked next to John, our new family member and the projected hero of my novel.

"Remember when Tom Sawyer and Becky Thatcher got lost in the cave?" I asked him. "Doesn't this remind you of that?"

He nodded. "Yep, I remember when they were in the cave and Injun Joe was after them." Well then, why didn't he catch on to the rest of the story? Why wasn't he offering me special glances as Tom did Becky, holding out his hand to lead me in the crepuscular light? Was John dumb, or was I?

We took time out from field trips to swim at Paradise Beach on Hog Island. No other living soul was there, but other kinds of life were plentiful. Our swims to and from the raft were greatly accelerated by the attention of sucker sharks.

"Those aren't really sharks," Nana explained to us quietly, "They attach themselves to bellies of sharks and tag along for the ride. The myth is that they kept ships afloat in the Middle Ages, saving them from shipwreck."

Nana's words of wisdom notwithstanding, when sucker sharks came kissing along our naked arms and legs, attaching to us, we shrieked and thrashed and tumbled out on the white sand in near hysteria. A shark was a shark.

Willy found a sleeping land crab and poked him into activity, crouching on his haunches as the crab rose up on its hind legs and achieved a frightening height of almost two feet. The two opponents faced each other in silence, feinting, darting, retreating, circling. The crab, bored, scuttled under a coral shelf, leading Willy to a pile of shells tucked into coral crannies. Such a profusion of portable treasures led to only one conclusion—collections! We walked back across Hog Island to our launch, laden with our new treasures, our hats, handkerchiefs, and towels filled with exotica. There were two drawbacks to our collections: We had very little space to store anything on board, and most of the shells were inhabited. Once aboard, the inhabitants crawled off to find new quarters, only to get lost, die, and stink.

On our second day in port, Sims and Smitty put up the awning. This heavy canvas was spread over the boom and tied to stanchions at the sides of the ship. Shaded by it, we lolled on deck. Our new tent house let me start up a novel line of thought—I was going on a long journey as a sailor, ending up in Persia where I lived as a houri in John's tented harem.

After every lunch we had rest period, a time cherished by Nana and Mother, and so made obligatory for the rest of us. One afternoon, I was stretched out on the top of the deckhouse reading *Anthony Adverse*. Quita and Willy were playing on the deck below me. They'd invented a new game called "Prisoner." The little shells from the new collections were lined up in rows. They were the prisoners. A big sea urchin shell was the jailer. He was bossing the prisoners around. The boys were below reading. I saw Nana turn the collar of her green seersucker dress inside out to keep it clean and her neck cool. She and mother were lying nearby on canvas cushions. Mother was speaking softly to Nana.

"You know how worried I've been about Ralf? He was so depressed after that Bellanca fiasco. Remember how he used to mope around? He never seemed to be able to pick himself up, but now I think this trip is really occupying his mind, and he's alive again. I think he's earned new respect from the children and all those men down at the Yacht Club. That's so important, don't you think?"

Nana didn't respond. Mother continued.

"And I did like the way he treated the little girls during the storm, tucking them in like that and fussing over them. He was in charge again."

I was waiting for her to talk about "The Other Woman," since I assumed she was also relieved to know that Pa was on the high seas and far from the commuter train to New York, but this was not mentioned. Was it an unmentionable?

I was surprised to hear Mother confess that she had worried about Pa when he was fired. I hadn't noticed that. I only remembered that astonishing crying act about the New York woman and all the bickering. That she should express such warm love was something new for me to take into consideration. And another thing baffled me. I never thought I had respect for Pa, much less lost it. And I didn't have disrespect for him either. I argued with him for fun. He was just Pa, my father.

Mother's voice dropped even further as she changed the subject abruptly with no transition, a well-established habit of hers, and declared, "I don't trust that Charlie. What kind of a cook is he? We've been here for days and I order fresh vegetables and fruits, and we still get canned peas, canned pears, always canned food. I asked nicely for plain fruit for dessert but he serves us blueberry pie from canned blueberries. His answers to me are rude. Really!" This was said in the same tone of voice she used when she was mad at Pa. I guessed Mother's left eyebrow was rising, that sure sign of a threatening storm, but I didn't want to look at her for fear of closing down their conversation.

"Well," Nana interjected soothingly, "the children don't mind. How they defended Charlie's pie against the pieces we were served at that restaurant last night! Didn't Willy have a flea on his piece there?"

The discussion was growing boring. I put down *Anthony Adverse* and picked up my journal. I was seven years old when I first began writing a life history. I was sick then, as usual, and the sun was shining. The room had just been dry mopped, and I was in my bed, propped up by pillows, alone in the room, staring at myriad sparkles of dust—a cloud slowly, softly rising on the ray of sunshine over my bed. I focused on one infinitesimal speck and gave it a name. As the speck rose up out of the beam of light, I decided to write the story of its adventures, following it magically out into the wide unknown and mysterious far-off world. Now, at thirteen, I was going to write about my own going out into the world. I had become my speck of dust and I would write about my own adventures. I had risen up out of my perpetual sickbed and set forth in the sunlight into the unknown. I would write my life story. I soon found out, regretfully, that this took a lot of time, time that I could have used playing around, but I persevered. I wrote down each day's experience in my journal.

After a while, I got up to stretch and walked forward to talk to Ted, our mess boy from Nantucket. I sat down on the hatch cover beside him. All the crew had been on shore leave, and I was curious about what they did when they went ashore. I noted with pleasure that Pa had taken Ted aside before he left the ship and given him a wad of bills. Pa noticed that I saw this exchange and took me to the stern, explaining, "We agreed at the outset of the trip that Ted wouldn't be on salary, so now I just want to be sure he has a good time ashore." Pa followed this procedure at every port.

Ted sat silently splicing rope. I decided I had to ask him directly about his adventures. "So," I began, "how was Nassau last night?" Ted looked at me and smiled. "Well, Sims and I hired a 'coachie', a seagoing hack if I ever saw one." He stopped and lit a cigarette. "We drove out into the country where we met a march. Did you kids know it was Guy Fawkes Day? Your Pa teach you about that? Well, that was some mob, beating drums, ringing bells, and they carried an effigy of Guy Fawkes. They kept crushing in on us demanding cigarettes. I thought they'd sweep us off the road, horse, coach, and all, but I kept them calm by shaking hands with Guy Fawkes and playing the fool. When we got back to town, the mobs were out of hand. Did you hear the racket out here? Let me tell you, the jails were full last night, but in spite of it all, we managed to get a cool glass of beer before we came back aboard. It was a great night, all in all."

Charlie stuck his head up the forward companionway at that moment and demanded Ted's assistance, and I got up and moved back to the stern.

That night Mother let us bring our mattresses on deck so we could sleep in the cool air. On shore a police band played for little black girls in cotton dresses dancing around a Maypole, but I was back in Persia, in the tented home of houris.

6

Our Classical Education Begins

P A'S MUCH-HERALDED schooling began in earnest after we left Nassau. He was sure the proper classical education he was about to deliver would lead us to good living, delight our souls, and keep us going onward and upward forever. His brand of education would not only increase our knowledge but would also provide our minds with the necessary tools for creative activity. Immortality would come to us when we recognized our own genius, our ability to create and re-create and live forever through brotherhood with all men and women through all time. Since God, the divine engineer, had invented the universe and then stepped away, our job was to discover His laws so we could make His universe run efficiently. God, after all, was off doing other things (I never could figure out where He'd gone) and needed us to run the world on our own and do it well. To Pa, our souls and God's mind were duplicates. It followed that education could never be dull or sterile. Education was fruition and joy. He quoted Emerson: "Thought is the blossom, language the bud; action the fruit behind."

Remembering his classes at his public high school in Brookline, Massachusetts, and at Harvard, Pa set out to give us a disciplined, rigorous consumption of material with plenty of memorizing. He thought mathematics, English, history, and Greek and Latin should be taught at the earliest possible age. Other foreign languages and science were not of immediate concern. The teachers at our progressive school had skipped some of these subjects, however. They believed their pupils would ripen through some inner, propelling growth and should not be disturbed or distracted by forced study or overwork. They wanted us to be comfortable about ourselves, enjoying every day, learning best through self-expression in free activity. At our progressive school, we absorbed math functions by building and running a store, The Pooh Store, selling candied apples and crackers to our schoolmates, watching profits and loss. Field trips to steel refineries and the Campbell Soup factory gave us a glimpse of the world of work. I knew school with Pa would be different. He always said it would be, but I was innocently unaware that these two schools of educational philosophy would crash into each other at our saloon table, giving my brain a jolting concussion.

School started each morning as soon as the table was cleared of breakfast dishes and our chores accomplished. Pa's pupils sat around the dining table with texts, lined pads, and pencils rising and falling before us. Pa was at the head of the table in his captain's chair. He started our lessons, that first day out of Nassau, with instructions and work for Al and John in Latin. Willy and Quita were doing appropriate arithmetic for their age, and I was at the end of the table on the corner couch with my algebra book before me. Algebra was new to me. I had few mathematical skills, having been absent so often from school because of my asthma; and, when in school, picking up random math techniques when serving behind the counter of The Pooh Store. I really did not know my times tables. Nevertheless, I wanted to learn algebra. I liked to explore the unknown. I skimmed the first pages of the text that explained the use of letters as symbols of numbers in their relationships and found one problem I liked a lot. I concentrated my powers on it to be ready for Pa when my turn came.

A man was paddling up a river at so many miles an hour and the current was flowing against him at so many miles an hour, so how long would it take him to get from one point to the other? I had the man well in mind as Pa came to my end of the table. My man was stripped to the waist, tall, well-built, deeply tanned. The river was in the tropics, filled with floating logs and muddy—the Amazon perhaps. The banks were lush, dangerous, with dank jungles spreading out as far as the eye could see. Inhabited, yes, of course, by the family and friends of my pickled savage, George. Would these savages catch the man making his way up river? Would the piranhas eat him if he tipped over? Would it work against him if he paddled into a back-eddy? What if a log swerved his bow out of the current? Who was meeting this handsome man, sweating in the tropic heat? What was his designated end? My mind was racing with variables, no letters yet, as Pa leaned over me.

"Well, Noonsie, let's solve this problem. Transcribe it, please, into letters so we can know the time factor."

I stared at him dumbly. He made another attempt, this time with pad and pencil, to introduce me to symbols of quantities and magnitudes and operations and their relations. I went on staring at him without comprehension. He had broken the spell of my precious adventure. His face began to show disgust, a look I had not run into before in a teacher. What vague grasp I had of skimmed directions disappeared as Pa and I suffered mutual shock trying to get that man up the river, each in his or her own inimically differing logical way. Finally, I wept in despair for being so stupid, so inadequate, and so enraged at my father for his inability to get to the core of the problem. Pa hated tears. He skirted sorrows. He took me gently by the arm, leading me to Mother in her stateroom.

As we walked the short passage, he quoted Emerson yet again, "Our greatest glory is not in never failing, but in rising up every time we fail." I sniveled in response. "Carol, Nina is having a hard time with her algebra. Here try her out on this," he said, handing over a storybook with pretty pictures written in French. She looked at it and looked at Pa with a sweet smile. She wasn't used to seeing Pa fail with his children or being trusted to teach one of them an academic subject. He had come to her for help, and she was pleased. She sat me on her stiff triangular bench, handed me the textbook and announced with authority, "I will teach you French." And she did.

We forgot all about classical education when we emerged on deck after lunch out in the sunshine ready for vocational training. Pa insisted that each one of us share responsibility for the ship, so we were soon part of the working crew. The patient captain taught us our first lesson: how you get to where you want to go. He lined us up and instructed us quietly in the use of the sextant, the mysteries of "shooting the sun," and how to navigate. Then he went on to explain the flowering petals of the compass rose under the brass binnacle in front of the wheel. "Now, Alfred, you start. Show us how you can steer this ship correctly. Keep that lubber line steady and take us southeast by south, a half south. O.K., hold it there. Don't let it wobble off course. And remember: The compass never lies." He surveyed his pupils. "Willy, what did I just tell you?"

"The compass never lies."

"Good. Never forget that. It may be the most important lesson you'll learn on this trip."

All the young were soon steering the ship on daytime watches. Willy, sitting on the deck housing, had to use his toes as well as his hands to turn the big wheel. It took skill and strength to keep the little figures of the compass rolling under the shiny binnacle, directly under the true line that marked our course. The force of the wind, the current and the strength of waves against the prow kept pushing the big schooner off course. We had to concentrate and physically fight to make the *Blue Dolphin* follow the path the captain commanded.

Pa, busy with navigation and being in charge, didn't seem to bother with Mother's contrasting influence on our education (when she wasn't under instruction to teach a formal subject like French). She wanted us to grow on our own. Forget the drill. Afternoons were her time to teach.

"Here, little girls, I'll let you use my good sketch paper. Take these pastels and colored pencils and draw me something. Willy, you can draw, too."

Willy covered his pages with explosions, guns, rockets, and crashing airplanes, foreshadowing the day when he would be a lone pilot in a Grumman F6F Hellcat training to fly off the deck of an aircraft carrier in World War II. Willy also liked to invent ingenious objects out of string, matchsticks, and the wooden spools of thread that ultimately looked like tractors.

Mother shook her head when I showed her my drawings. I drew floor plans of square houses. The first floor always had a large ballroom and a smaller music room. "Nina, why do you always draw compositions that are so static? I keep telling you to use dynamic symmetry." Her tone was one of patience tried. "Organize your drawings so that they are slightly off balance to hold attention and make the mind search for new stability. Your productions are forever square. Boring."

Mother's repeatedly calling Quita and me "little girls," especially right there in front of the men on watch, made me mad. I wasn't a little girl. I was a woman. I had "the curse." When would she ever catch on? This "little girl" was in no mood to hear her criticisms of my handiwork. I growled as Mother moved over to Quita with relief, knowing that Quita had the principle of dynamic symmetry without even having to be taught. I received approval only when Quita helped me draw scenes of green palm trees and sandy beaches that we then transferred onto cloth to make into cross-stitched samplers.

Left to ourselves in the late afternoon, we quickly established a routine of games, usually played below in the saloon. We kept up roulette and added poker. I relied on George, mounted there on the wall above us, to intercede for me. We did a lot of roughhousing, knocking each other about. Willy and I had a daily wrestling match on deck by the binnacle. Each one of us was able to tie the other up in knots, taking advantage of double-jointedness, urged on by Al who had seen professional wrestling matches at the Nantucket Fairgrounds, where he'd cheered Mountain Man as he fought The Yellow Peril. "Rub his back!" Al would shout, or "Give her the knuckles!" Willy grew so adept in defending his fat little self against his big brother and sister that, in due course, he became the interscholastic wrestling champion of Philadelphia.

Just as I was getting to be the wrestling champion of the ship, Ma stopped me. She took me aside, after I had pinned Willy and lay on top of him, and whispered, "Nina, you'll have to stop this wrestling, that positioning, especially here in front of the men." I liked her conspiratorial tone, but had no idea what she was talking about. That night, picking up *Anthony Adverse*, I read: "On the bed the youth and the young girl slept as

one in being, their curls and legs tangled together as if they lay on an island beach washed by the ocean of Nirvana." I never wrestled with Willy
again. I could see there was more to wrestling than our deck tangling and
began to contemplate exploring that other ocean, Nirvana.

For all of us the most pleasant teaching and learning came with the
constant reading aloud by Nana and Pa. Nana read before supper and Pa
took over in the evening. The first book Pa read was Coleridge's *Rime of
the Ancient Mariner*. We sailed along at dusk, grouped around Pa on deck
as he read:

> *The ship was cheered, the harbor cleared;*
> *Merrily did we drop*
> *Below the kirk, below the hill,*
> *Below the lighthouse top.*
> *And now the stormblast came,*
> *And he was tyrannous and strong;*
> *He struck with his o'ertaking wings,*
> *And chased us south along.*

I stirred comfortably on my canvas pillow. How close we were, the
Mariner and I, so far . . . go on, go on, Pa, don't stop . . . that noise you
just heard—that's just the sail luffing as the wind slacks. Pa picked up
again, swooping majestically over the waves of the ballad line:

> *And now there came both mist and snow,*
> *And it grew wondrous cold;*
> *And ice, mast-high, came floating by,*
> *As green as emerald.*
> *The ice was here,*
> *The ice was there,*
> *The ice was all around;*
> *It cracked and howled,*
> *And roared and howled,*
> *Like noises in a swound!*

"Are we g-g-gong to g-g-get into ice?" asked a frightened Quita.

"The Mariner went too far, Quita," said Pa, hastening to allay her fears. "He has gone on down to the South Pole, around the Horn. We won't go that far. We're going through the Panama Canal." A short intermission followed while Pa gave us a brief geography lesson. Quita was ready to continue.

Yea, slimy things did crawl with legs
Upon the slimy sea. . . .
The water, like a witch's oils,
Burned green, and blue, and white.

Pa warmed to the horror of the ghost ship sailing by, of death and the mate casting the die on the deck, and the Mariner sucking blood from his arm to slake his thirst. Shy, sensitive Quita visibly paled and interrupted the reading.

"Is th-th-this . . . t-t-r-r-ue?" I glanced at her. This reading was awakening the dark forces that swept through her dreaming mind in the darkness of Nana's cabin. The next night, at supper, Quita toyed with her food and turned her head with tight closed lips when Mother, worried, pressed another bit of canned peas on her.

7

Discovering America

W E WERE APPROACHING Watling, or San Salvador Island, in the Bahamas, when Pa took up another important aspect of our education: making sure we knew the history of each port we visited.

"History," intoned Pa, as we gathered to go below for supper, "is the greatest source of truth. The march of progress becomes reality before your eyes. And, by the way, if you want to know how people think about their country, just read the history books they teach in their schools. Now, come on, children. We'll take our seats and have a history lesson about San Salvador, Christopher Columbus, and his discoveries of the New Indies."

Pa's history lesson, however, was briefly interrupted. The wind was pushing the water into curling heaps, so when we came below we found the books thrown out on the floor again, and Al, arriving last and struggling to take off his sweatshirt, lost his balance and staggered against the tipping table. Glasses of milk slid to the floor accompanied by clattering silverware, plates, honey jars, butter, and molasses. A clucking Charlie emerged from the galley and, with a laughing Ted, cleaned us up. We made a chain gang and soon had the books behind racks and the floor tidied as we readied ourselves for San Salvador and Columbus. It was too rough to sit in chairs so Al and John crowded in with Quita, Willy, and me on the long bench running against the side of the ship. All went well until a particularly high wave tossed the ship over on its side and sent the table hard on our knees. This time, two cups of hot cocoa flew into Quita's and my faces, and a piece of mince pie fell neatly into my lap.

Not to be held back by sea or storm, Pa continued with his lesson.

"Before you can understand why Columbus set off in the *Niña*, *Pinta*, and *Santa Maria*, you have to know what was going on in Spain in the fifteenth century."

How like Pa, I thought. He keeps going backward as if he had to have a long running start before he could leap into the present. Why did it take him all that time to get to the exciting part, the here and now? I was having no trouble at all in being Columbus or one of his crew, so I wanted to get on with the landing, what with the food flying here and there and all five children squashed together.

"Spain was in a depression. King Ferdinand of Aragon and Queen Isabella of Castile joined their kingdoms and fought the gloom of the period by experimenting with expansion and discovery, thus changing the course of history, leading their country and all of Europe to prosperous, triumphant times."

Pa digressed again to imply that our little family was doing the right thing by our national depression too, and then, at last, we got to the good part.

"The trip across the unknown ocean had been hard. Their ships were even smaller than ours, you know. The *Santa Maria* was only seventy-five feet long. Mutiny was brewing. A gale was blowing up. Now Columbus was a quiet man, redheaded, you know, and he was trying to calm his men by promising to turn back to Spain if they didn't find land in three days. He also promised a large bounty for the first man to sight land. He knew what he was doing, for he had picked up a new scent in the air, and new, strange birds had appeared. At dusk, Columbus won his own reward by sighting a light on San Salvador. The rejoicing on the caravels was great, but Columbus decided not to anchor for fear of reefs, so they hove to, working back and forth along the coast awaiting dawn."

"You know what?" I chirped in, "I wrote up my journal this afternoon and put in about those weird birds that flew by, the ones with yellow wings and striped bellies. Remember? I bet those were the same birds that clued Columbus to the approach of land."

"Mr. Chandler," asked John, "Are you going to give Mr. Doyle a reward? He sighted San Salvador at dusk."

"He who knows history does not have to repeat it," replied Pa.

But we did repeat a good deal of history. We, too, hove to off shore, watching the blinking lights of a village, the wind blowing too hard to anchor. "That island looks just like Nantucket," Ted said, rather wistfully, as he brought us warm newly baked bread.

Right after breakfast, Pa announced, "It's time for the lesson of the day. We will now go meet the natives!" The natives had gathered on the shore to eye our arrival as they had for Columbus. I was disappointed to see that they were properly dressed, not naked as they had been when Columbus landed. Three little dugouts had come to our ship, one with sail, the others sculled. Nana, Mother, and I went in a dugout while Al, John, Quita, Willy, Pa, Sims, and Smitty went off in our long boat. I remembered from an old history book that the Spaniards had come ashore armed and carrying the tall banners of Ferdinand and Isabella marked with F and Y on each side of a cross and a crown over each initial. I wanted to visualize myself under such a banner, but having Mother and Nana on each side of me on the thwart in their simple dresses, brown lisle stockings, and sensible brown leather shoes kept me firmly in the present.

We were greeted with the same dignified warmth that Columbus described. Like Columbus, we found the natives to be unusually handsome and friendly. No white people lived on this island with the exception of the Catholic priest, Father Dennis, who was off the island at the time. Columbus and his men traded beads. John tried taking a photograph. Beads had gone over better, however. The camera frightened a little girl who ran and hid behind her mother. We walked to the great lake that Columbus described and watched the wind-driven foam pile up on the far shore.

From that day forward, every celebration of Columbus Day has bought back rich, almost palpable memories, including the scent of the dainty flowers that Nana and Quita bought back to the ship. I know what it is to discover America.

8

Field Trips
and Other Explorations

As we prepared to leave San Salvador, Captain, maneuvering the ship to run in towards shore to pick up some of the family, who were off swimming, veered off to leeward ready to jibe and reach back. As he gained speed, a sudden sickening lurch shook us. The ship rose up out of the water, teetering, unbalanced.

"Oh Lord!" screamed Nana, holding onto her straw hat, "Stop that!"

"Jesus!" groaned Captain, seizing the wheel that had spun out of his hands. "Chief! Chief! Full speed ahead! Sims! Smitty! Ready to come over! Coming over! Hard a lee!"

Busy writing in my journal on the deckhouse, I dropped my pencil and stared at the sea, expecting a giant octopus to emerge. I thought he had gripped our keel and would pick up our ship, dashing us to oblivion.

"Sir!", snapped Nana, "that was coral. You have ruined the bottom of this ship!"

"Oh, no, Madam," answered the mollifying Captain, "That was sand. Cleaned the barnacles off our bottom. Good thing. Yes, I know, I know. It was a scare, but we've been lucky again."

Early the next morning we reached Landrail Point on Crooked Island and found that our schooling routines would be infinitely varied. I was learning that Pa could be generously flexible in spite of his commitment to routine classical education. Two friendly men had rowed out to greet us; they took charge of our long boat and rowed us to a tiny beach, the only landing place along the jagged coral coast. The usual band of curious children awaited our landing. We set off, single file, to walk to town about a half mile away, each with his own escort. Pa led the way, joined by a man who introduced himself as Mr. MacFarland.

"How did you ever get a Scottish name like that?" inquired Pa.

"Well, sir, many years ago a Scot, name of MacFarland, came out here to this island, and when he left there were quite a few Scots named Mac-Farland in these parts." Pa laughed, shook his hand warmly, and invited him out to spend the next day on our ship.

There were a few problems with this man's statement that I didn't quite get. How many MacFarlands? All by one wife? If not, by whom? Pa seemed to know. Why didn't I?

Willy came next in our marching line, surrounded by a band of little boys, then Al, John, Quita, and me. The girl who attached herself to me asked me my name.

"My name is Nina," I answered.

Like a swarm of buzzing gnats, a growing band of girls moved around me, humming "Ninaninaninanina . . ." The girls turned to surround Quita.

"What's your name?

Quita shut down in shyness and sidled closer to me. She could not answer. She stood and smiled quizzically, her brows tight. The girls were puzzled and turned to me.

"Why don't she talk? Don't she like to talk? Ax her to tell us."

"She's shy and her name is Quita."

The girls began to hum a dancing welcome for her too. Mother and Nana followed us. I could hear Mother telling a comfortable looking woman all about Sophie. A lugubrious old man had attached himself to Nana, reciting the oft-told horrors of recent hurricanes and tidal waves.

Our history teacher, "Mr. Chandler," spotted a likely-looking ruin for class discussion, so we detoured off the road, Pa instructing us all the while on triangular trade routes, how the ships carried slaves from Africa to these islands and then came on to New England with rum and sugar. He told us about the cultural development of the islands, how the plantation system worked, how English traditions of law and order were rooted here, all planted by the settlers. Pa made us understand this with our mind's eye. Our eyes caught the flicker of green light from a lizard darting across our path and the gentle gossamer flight of dainty butterflies that drifted beside us.

Up early the following morning, I was ready for new exploration and lessons. Darting out of my stateroom, I scrambled up the companionway and shrieked. There, poised on the companionway sill, coming at me, was a huge land turtle. Of course, I was chagrined to realize, a stuffed turtle. Placed there by Sims and Smitty, it had duped me. They stood by the wheel, laughing at me. I tried to regain dignity by admiring their find, but quickly turned to meet five black men, including Mr. MacFarland. They seemed to be settling down for a morning visit. Two more men were tied up astern, fishing from their dugout. Obviously, fishing was the morning lesson, so out came our lines. We applied ourselves without comment, happy to be relieved of class work at the saloon table.

Quita was the triumphant one on this day. She pulled in a metallic blue parrotfish, looking disarmingly like a frightened, open-mouthed Roman senator. "Just the color of Mary Morris's blue delphinium in the box garden!" exclaimed Nana, delighted by its iridescent glistening. This remark, and the memories it brought to Quita, led her to her magic world of artistic creation. She walked quietly and politely over to Mr. MacFarland, and asked him to scale the fish. Then she ran below and opened our bureau drawer with the collection of tiny "prisoner" shells hidden in the corner, selecting those suited to her scheme. Like a medieval miniaturist, she sat on the deckhouse with her dazzling specks of color about her, the bright blue scales, red scales from Al's snapper, tones of tan and brown from John's grouper. She designed a tiny garden of flowers set in a mosaic of shells, pasted for posterity on the stiff cardboard taken from Pa's starched shirt. When she finished, and we had all admired her delicate work, she wrapped her creation in tissue paper and saved it to send to Sophie at the next mail port.

That afternoon, Pa and the boys sailed to town in a loose-footed sailing craft borrowed from our native friends. They planed over the rollers toward shore, an exciting new sailing experience for them. On their return, they reported on their visit to a small village. Only one house had an intact roof following the last hurricane, maybe the same hurricane we had lived through. Best of all, they returned with large quantities of fresh food. That night we had Sunday dinner on Monday night, fresh-killed chicken, fresh squash, new potatoes and fresh, ripe cherries. Mother was triumphant.

Having spent a lot of her life on a farm, Mother was convinced that fresh food was not only easily available at all times, but absolutely essential for her children's growing bodies. She was sure that produce in cans lost vitamin content and absorbed injurious elements from the tin that would kill us off young, if not poison us overnight.

But then there was Charlie. Charlie cooked three meals a day for fifteen people at staggered intervals, forty-five servings a day. He cooked in a tiny galley over a coal-burning six-burner stove with the temperatures in the galley climbing towards 120 degrees. He stood in his cramped space, his lean body bent, dressed in his ever-faithful blue carpet slippers, his stained white trousers and his huge, all-encompassing white apron. With appropriate swear words for additional flavoring, he cooked our meals. He did all the baking, loaves and loaves of bread, rows and rows of pies, in and out of the oven all day long. Understandably, then, he was in no mood to fuss with finicky lettuces and greens, or bother paring vegetables and cutting fruit. S. S. Pierce provided such food in tins ready to eat. After a few weeks of heavy, starchy meals, with fresh vegetables burned or cooked into a dreary wilt, Mother and Charlie were barely able to speak to each other.

"He did it on purpose, the wretch! Ruined that meal!" Mother would exclaim in earshot of Charlie. We children tried to cover up her indignation with loud conversation. Pa didn't say much, apparently enjoying the shift of direction of Mother's invective. He made it clear, however, in soft tones directed at us, that he sympathized with Charlie.

In the end, it was Ted who became the peacemaker. He offered to take all of Mother's menus, her problems of supply, and her suggestions about cooking fresh vegetables to Charlie in writing. Any remarks Charlie might want to relay to Mother were digested, translated and cleaned up by the understanding Ted and delivered to Ma in the stern. This plan worked so effectively it continued for the entire voyage. Though confined together on a hundred-foot-long ship, Mother and Charlie rarely encountered or spoke to each other again.

And it was the magic Ted who also somehow managed to get permission from our vigilant mother to take Quita and me into the forbidden territory of the crew's quarters. He bellowed the announcement that women were coming as he led us forward past the huge 110 H. P. Cooper Bessemer diesel engine filling the center of the ship, past the captain's port cabin with its own head, and into Charlie's galley. Ted spoke with authority.

"You can see there is no room here. You could swing a cat by its tail and endanger all of its nine lives at once in this space. Look over here to port: here's the water tank, and all this space is for storage. Coal there is stored next to our sink, just to remind me that dirt is always near me to clean up." The six-burner stove stood amidships before the mainmast. As we moved to the starboard side, Ted continued his travelogue. "Now here's the electric fridge and ice machine. It's run by a diesel-generating outfit, too, like the main engine. Get past this mess table and you can look into the fo'c's'le—that's where I sleep, on one of those upper bunks. All the rest of the space, from past the head to the bow of this ship, is filled with anchor chain. I don't see why they didn't make my berth longer. That would have lessened the space for the anchor chain that we have to pull up by hand at each port. The damned thing weighs a ton, you know. Now if you go down that little corridor to starboard, you get to Charlie and Chief's cabin. They live in style."

That afternoon, we sailed south again. The wind came up and drove us by two enormous coral rocks with surf crashing ominously over them. Off to leeward we saw the symmetrical abstract pylon of a lighthouse banded by three red stripes and with cubes of bungalows at its base. Since we had slacked on our morning schooling, we were put to Latin and mathematics before supper. When the stars sparkled in the clear black sky that night, Nana told us again about the constellations. I had loved standing out on the lawn at Dalhousie barefoot in the cool night dew listening to Nana describe the figures in the stars. Now she was introducing us to the Southern Giants, the Scorpion and the Wolf. Swift, jagged heat lightning caught the line of my vision and threw it back to the horizon.

9

Love Lessons

I WAS UP at six the next morning. I'd studied our route the night before and noted that we would pass Great Iguana Light at dawn. I ran eagerly on deck hoping to catch a glimpse of it. I was disappointed. We had hit an oily calm and were moving slowly, slowly, ghosting along under the power of our small throbbing auxiliary. Already the sun held sway over the sky and sea. Not a cloud absorbed the glare, not a piece of land punctured the shimmering light waves on the horizon. Our sails were useless, slatting and flapping. The pennants hung limp from the mastheads. I looked disconsolately at a tanker rapidly overtaking us from the stern. My envy made me scornful of the powerful motors that drove the tanker's bow through the sheer blue silk sea with its knifelike slice. Off to starboard, a large liner marked off its miles while we creaked along perspiring, limp in the heat. Beads of sweat rose on the leather seats in the saloon.

Nevertheless, the rule held. School started after breakfast. We obediently went to the table for our studies. The temperature was 108 degrees in the fo'c's'le, 90 degrees in the airless saloon, but study we must. Pa, finally, grasping that the heat was dulling our minds, took pity on us, excused classes early and after a light lunch, let us read on deck. We were admonished to be extra quiet, for the men off watch were sleeping in the lifeboats, recovering from a sleepless night up forward.

Toward the end of naptime, Pa came over to me where I sat alone by the bowsprit, absorbed by Anthony Adverse's newest love affair. He squatted beside me.

"Nina," he was almost whispering, although no one was in earshot. He wasn't looking at me. His gaze seemed to be on a far horizon.

"Your mother tells me she was upset about my being in New York with my friend, and that she told you about it." Told me! She'd been sobbing. There was a difference. "I don't want you to have any misperceptions about my behavior. Let me assure you, there was no hanky-panky." He stopped and studied my face to gauge my reaction. "The lady I was visiting," he continued, "is an old dear friend of mine from my Brookline childhood. She used to come to our dancing class that was held in our house on Washington Street. She's a physician and practices in New York, and I do love to check in on her when I can. That's what you do with friends. Keep track of them. But really, your mother has no cause whatsoever to be upset about these visits." There were a few moments of silence. Then he added in a softer tone, "I just wanted you to know so you wouldn't worry." I was embarrassed. I said nothing and just smiled a distancing but accepting smile, not that he was looking at me. Pa had never revealed anything about his private life to me before. I didn't want to know about it. And what was "hanky-panky" anyway? Why didn't he understand that I hadn't been worried? I was just curious about what would make Ma cry. Pa patted me on the shoulder and slipped off to the stern.

Did Ma really think Pa, my father, who, as far as I was concerned, was a sexless object, was in love with someone else and playing around with sex? Watching the rhythmic waves, lulled by their slap-slap sound against the bow, my mind drifted off to another love affair of a different kind altogether, my unrequited passion for Leopold Stokowski.

Long ago, back in Delaware, when my asthmatic breathing was under control, Mother would take me on Friday afternoons to Symphony Hall in Philadelphia to hear the Philadelphia Orchestra. Nana had subscription tickets for a box lined with dark red damask and with red velvet chairs. This box was the first in the circle and overlooked the stage. I could look into the wings too. I was sure I was now old enough to be seriously in love with Leopold Stokowski, the orchestra's floridly handsome conductor. But Mother spoiled my dreams by telling me in whispers, with a slight lascivious smile, about Stokowski's love affair with the beautiful tall woman who strode down the aisle below us in a floor-length mink coat just before the music started, the house lights dimming. She presented an insurmountable problem to me. How would Stokowski ever notice me with that elegant creature right at his feet? Up on my red velvet perch, looking down, I would kick my sensible brown brogues against the silky damask and dream up a fire in the wings that only I could spot. Before his girlfriend could notice, I would sound the alarm and save Stokowski. He would have to reward me, wouldn't he? And then, a splash of cold spray hit my face. I went back to reading about Anthony Adverse, my father having long since left my mind.

By 4:30, the children could be contained no longer. We exploded into action and followed the well-laid plans we'd been hatching all day long. We raced below and put on bathing suits. Back on deck we tied ropes to bucket handles and then knotted the other rope ends around our waists. Flinging the buckets overboard, we filled them and hauled them back in, ready to douse each other with shrieks of glee. Oh glorious relief! We lay on deck, holding our noses, rolling, trying to line up every plane of our bodies for a cooling wash. Willy poured water on the deck, threw himself on his knees, and slithered down the slope to the scuppers, and we all imitated him. Finally, the decibels reached too penetrating a pitch, and we were ordered below to dress for supper. Al and John reappeared self-consciously in khaki shorts, a change from their long pants.

"Boy Scouts! Boy Scouts! Nyaa, Nyaa, Nyaa!" I hooted. With great pleasure, I noticed that John was blushing through his sunburn. I did have power over him after all.

That night, after reading, we children huddled together on the deckhouse and began to tell each other stories. We started with simple ghost stories, remembered from sessions in deep dark closets at home. This storytelling hour, with the grownups far in the stern, became one of our happiest times. Al was the star creator. As the voyage went on, he led us through the serial adventures of Bilgewater in Boarding School, Wild and

Wooly at Sea and then the epic Wrinklebelly saga—Wrinklebelly and the Giant Ants, Wrinklebelly in Africa, on and on with Wrinklebelly.

As we listened this night to Al solve a murder, a huge cloud formed dead ahead, looking like a black velour curtain, ready at any moment to be thrust over us and smother us.

"So, the dead man's body is on a narrow bed in a small, square bedroom." Al said, "His eyes are popping out and his tongue is hanging down his jaw. No evidence of violence. No blood. So what killed him?" No one could answer. "Carbon monoxide, that's what killed him. It was piped up through the spring and mattress right under the pillow."

At that moment, John, sensing the story over and wanting to exorcise the mood, sprang to his feet, hunched his shoulders, swung his arms like an ape, and was King Kong. We shrieked and scuttled off in a spray of activated children. Quita fell over a chair in the saloon and wailed. I jarred the censorious Mr. Doyle, standing at the chart table, as I rushed past him into the damp slicker closet, slamming the door and holding my breath to keep out the smell of salt, sweat, rubber, and any carbon monoxide that might be piped in, transfixed by the sheer joy of continuing the ghostly horror and hoping I was pursued by John.

A cry, "All hands!" bought children and crew together on deck. The black velour curtain was indeed coming down on us. Captain, fearing a wind squall, shouted out his command: "Lower all sails!" I was disappointed when only rain and sparklers of heat lightning came, but the rain cooled our bodies and our ardor, and we were ready for bed.

10

We Lay Siege
to La Citadelle

Q UITA, NOW BACK in her bunk below me, was struggling impatiently
with the rope of her wrapper. The electrical current of landfall running through the ship had awakened her. She transmitted the charge to
me in the dim dawn. I hurried up the companionway behind her,
whistling in awe at the sight of mountains, mounds of mystery, rising up
before us out of the murky brown sea. Haiti, purple and pink in the light
of the rising sun, stood silent under cumulus clouds towering in clumps
over the mountains. These clouds had the distinct shape and color of the
familiar illustrations of N. C. Wyeth. We were running along the coast
heading for the harbor of Cap-Haitien. Still eight miles off the island, we
submitted peacefully to the order to go below, get dressed, and eat breakfast, which we did hurriedly so we could run on deck again to wonder at
this new grandeur before us.

We sailed past a three-masted barkentine riding at anchor under the
great green mountain of Morne Glorie and prepared to drop anchor ourselves. Before we could do this, however, we had to follow the usual proto-
col and wait for the harbor master's inspection of our ship. He was rowed
out to us, sitting sedately in the stern of the boat, black and stunning in
his immaculate white uniform, his eyes obscured behind enormous
tortoiseshell sunglasses. I squinted at another boat following the harbor

master, the one carrying the port doctor, imagining him to be a French colonial official in a galley manned by sweating slaves. Illusion evaporated when he stepped on board, however. He was a uniformed American Marine, Dr. Monc.

"Pa, Pa," I badgered the poor man, "why an American doctor? How come he's in uniform? Is he a Marine? How come? How come American Marines are here now?"

I noticed that the uniformed Marine was looking equally puzzled by finding a boatload of children in his port.

"Oh, Nina," Pa finally answered in exasperation, "I can't explain it all now. Later, child, later. Quick summary: Haiti's been broke since the slave revolutions, so our past president, Hoover, sent a special commission down here from the States to study the problem of firming up a democratic government. These Marines are backing up that commission."

Once ashore, the children were again allowed to go their own way while grownups did grown-up things. We said a polite goodbye to Dr. Monc, who had accompanied us ashore and was directing Ma, Pa, and Nana to the bank, as we sauntered toward the main street, hopping across puddles, stopping a moment to watch a freighter unload, absorbing the heat, the stench, the effect of great and ceaseless activity. Al pointed to the sidewalks two feet below the roadway.

"They keep roads up so high so they'll stay dry during the rainy season," he said authoritatively. "And see that ditch along the side of the road? Take a deep breath. That, kiddos, is an open sewer. If you have lots of rain plus running sewers, you need elevated roads. Right?"

If we didn't have Pa to teach us, we always had Al. Quita nudged me in the ribs and whispered, "Look!" A straight-backed woman in a loose cotton dress strode by with a bucket of water on her head, her arms swinging by her side.

The main street led us to an open market encircled by colonnaded buildings. As always, a crowd of children gathered around us. A boy stopped Willy and asked him if he could shine his shoes. Willy said sure. We all stopped and waited. A rival shoeshine boy came running up and claimed the other foot. The shoeshine boys began a fistfight, declaring war in loud Creole. A slugging brawl grew as more and more children took sides and entered the scrum. We took Willy by the hand quietly and slowly receded from the scene. No one noticed our departure. This behavior struck me as very different from the gang of kids we'd played with in Nassau. If Haitian kids were that rough, no wonder they needed Marines.

Al shepherded us to the bank, where we found Nana. We walked with her toward the center of the market in the hope of catching a breeze. Nana was fanning herself with a newspaper, her face flushed by the heavy wool blanket of heat around her. We watched a thermometer crawling slowly past 95 degrees. As soon as we stood still, four beggars approached us, followed by loud boys, strays from our shoeshine gang, and quiet, curious older natives, silently staring.

"Shoo!" shouted Nana, waving her newspaper in a wide sweep. The tiny imperial woman made herself understood. The crowd dispersed. We were left alone to watch the small donkeys sauntering by loaded with straw mats and old women sitting on top. "Ooo, look at her," I whispered to Quita, pointing to a sad-faced woman with the swollen legs of elephantiasis. Occasionally we would see a car race down an adjacent street, seemingly propelled by its horn as it maneuvered through the crowds on the narrow elevated tightrope of a road.

After lunch on the *Blue Dolphin*, we had the obligatory siesta. Siestas were beginning to make sense to me. It was simply too hot to move about under the noon-hour sun of the tropics. Willy spent his naptime sitting cross-legged on deck stringing shells together on a length of marlin. He terminated naptime when he jumped to his feet, dragging the clattering shells behind him, racing around and around the deckhouse, making explosive engine noises all the while.

Alert again, looking at shimmering heat waves over the water, we prepared for a visit with Dr. Monc and his family for an afternoon swim. The Moncs met us at the dock and drove us to the Marines' living quarters behind the native town, which was isolated by old, walled fortifications.

The parents handled the formalities, and I began to be bothered by the meaning of so many walls, barricades, divisions and subdivisions. Why so many partitions? I wondered why men and women were separated in the dressing rooms, the natives from the Marines, the rich from the poor. This place seemed corroded by a fear that necessitated barriers. The French, years ago, must have been scared like this, too, in their fortress palaces, building walls against the hate of the subjugated natives and slaves.

We frolicked in the cooling waters, behind nets (more guarding barriers) sunk to keep out sharks and barracudas. Kate, the Moncs' daughter, about Quita's age, who thought we were grand coming all the way from America in such a little ship, particularly delighted us. We began showing off before the admiring American children, exaggerating the terrors of the hurricane. Back at the Moncs' cool stone house, the young were kept quiet with fresh lemonade and ancient Sunday funny papers while the grownups sat back and talked. We lay on our stomachs, leaning on elbows, our heels kicking. Occasionally, I let Pa's and Dr. Monc's conversation sift into my mind. They were talking about the gradual withdrawal of Marines from Haiti. Dr. Monc was not optimistic, I gathered. He wasn't sure that diplomatic discourse would be effective in replacing military might.

That night, at supper, I asked Pa, "Why are the people so poor and angry here? On the other islands, the natives had hardships, but they had dignity, and they just seemed good and peaceful, and so welcoming, too. How come?" This was Pa's opportunity for prolonged discourse. But that was all right. I was genuinely puzzled. He began waxing eloquent on the Paris of the New World, beginning, of course, with a discourse on Paris of the Old World.

"It all started with the French and English wanting this little island of Haiti for their empires. This island was their jewel of contention. Both countries needed to control it. The French had ownership first. In a magnanimous gesture, they freed the slaves, hoping that in return the slaves would help them keep the island. But the slaves did no such thing. They took their freedom, organized the ex-slaves and natives, and engineered a terrible revolt, driving out the French and setting up a series of dictatorships. Their new rulers, now, remember these names, because you'll hear a lot about them in the next few days, Toussaint L'Ouverture, Dessalines, and Henri Christophe, made a mistake. They mimicked the French. They copied their buildings, fortifications, dress and manners, everything." Pa went on to denounce the French, as he was apt to do.

"Revolutions," he snorted, "a disease of the French mind. I've seen this firsthand in France."

He made it clear that revolutions in France or anywhere else did not solve economic or social problems but led to dictators and binding bureaucracies like Napoleon's and the rigid society Pa had known during the war. Pa once again spelled out his bias for the English.

"Pay attention to parliamentary procedures and incremental change," he droned on. "It's good to have a large number of special-interest groups fighting for control because they have to barter out compromises." I was beginning to get the message: The French as a people and the French in Haiti had failed to become classical capitalists. They had not developed their trade, had not promoted individual initiative, had not provided capital and management that would create wealth for both producer and consumer, leading to full employment and other heavenly ends.

"The rich in Haiti," Pa explained, "especially the big landowners, just accumulated wealth for themselves and didn't let it move into the hands of the people. That's what they should have done. They were takers, not givers. But, pay attention now: Haiti is coming into a new era, thanks to the kindness of the United States and the effectiveness of the Monroe Doctrine. The American Marines are going to ensure a proper democracy for Haiti. The World Conference held just last June will lower tariffs and restore international trade. Haiti won't be isolated any more. She'll be part of our great interdependent world and everyone's going to flourish."

After supper, Pa continued the history lesson by reading aloud *Black Majesty*, a novel about Henri Christophe, but his voice soon tired after all the talking he'd done that day, so he put down the book saying, "That's it for tonight." Al, John, and I were now free to go forward and sit on deck with Mr. Doyle, Chief, Sims, and Ted, to listen to a different set of stories.

Tonight, it was Ted, recounting his adventures ashore.

"Last night in port, kids," he began, "well, Smitty and I met this Marine in one of the local pubs. We conducted a scientific experiment. You might want to write it up for your Father's science course tomorrow, Nina. You interested?"

I was always interested in Ted's tales. He made me feel as if I was one of the crew, as if I, too, were grown up and lived in a man's world.

"Well, we took this glass of water that we found on the table. This was drinking water, you understand, left there for that purpose. If you looked very closely, you could see tiny wrigglers moving around in the water. First, we tried heating the water over the oil lamp on the table, but that only made the wrigglers move faster. When a good stiff dose of whisky went in the water, this had no visible effect, so we gave up our research and went down to the Marine barracks. Here we began another scientific experiment. Don't write this one up for your father. Smitty and I tried to drink two Marines under the table. Result? Failure. They'd had more practice."

The next day we put our sandwiches in paper bags and started off on our field trip. We were going to see King Christophe's Palais Sans-Souci at the foot of the far mountain and climb to his great fortress, La Citadelle, high on the mountaintop. We drove off in two old open touring cars for the hour-long trip to Milo, a town at the base of the mountain. We splashed through deep mud puddles, honking our way through clusters of donkeys, hogs, mules, horses, dogs, and chickens; past old people bent and still before their thatched mud huts with puff-bellied, pop-eyed naked children at their feet. Maybe, I thought, maybe free trade and open seas protected by a strong navy and the U.S. Marines could correct this poverty, but as I watched it go by, it seemed eternal and unchangeable.

In Milo we drove up to a set of low buildings strung together in sensible propinquity—a rest house, a barracks, and a jail. An old woman carrying cups of steaming black coffee laced with rum came from the rest house and joined us. We gulped this down, despite the bitter taste of the coffee. Willy licked his lips in appreciation of being grown-up and drinking rum. Four diminutive donkeys, three sway-backed mules, and one white horse were led out for us to select as our mounts. Nana claimed the white horse, of course. We children scrutinized the donkeys and mules, finally settling on the ones we wanted. The rum began to take effect. We leaped on our steeds and shouted, "*Allez!*" Our steeds had had no stimulating rum, however, and did not even consider moving. The guides had to whip and goad the animals to make them take their first step.

Our safari wound its way though the little town of Milo and down an avenue of old and new churches until we came upon the decaying palace of King Henri and his consort, Queen Charlotte. Great reaches of long, ascending staircases with delicate stone balustrades led up to the level of the palace proper with its repeating archways. The crumbling ruins of the upper stories were scattered everywhere. Creeping over the stairs, reaching into the arches, trailing around the monuments, covering the stone chairs were the powerful green tentacles of an omnivorous jungle, stronger by far than man or the monuments he considered enduring. The gloomy emptiness of the ruined building, the defeat of man's schemes by a force as inevitable and powerful as my more familiar sea, filled me with an increasingly profound respect for nature's power.

Eager to reach the mountaintop, we did not linger. We began our assault, marching triumphantly, a proud troop, through a tumbling archway, and submerged instantly into the jungle—damp, thick undergrowth with spiky hulks of banana trees and a delicate rustling tracery of bamboo over our heads. Nana, following a guide, led the family parade on her white horse. We came after the queen in single file.

We had to cross a stream where three women on their knees washed, beat, and slapped tattered strips of cloth and bleached cotton dresses against the rounded rocks. Their hair was yellow and matted, rubbed, we learned later, with dried manure, a religious practice. They did not stop their washing as we splashed past them. They did not even look up. Alarmed, I recognized these sullen, secretive women as the ladies of the palace, the ladies of pleasure, the noble ladies, now, in this stretch of time, moved out of their palace and kingdom, the ladies-in-waiting, but really waiting, waiting, waiting for the propitious moment of return. I kicked my mule, trying to hurry into the darkness of the protective jungle.

"Say!" called John from the rear, his thick black hair jouncing over his thick, raised eyebrows, riding up behind Pa, "Call the Society for the Prevention of Cruelty to Dumb Animals. Look at your father's poor mule!" Indeed, the poor mule appeared to be having great difficulties supporting Pa's 230-pound frame.

We moved from the jungle to a narrow treacherous path along mountain ridges. John's donkey seemed to keep his balance better if he teetered on the very edge of a precipice, but John did not mind. The rum had eased him into a detached state of mind. He was humming.

The winding, rising path brought us out on a high plateau where we stopped to look down on the green, cultivated, criss-crossed patterns of the plantations below us. We contemplated the plateau we must cross to get to our destination, a mountain that ascended into a wreath of clouds.

"*Allez! Allez! Allez!*" shouted the guides, running up behind our mounts and lashing them. We were pushed along the path, through a field of grass, yellow in the sun, rippling in the heat of the day. We glimpsed a tall black man at the edge of this field, stripped to his waist, singing his way through the grass, cutting a wide swath with a long, swinging scythe, chanting a plaintive calypso lament in a wailing high falsetto voice, the notes ringing clear in the still air.

"Giddyup, Lizzie, you'll make it in second!" commanded Willy, addressing his donkey, who was as round as he. The donkey, noting the gentle voice behind his ear, came to a lulled stop.

"Aw, Ma, my one horsepower has stopped," whined Willy, just as a guide ran up and kicked the poor mule until the pair stumbled on together.

"Ride 'em, cowboy!" yelled the happy boy.

We re-entered the jungle. Orange trees heavy with fruit lined our path. The guides took sticks and knocked off fruit, filling their hats with ripe oranges and passing them around to us to suck. They also pulled down ripe bananas, small green-brown ones, and handed them first to Nana and then to us, calling them "feegs."

Gradually, as we climbed up and up, twisting and turning, we rose out of the jungle and came into a cold, foggy land of rocks and bristling undergrowth. No trees, no people, no birds, no animals. We were in an arid world on a distant moon, separated from our own orbit by time and new, cold space. As the loneliness of the heights filled us, the huge fortress suddenly thrust its high ramparts through the blowing white clouds. The gray walls loomed over us with such abruptness that I thought I saw the shrouded mass move toward us.

Having read several Scott novels, we had definite ideas on how to enter a well-defended castle fortress, and we were going to proceed with them, even though this fortress was deserted. We massed our forces at the iron-studded wooden gate, tethered our noble beasts, and marched in a phalanx across what had been a moat, then on through the gaping once-portcullised entrance to the wide stairs, which led to an impressive hall. The ghostly quiet of the place stilled us. Walls dripped, green with slime. Mysterious mazelike passages led off through arched doorways into the fetid darkness. We banded close together so that neither the crumbling bulk of stone nor the ghosts would grip us and carry us down to the dungeons. Our voices, grown louder to bolster our courage, returned to frighten us in reverberating echoes, words taunting themselves. We wandered from courtyard to courtyard, coming through a lovely arch into a dried-up inner moat. Its drawbridge had decayed, so we could not cross it with style but had to scramble down the ditch and crawl up the other side.

We moved upward through the ruin, instinctively trying to get to fresh air and leave the atmosphere of decay and death pervading the hollow, silent rooms. Quita and I held hands as we trudged up three flights of slippery, wet stairs in the dark. We emerged into a wide, light room with a cannon at every window, then more stairs, then another large space, tiled and terraced.

We decided this must have been the great court. An empty fountain graced one end. In the center, stood the tomb of the dictator. We agreed to lunch here and sat by the tomb, eating our sandwiches from the brown paper bags, while one of our guides who spoke English told us about Henri Christophe. He had committed suicide, the guide said, when he knew he was defeated. He ordered the grave we sat by to be dug, then filled with wet cement. He stood at the base of the grave and shot himself in the head with a silver bullet, falling into the wet concrete. No one would ever be able to steal and desecrate his body. Quita stopped eating.

The guide went on to describe the troops, so well trained that, when ordered to march to the edge of the ramparts, fell right to their deaths on the rocks below if no one ordered them to turn. None of us spoke. I stared at the tomb, a skeleton within a skeleton.

Anxious to break away from the grim storyteller, we decided to cloak ourselves with bravery and go find the dungeons. Down we went, back through the great thick walls, into darkness, water dripping on our heads, past the powder house and into a lower hall. We stopped, curious, grouped around a wide hole about four feet in diameter in the middle of the floor. Dropping on our knees around the opening, we listened as John dropped a stone and waited a long time before a watery splash let us know the distance to the bottom. Just then, one of the guides came running down the stairs, his echoing steps following him in the dim light. He announced that it was raining, and we must begin our descent of the mountain. We were not reluctant to leave these slimy walls and return home. Somehow, reading about wars and revolutions in castles was easier than feeling the real grip of them closing around you.

Al reached his donkey first and actually made the donkey gallop. He waved his whip around his head, his gob hat raked back on his head. Although his mount was so short and round that Al's feet scraped the ground, with the cry of "*Allez!*" he led the charge down the mountainside.

I was at the end of the line. Halfway down, my donkey stopped and began grazing. No one seemed to notice that I had dropped out of sight, and suddenly I was alone in the jungle with only this animal for company. My mind began roaring with the noise of native uprisings. Lurid pictures rushed by of kidnap and torture by bandits. Our guide had told us bandits were thick in these mountains. A voodoo drumbeat began somewhere in the back of my mind. I slipped out of the saddle and grabbed the reins. I tugged and moaned and pleaded in the French that Mother had taught me, trying to be quiet but persistent, not loud enough to betray my whereabouts, but enough to make my point to this balking, grazing beast.

Finally, Mother noticed my absence and sent a guide back to kick the animal down the slopes. At the rest house, tired and stiff, we had another delicious portion of rum and thick black coffee. Driving home, Willy, intoxicated by rum and exhaustion, called every passing thing, "mulie, mulie, mulie." No one could hush him.

Back on shipboard, after dark, Captain greeted us. He had his own adventure to tell. Late in the afternoon, three gigantic waterspouts had whirled down the harbor toward the ship. He called all hands to slam ports and hatches closed, and, just as our beautiful ship, our home, our school, was about to be sucked up into the skies, the spouts veered off and spent themselves out at sea.

As I listened to Captain, I was glad we were saved but mad that I had been so close to a disaster and missed it. I looked down the harbor and imagined our ship rising in the air. I would somehow rise with it and descend unharmed. If we had been allowed to read the *Wizard of Oz*, I would have compared myself to Dorothy, but Pa had declared that book trash, so none of us had ever bothered to read it.

11

Wrinklebelly

W E WERE OFF on a four-day run down to our first major city, San Juan in Puerto Rico. These were four days of fine sailing, spanking wind, and no storms. Pa, with great patience, was finally making progress teaching me algebra. But his success with me did not extend to all his pupils. He was beginning to realize that Quita and Willy were floundering under his tutelage. Quita was afflicted with the family curse of dyslexia; and in spite of the fact that Pa was dyslexic himself, he couldn't figure out how to teach her. Willy, on the other hand, wasn't old enough to appreciate Pa's disciplined thinking and expectations. Just as Pa had handed me over to Mother to learn French, so he walked Quita and Willy back to Nana's cabin and suggested Nana take over their education for a while. Nana, like Mother, was delighted. She started by reading them *The Child's History of the World* by Hillier. It began with a description of the solar system and moved on to the formation of the earth before it came anywhere near the history of the people on it. Like Pa, she felt we all needed background before we hit the key topic.

The first afternoon out of Haiti, during naptime, I rested my muscles, newly stiffened by riding. Vague memories of cold, damp wind blowing down from the hills of Delaware and whining through the weather stripping at home, of numbed fingers under wet leather mittens, of chaos surrounding five children getting off to school in the early morning, being fed, matching and clicking on galoshes, collecting homework—all those almost forgotten wintry aspects of life—drifted through my mind. I stretched catlike, eyeing the sunlight glancing off the green water.

A call from Nana to Willy interrupted my reverie. "Willy, where are you? Time for my lesson!" Willy separated himself from building a cockroach trap and went to join her in the stern where she sat under her straw hat on a folding canvas chair. He was teaching her to shoot craps. This was serious business. Nana leaned over to cast her die. Willy was on his knees before her, his long-visored fishing cap swiveled around backwards. Neither one of them smiled. They hardly spoke, except to clear up terminology, Willy explaining "Ada from Decatur" and "snake eyes." They just bent towards each other, concentrating, and rolled the ivories.

Chief called us children now that naptime was over and invited us amidships to test an experiment he'd perfected. He was anxious to redeem himself after forgetting to turn off the oil cocks that morning, which resulted in oil flooding through the wall from the engine into the saloon. The heavy stench of that black oil had been awful. The children complained loudly and made retching noises, while Nana repeatedly dove to the rail and spat. Now Chief was beckoning us to show us how he'd rigged a hose that had enough power to push Willy around the deck. We invented a game of water baseball, using Will as the ball. Exhausted after a while, we went below and relaxed with our daily afternoon roulette game.

During this stretch at sea, Al began the latest installment of his Wrinklebelly saga. After supper and Pa's reading, the five children, wrapped in blankets, sat close together on the top of the deckhouse and listened to Al as if our lives depended on every word he said. At fifteen, brother Alfred did not make a strong immediate impression. His advisor at Exeter, who later would have him in his charge for two years, found, apologetically, that after a few years' time, he could not visualize the boy. He remembered him only as a "quiet, retiring sort of chap with terrible handwriting." Al was not tall and he stooped. He mumbled when he talked and moved in a loose-jointed shuffle. He never forced himself into groups but camouflaged himself, staying at the edge, watching, taking mental notes, making incisive, analytic conclusions about what was going on. His thick black hair stood up in stiff curls above his high forehead. His eyes were big, his mouth large and soft, and his chin receded. But if you were in Alfie's confidence, and if Alfie was excited about an idea he was working out, you were face to face with the beauty, dazzle, and power of cerebral electricity. He would grow so excited that tears of joy and passion filled his eyes. He talked faster and faster until he was almost incomprehensible. Running all through his talk was a bubbling humor. He was a laughing boy and kind in his laughter.

Wrinklebelly was clearly Willy, our chubby little brother. The other characters were Willy's and Al's friends at home. When the story began, bombs had just wiped out New York in a great world war. Noxious vapors from gases, sewers, and decomposed bodies had finished off those inhabitants who had lived through the bombings. The city was a lifeless junk heap. From far to the north, untouched by gases washed away in the clear currents of polar air, came a tribe of nomadic Russians, led by two men— one small, who had the brains for leadership, and one big, big enough to beat everyone into obedience. As they approached the city of New York, they found it in desolation, smoke rising from shattered ruins of great skyscrapers.

Deep down in the bowels of the subway system cowered the sole survivors of the terrible destruction: Wrinklebelly and his friends. Fortunately, Wrinklebelly was a genius with the switches and electric mechanisms of the subway system, and he puttered around long enough to get one car to go.

In spite of the stench and the horror of appearing above the surface of the earth, the brave little band felt they must explore the possibilities of escape from the holocaust. Wandering through the debris, wearing improvised gas masks, they met the nomadic Russians and managed (by intuition, sign language, and by talking primarily to the small, bright leader) to become allies.

Resuming their walk, they reached the remnants of the Empire State Building and climbed to the top to view the ruins of the city. What they saw brought panic, for marching over the horizon was an army of giant ants, each the size of a freight car. Now, these ants had been grown in the central part of deepest, darkest Africa, where a mad scientist from New York, enraged at mankind for slighting his inventions, had fled. He trained the giant ants and bred them with human intelligence, swearing they would finish off the human race. What he had not reckoned with in his scheme to destroy mankind was that ants with human intelligence would turn first on their master and creator. This the ants did. They ate up the mad scientist and set off to New York to see the sights.

When Wrinklebelly saw these ants swarming across White Plains, hungry and eager to eat the 7,454,996 corpses, he was quick to realize that giant ants might not distinguish between the living and the dead. So he proposed immediate flight. His girlfriend, Peggy Rankin, fainted but was quickly revived by the anxious leader. They all ran down to their subway car, warning the Russians as they went. The Russians, who were slow on the uptake and did not follow, were left to fight it out with the ants.

Once back in their subway car, Wrinklebelly and his followers headed out through the maze of tracks with the aid of a handy crowbar to throw switches and a map of the IRT System snatched off the wall of the subway station. They headed for Floyd Bennett Field, where they found an autogiro that had not been smashed to pieces by bombs. Fortunately, Wrinklebelly knew how to fly. (This was logical to Al's audience because Pa's pilot, when flying the company Bellanca six-seated plane, let us sit next to him and hold the stick, assuring us that we were really flying the plane). The brave band climbed in and hopped off to New Jersey to refuel at the refineries. They glanced back to see a battalion of giant ants crunching across the highways toward them, waving their antennae in the excitement, hoping to trap the escaping prey with their hairy wildly flaying feet.

"Alfred, Nina, Quita, Willy, John. Time for bed, children. Hop to!" Grownups were never good at timing. Why did we have to stop now, just when things were getting good? But obedient to command, with the customary feeble groan of protest, we stood up and prepared for bed, each one of us trying to finish that chapter in our own imaginations.

12

City Life Experienced
and Rejected

To A COUNTRY CHILD, a city is a formidable and ominous place. I still approach a city with timidity, an excitement edged with fear. I am never certain if I will be able to conform to the expectations of that voiceless but noisy, ever-moving line of people circulating through the tunnel-like streets. So far, with the possible exception of the quiet town of Nassau, our visits on this trip had been to small, sleepy ports. We'd meet a few people at a time and enter briefly and comfortably into their lives. San Juan and Puerto Rico would be a sharp contrast. San Juan was a city, Puerto Rico Americanized. We were about to be challenged.

We sailed into San Juan's harbor past the old fort, Morro Castle, its ancient walls orange in the late afternoon light, with swirls of gray-green lichen running down to the lawns at their bases. We passed a bell buoy that reminded Pa of one of his most important wishes. "Don't forget," he shouted out, "I want to be buried under the bell buoy at the end of the jetties in Nantucket. I want to watch those pennies everyone throws there for luck. I want to see that copper lucre come spiraling down on top of me!" He didn't need to remind us. We'd heard this request many times before, but it was nice seeing old familiar bell buoys again.

Now we were gazing at the city, at the jumble of shacks that made up the slums, the gleaming white and pink skyscrapers, the green, red and blue residences, the great dome of the Government House—and beyond, the purple mountains behind the city. We anchored at dusk. Lights were coming on, dancing excitedly, awakened by the last caressing fingers of the sun's rays. We could hear horns blowing, sirens wailing. Tiny ferries scooting around the rows of docks made us laugh; they looked like our pets, the cockroaches, who made their home with us.

As the darkness deepened and city lights calmed down to a steady glow, the water came alive with light. This was paradox indeed, sparks going off under water! Delighted with this phosphorescence, Willy heaved a bucket overboard to scoop up some of this fireworks display. We could follow the paths of the specks of fish in the bucket as they left tracks of light behind them. Then he had a better idea. He called Quita and me to the head, closed the door, turned off the light, climbed the steps up to the tub, pulled out the plug, and let the sea rush in. We stayed there until suppertime watching tiny brilliant fish pop through the plughole, lighting their way through the black water. We added to the blaze by running our fingers under the water, turning them into sparklers. Spellbound, we never heard Mother calling us to come eat. The spectacle ended when she threw open the door and blinded us with the glare of artificial light.

At six the next morning, the San Juan reception committees began to arrive. First, a fat port doctor—grumpy and impolite—heaved himself on board. The next boat brought out the lanky cheerful pilot with a friend. The friend gossiped with Al, John, and me while the pilot talked business with Captain. Then came another boat with an inspector who spent most of his visit next to Willy on the leather sofa in the saloon describing the Columbus Day parade and the celebrations in San Juan the day before. John, standing beside me, waiting for breakfast, watched yet another boat arriving and declared he'd invented a new theorem: A city's size could be determined by the number of bureaucrats necessary to register a ship's entry into port. This latest boat drew alongside bearing a real welcoming committee, friends of the captain's, a Mr. and Mrs. Towers, who were to be our hospitable guides and friends for the length of our stay.

We had been at sea for almost a month, confined to the cramped world of our little ship. San Juan was to be a vacation from life on board.

We would even stay at a hotel. None of us could remember ever staying in a hotel before, so we were excited. We would take the first hot, freshwater, soapy baths we'd had in a month. We would sleep in beds that we could exit from either side, and maids would make them. "Civilization" was eagerly anticipated. I shut myself in my stateroom and practiced sophisticated facial expressions before my hand mirror, working up the drooping-eyelid look I fancied drew John into my power—although this enormous faith I had in the eyes as the locus of seduction was based on no evidence whatsoever.

Not only was this our first city, but it was also to be our first major mail port. On landing, we went directly to the National City Bank, our designated mailing address. We were bewildered and deeply disappointed. Not one piece of mail awaited us. Pa excused himself from the moaners and ran across the street to another bank. In a minute or two, we saw Pa emerge beaming and beckoning to us, so we trudged over. He introduced us to the president of the bank, Mr. Carrion, an old friend. The two men had worked together building railroads in Cuba for the Baldwin Locomotive Works. There followed a boisterous reunion and long introductions, as Pa detailed our names, ages, relationships, and every possible accomplishment that any of us had ever achieved. In the warmth and generosity of Mr. Carrion, we forgot the sorrow of not hearing from home.

He drove us off right away for a tour of the city in his brand-new car, a pink Buick, which just suited my drooping-eyelid look. Our destination was his home, a one-story stucco Spanish-style house in the suburbs overlooking the sea. Here we met his Spanish wife and seven dark-eyed children. The house intrigued me because the windows had no glass; only wrought-iron grills covered them. Mr. Carrion offered us an old Lincoln for our own use and then led us all to our hotel.

Ma, Pa, and Nana checked in and gave directions about the luggage while the five children split and made quick exploratory sorties, reporting back half an hour later to our rooms to share our findings. John had found a beer garden surrounded by slatted walls. I found three dining rooms, each one successively grander than the last. Al made the best discovery, a large swimming pool on the edge of the ocean. So far, we were excited by the prospects of "civilization" and hotel living.

But then I found my mind repeatedly returning to unsettling details. I had picked up the hotel brochure at the front desk. They were calling this place the American Riviera, the Switzerland of the Tropics, the Isle of Enchantment. The hotel and surroundings did not match my idea of the Riviera or Switzerland—not that I'd ever been to either place—but I'd certainly seen a lot of pictures and read a lot of books. After all, Anthony Adverse had started out in Switzerland, so I was pretty familiar with the territory. Should I conclude that this place was fake? If so, what did that do to the thoughts we had about "civilization"? Further, I was bothered by so much repetition—the rows of beaded chandeliers, the rows of white-clothed tables; everything came in rows. Did these people think that grandeur was achieved by duplication, row upon row?

Then came the shock of the Rotarians. The maître d' had placed us next to their table. Their raucous mumbo-jumbo made me want to run back to the gentle sounds of our ship. Ship sounds were enticing; Rotarian noises made no apparent sense. I had to ask myself—was I just nit-picking, or was I misperceiving, perhaps, because I was a rube from the country?

These dislocating concerns left me when we went to tea at the Towers. We rejoiced in the freshly squeezed grapefruit juice, shrieked at the huge toad that jumped against John's leg in the garden, and were amazed at the fury of the tropical downpour that hit us on our way home. Unfortunately, the windows in Mr. Carrion's old Lincoln had long since given up on mobility. They rested comfortably in the down position, and we arrived back at the hotel drenched. That night we went to the movies, laughed at *Flip the Frog,* and cried over *Tugboat Annie.*

The next day, Mr. Carrion's handsome, quiet-mannered son directed us through Morro Castle, a fine fortress, of course, but after our conquest of the Citadelle in Haiti, not much in our eyes. The authorities had prettied it up to attract tourists. The guards, clad in modern uniforms, did not match the lichen. The surrounding golf greens and tennis courts made the hoary old fortress seem out of place. There was even a guest book, in which we dutifully signed our names. And rope barricades kept us from launching into games of our own devising. We could have divided ourselves into two teams, soldiers defending themselves from the attacks of marauding pirates, but such imaginative projects were clearly not in order. This tour of a fort made our history lesson more like conventional schooling, not the new kind of participatory history that had us hooked.

Driving away, we came to an ancient Spanish cemetery shining in the sun. Quita and I begged to stop and see it. We loved cemeteries. We used to spend a lot of time in the old graveyard behind our house in Nantucket and liked to make up stories about the people lying there under the headstones. We had only slim clues to go by, family relationships, spans of life, tone of epitaphs, but we had no end of imagination to fill the gaps. One family plot, the Starbucks', had particularly charmed us. Twenty-five Starbucks were neatly lined up behind a wrought-iron rail. They were identified by name and date only, save one. This thirty-six-year-old Starbuck was memorable for one thing. He, it was noted, died in Brooklyn, New York. Was that why he was placed at the very back of the far corner?

We grieved for Joseph Folger, who drowned at Mendocino, California, at the age of forty-two. We constructed a life for Charles Macy of the Eighteenth Massachusetts Volunteer Militia. He had died at Andersonville Prison during the Civil War. We pondered the Clark family. Charlie Clark lived for most of the nineteenth century, had three wives, a whole string of dead babies, and a mother named Jerusha. And then there were slabs in memory of the lads who were lost at sea during the great whaling era. Some were only our age.

Mr. Carrion obligingly stopped the car. As we walked through the gate of the tropical cemetery behind the white walls, our breaths drew in in admiration. The white, baroque wedding-cake statues of marble, the tall tombs and ornate shrines were a far cry from the quiet, gray granite of Quaker New England, the gentle weeping willows and simple urns etched on the moss-covered stones, marking the last resting places of our friends the Starbucks and the Macys.

Our major island expedition began that afternoon, a circling tour of the island with an overnight stay at Coamo Springs. We wound around and around the narrow mountain roads, gasping at each hairpin turn, contemplating the prospect of instant death. The road edged along cliffs and precipices with no guardrail. Our old Lincoln was top-heavy and just too long to take the curves easily. Approaching drivers didn't seem to mind any set of rules we could fathom, and Pa, our driver, didn't help. He kept taking one hand off the wheel, waving with sudden enthusiasm, and shouting.

"There! There!" he would cry out, "Look what's coming! A real arch, an ancient arch. Now that's a great feat of engineering, and you won't see anything like that again for a long time." But then another arch would appear around the next bend.

We arrived, exhausted, at Coamo Springs after dark. The Spanish landlord came out to greet us and led us to our rooms, which were strung along a wooden porch. He brought us pineapple juice and piña colada to drink. Later, under the trees, in the cool of the evening, we dined and were allowed to drink red wine with our Spanish meal. My drooping-eyelid look developed a sudden new authenticity.

Before breakfast, we dressed in bathing suits and ran down a long flight of stone steps to a small indoor sulfur pool. The smell was nauseating, the tiny sunken room dark and airless. The others were about to retreat when I persuaded them that swimming in sulfur water was stylish. Anthony Adverse talked a lot about spas and sulfur. I told them to grow up and be sophisticated, but even I, I must admit, was relieved to get out of the pool and onto the lawn where we listened to a nightingale and played with a tame monkey.

On our day's drive back to San Juan, Nana took over the history lesson with gusto. Her husband, Major Ramsay, had landed in Puerto Rico with American troops in the Spanish-American War. We went right to the spot where he came ashore in Guanica. I could easily picture him wading up the beach, for Nana had a large photograph of Grandfather on her bedside table in his bemedaled Army uniform, the one he certainly must have worn for the conquest. Since we were there, as was the second largest sugar mill in the world, Pa gave us a lecture on economics and, for extra credit, had us take a tour of the buildings. We stopped at the United

States Military base to pay our respects and were invited to lunch by the wife of one of the officers. "Perfection!" exclaimed Nana, as she finished off a second helping of green-bean salad; and off we went again, driving for five hours through great mountain ranges and arriving, finally, at the hotel at midnight.

The next day was set aside for reprovisioning the ship. Ma and Pa went downtown, Chandlers to chandlers, to put in the order. Nana stayed at the hotel and read aloud to us. The story had been evolving for about an hour when she suddenly grabbed her head with her hands and moaned, "Oh! Help me! I must lie down. Sparks are going off in my head."

We led her to her bed and stood in a row at its foot, bewildered— what, after all, did we know about dealing with madwomen—watching, as she stiffened with fright, grabbing the side of the bed.

"Help! Hold me! I'm falling!" she screamed.

Mother returned and took over, shooing us away to the pool. We found it deserted and started a complicated game of follow-the-leader. We had just finished falling off in a line into the shallow end of the pool when we realized Willy was not there. We found him bobbing in the water at the other end of the pool, sobbing. He had lost his balance on the high diving board and had fallen, not into the water, but onto the sandy concrete rimming the pool. From there, he had rolled off into the water. As we pulled him out, we exclaimed with horror. Both his legs were bleeding. The concrete had stripped off long stripes of skin.

"But my arm . . ." he moaned. John and I looked at the arm, looked at each other, and shook our heads in mutual dismay. A protruding bone pushed up the skin near the wrist.

"Willy," I said confidently, holding the limp hand, "I have always heard that if you can move your hand your arm is not broken. Now, look," I said, gently rotating the hand around the all-too-obvious projecting bone. "You see, you can move it. It's okay. Honest."

My Florence Nightingale act was a flop and turned Willy even whiter. Alfred and John carried him up to our hotel room and laid him on the bed next to Nana. Mother summoned the doctor and began to wear that cool, remote look of the completely distraught person. She'd been dressing to descend into the foyer to greet the Carrions and Towers for a tea party. We children were sent down instead to be the welcoming committee, leaving Pa and Ma standing at the end of a bed holding hands and whispering to each other, trying to deal with multiple disasters.

Pa took Will off to the hospital. There he was cleaned up and his arm put into a cast that was to stay on until we reached Panama, six weeks later. A doctor came to the hotel and diagnosed Nana's trouble as "mountain sickness," a disturbance of the fluid in the inner ear and a result of our rocking ride over the mountains. She had lost her sense of equilibrium and felt as if she were falling in space. Mother suggested that the doctor check Alfred because of his unaccountable pains during the past weeks, and he found a serious hernia. Since surgery did not fit our schedule, the doctor recommended that Al do no pulling or lifting.

By this time we all wanted to go home, home to our ship. The city was threatening. We wanted the safety of our familiar space and routine. Before returning on board, however, Al, John, and I found time to see the movie *Reunion in Vienna* that was preceded by the newsreel *The Eyes and Ears of the World*. We watched goose-stepping soldiers saluting Mussolini on his balcony. We laughed. Mussolini was almost as good as Charlie Chaplin.

We were prepared to leave the next day, Sunday, but John woke up with bad pains and chills and fever. By afternoon, we sat hushed on the deck as John's condition worsened. After supper, he had a temperature of 104 degrees. Pa fetched the doctor again. The doctor didn't seem to mind coming out to the ship on a Sunday night, but he diagnosed a case of sunstroke. "At this rate," he called back, as he left in the launch, "I'll see you again tomorrow!" Fortunately, no new illness hit during the night, but the doctor came anyway to clear us for departure. We sailed south that afternoon, as fast as the sails and motor combined could carry us. Ma and Pa stood at the stern holding hands again. We'd had quite enough of "civilization" for the time being.

13

Naval Warfare
and Little Rosie

CONTINUING OUR EQUIVALENT of the grand tour of Europe in tropical
settings, we swept down the Leeward and Windward Islands. We
were to make a succession of spot landings, going from culture to culture,
imbibing history. Still suffering from our Puerto Rico hangover and
wanting to avoid another American port, we touched in at St. Thomas,
once Danish, now American. We got a glimpse of five little Danish girls
in high straw hats and long dresses, golden in the sun, their plaited blond
hair swinging down their backs, a contrast to the dark-eyed, black-haired
children of Spanish Puerto Rico.

We also celebrated Thanksgiving. Charlie had picked up a stringy
turkey at St. Thomas and presented us with canned cranberry sauce to go
along with it, giving to Pa one can all for himself. Pa claimed that he
qualified for this distinction because he was born and bred a Bostonian,
and cranberries at Thanksgiving were distinctly Bostonian. We ended the
meal with pies of canned pumpkin covered with strawberry jam. Charlie
put strawberry jam on every dessert he concocted—a mark, he clearly felt,
of his creative genius.

On the first day of December, we anchored off St. Kitts and took our
launch to Basseterre heading for a swim. We'd gone back to England, but
an England with tropical sugar plantations spread out for miles and miles.

Brimstone Hill, a great old fort, allegedly blown off the top of nearby Mount Misery, protected this so-called Gibraltar of the West Indies. I suggested to Pa that "Brimstone" and "Misery" cast a gloom over this port, but Pa paid no attention to me, for he was well under way on a splendid running lecture on local celebrities. He'd begun with Alexander Hamilton and his contribution to American history, moving on to the marriage of Lord and Lady Nelson, which had taken place on this island, and was winding up with the career of Josephine Bonaparte—who, he was pointing out, would have been better off staying here, since getting mixed up with the French usually turned out to be a mistake. I interrupted him. I said Josephine's life sounded pretty exciting; better than lolling around Brimstone and Misery. Pa looked down on me with scorn, but remained silent. He was already at work on the details of his next complicated lesson plan, a project he had given us hints about for several days.

The lesson began as we sailed south to Nevis, our next English port. Pa had requested the crew join the family on deck by the binnacle after breakfast. As we stood there together in the sun, all sails set, scudding along, he addressed us.

"Now we're going to learn about naval warfare," and so saying he opened up one of his favorite books, Alfred Thayer Mahan's *The Influence of Sea Power Upon History, 1660–1783.* "We're going to refight some of the battles between the English and French fleets for control of the Caribbean. We'll use these charts from the book to position our ships as they prepare their cannons. The *Blue Dolphin* will represent Admiral Hood's ship, and I'm Admiral Hood. We'll run through the actual maneuvers with our *Blue Dolphin*, using these batons to represent the other ships. You'll get a sense of how hard it was to win a naval battle as we tack and jibe. First, we're going to review some of the basic tactics the fleets used in these fights, which, by the way, are just the same as Nelson and the English fleet used at Trafalgar when they beat Napoleon. Captain has agreed to be deGrasse, and he's in charge of the French fleet. We'll pretend this is his boat."

So saying, Pa picked up a sail baton, a short flat wooden stick, from a pile by his side and laid it on the deckhouse. "I'll use one of these batons for each ship, including my own, although we'll run the maneuvers with the *Blue Dolphin* just to give you an idea how much work and thought went into these battles. Watch how I lay them out on the deckhouse. See: I'm copying Mahan's charts."

Pa went on with the drill. "The *Blue Dolphin* is now leading a fleet of twenty-two ships of the line, and we're about to meet deGrasses's thirty-three French ships of the line. You can each chose which boat you want to command. Place your baton according to the chart. The rest can represent the other ships. Divide yourselves up, now; take sides and a baton, all of you, for today we are going to fight the Battle of the Saintes."

Captain moved to the other side of the ship and saluted.

"You know from what I've been telling you," Pa continued, "the English have been chasing the French for several days. The most important thing in this era of naval warfare is paying attention to the wind, just like racing in Nantucket. The wind will determine if you are victorious. So both I, Admiral Hood, and Captain over there, Admiral deGrasse, and all of you lesser captains of the fleets have to pay attention to the direction, strength, variability, and signs of change in these great trade winds we're in now. Look at the clouds. What do they tell you? Then come tactics. We are going to have to learn how to handle ships of the line. Both sides will have to persevere in pursuing every advantage in maintaining striking position."

By this time, Al and John had taken on with enthusiasm the roles of captains of various ships, all English. The English were about to execute "crossing the T" to increase their range of cannon shot.

"This," pronounced Admiral Hood, "will be our major naval military tactic that will bring us victory." Captain, now French, sighed *"Oh, la, la!"* and gave sort of a helpless shrug.

In my now well-honed oppositional manner, I chose to be a captain of a French ship, the *Zélé*. I had been taken by the fate of the *Zélé* when Pa let me glance through Mahan's book. She was the bane of the French fleet. First, in the night, she rammed the *Jason*, another French ship, incapacitating her, sending her off to Guadaloupe the next day for repairs. As if that wasn't enough, the *Zélé* collided with the French flagship, commanded by DeGrasse. (Captain had a few words on my abilities.) DeGrasse ordered the *Astrée* to tow the *Zélé* out of sight, out of mind. He was now three ships short, and I was saved a lot of physical activity. I lolled on cushions pretending I was holed up in Guadaloupe. This left me free to comment on the English as they jibed, reached, tacked, and luffed, crossing that T.

In the meantime, a miserable English lieutenant, played by a grinning, somewhat diabolical Ted, muffed the English surprise attack. He was commanding a ship that was hove to in the dark and failed to get out of the way of another cruising English ship, captained by Smitty. Smitty's ship rammed into Ted's port side, creating a stunning amount of noise and confusion, alerting the French, and spreading the grin on Smitty's face.

Pa, Al, and John cheered in victory as the *Blue Dolphin*, now in lesson number two, had metamorphosed into an English ship, under the command of Rodney (Sims). They had sailed the new, dangerous, and tricky maneuver of "breaking the line" to capture the first French naval commander-in-chief to be taken in battle (Mr. Doyle), winning one of the greatest sea battles in history. The English stood and cheered in unison, but when they'd calmed down, I felt it imperative to stand up for the French, reminding the English that they weren't all that smart. Even Admiral Mahan scolded them for not capturing and chasing the rest of the French fleet. "Just 'cause you win," I stated with authority, savoring my recalcitrance, "doesn't mean you can relax."

The battle over and absorbed into our memories, we sailed on to Nevis, the dot of the exclamation point of St. Kitts, and reached it just in time for a swim. Two types of welcoming committee always greeted us when we came into a small port as an unscheduled ship. Curious residents grouped and scrutinized our arrival to judge if they'd accept our intrusion. And taxi drivers gathered to collect a fare. Here we were watched by a small band of Englishmen. A man and wife stepped forward, introduced themselves, and said they would be delighted to show us a good swimming spot. Just follow us, they said. We could hardly hear what they were saying because the drivers of two battered Ford touring cars were clamoring loudly for our attention. We divided ourselves between the two, but alas, only one car would start, so we all climbed into it and drove off as the jilted driver shouted curses after us, shaking his fist. The dust settled, the exhaust blew away, and we disappeared around a bend.

Our new friends, a Dr. and Mrs. Cramer, led us to a beach, a curve of white sand under a line of palm trees. We had the beach to ourselves. After our swim we went on to tea with the Cramers. Mother's internalized etiquette manual compelled her to pay back the hospitality, so the Cramers came to dinner on board the *Blue Dolphin*. Dr. Cramer kept us children circled around him all evening as he sang songs and showed us card tricks.

We sailed through the night under full sail and full moon, aiming for Dominica, another sample of England in the Caribbean. Pa began reading aloud a new Scott novel, *Quentin Durward*, and read all the next afternoon. At supper, the second night out, we were short with each other for no particular reason. An unspecified irritant seemed to be nagging us. The meal had begun normally enough. Al said the family grace with bowed head, "When one is served, all may eat," and immediately stuffed his canned beans in his mouth, but then Willy began whining about his seat in starvation corner just as Pa started up on Roosevelt.

"Little Rosie," Pa announced, "is a wretched populist." He made it sound as if Roosevelt had leprosy.

"When my father, your own grandfather," Pa went on, "when he was elected the First Selectman of the just-established Town of Brookline—he was one of the founders of Brookline, you know—well, your grandfather thought a lot about the best kind of government for the citizens of his town. He liked to tell me about Governor Hutchinson of Boston, who was involved in an election in 1770. Hutchinson knew there were only 1,500 legal voters in Boston yet 3,900 to 4,000 turned up to vote anyway. That's corrupt mob rule. Mobs, in turn, are usually controlled by tyrants. Roosevelt better be careful. He's using the mobs and ignoring the law."

"He's not ignoring the law." I said with great firmness, as if I knew. And besides, I was beginning to think law didn't matter much as long as you were doing good.

"Of course he's ignoring the law. Look at what he did with the banks. Closed them all down the minute he took office. Didn't even have the grace to wait for Congress to convene. Our founding fathers, suspecting men would not always act honorably, set up our government so there would be checks and balances: the Executive branch, Congress, and the Supreme Court. Our elected representatives, chosen fairly in popular elections, not like that one in Boston in 1770, should make the major legislative decisions. Roosevelt acted on his own without authority."

Al with his mouth full, grumbled, "Congress passed the legislation to close the banks as soon as it came into session."

"That's not the point. Law is law. We're not at war; he couldn't take that kind of action. Why didn't he let the states close the banks? It was in their jurisdiction. To take such immense federal power without using the law is redistributing the power to a few, not to many. Read James Madison."

I had no intention of reading anyone so boring and, anyway, Pa stopped talking when he had his full plate. He loved eating almost more than talking.

Mother's unease was palpable and, as always, unrelated to Pa's talk. Mother had been increasingly worried at mealtime, and this meal was no exception. Quita was not eating well. Unlike her bulky sisters, Quita was a small-boned, delicate, beautifully proportioned girl. At this meal, as before, she toyed with her food lackadaisically. To Mother this was like the red flag of a storm warning hoisted by the Coast Guard at Nantucket before a gale. A healthy child ate well. Mother urged and petted, threatened and cajoled, but Quita would not eat.

"It's Charlie's fault," muttered Ma, trusting Pa heard, "If only he would give us fresh vegetables, she'd eat."

Nana was not happy either. She sat glumly at her place, staring over our heads at a corner. She rubbed her stomach with the flat of her palm to ease her distress until she let out a healthy belch.

"Nana, my dear," said Pa, deciding Nana was easier to placate than Ma, "have some corned beef."

"Hmph," snorted Nana. "Meat. Well, I've had my corned beef, thank you. But see here," she addressed all of us now. "Don't you boys realize what has happened?" She always included Quita and me in the "boy" category, preferring boys to girls. "I have eaten my helping of corned beef decently and slowly, just as I like, and now I am ready for my canned vegetables. And where, please, are my canned vegetables?" She waved her hand in a sweep. "Gone. Gobbled up. There is none left. I do wish you would all be a bit more considerate and leave me just a little." She folded her hands in her lap. Silence blanketed our usual free-flowing supper conversation.

"Hey, folks!" called Sims down the companionway, "You should get up here and see the moon. It's just coming up over the edge of the ocean!"

Relieved to find ourselves excused from the bad mood we were settling into, we hurried on deck, all but Pa. Pa sat at his place at the end of the table and reached out to collect the bowls of unfinished, canned cherries in a semicircle around him. He always ate up the family leftovers when we departed from the table without finishing our meal. We called him the human garbage can . . . behind his back, of course.

"*Pax vobiscum!*" he called out as we left.

"*Nux vomica,*" I answered. I didn't know what that meant, but it was a favorite retort of Uncle Willie's and worth trying.

Out on deck, we lay quietly in the moonlight with no reading, no story telling, watching the sails billow out in the strong wind. I listened to the wind stroking the rigging like a bow on a giant cello playing a lament, a rich humming obbligato. Then I heard a wailing crescendo, a rising and falling in the solo line. The clanking of the block and tackle added percussive rhythm to the mournful piece.

We were sleepy, lulled by the swell, the concert in the rigging, and the churning of the sea. Suddenly we were jerked to our feet by a pistol shot in the night. I later recorded the sound in my Journal as a "CRASH!! Bang!! Clatter!! Bang!! RIP! RIP! CRASH! BANG SWISH!! SWASH!!" The men shot up out of the fo'c's'le into the moonlight in their boxer shorts and pajamas to join the watch on deck. Captain shouted orders, and in a moment all was still again. The jib pennant chain had parted and slashed the great full jib to shreds. Our speed was slowed, but our pulses were not.

14

Pa Goes to Jail

P A'S CONSISTENTLY HIGH estimation of the English had a marked drop when we landed at Dominica on a bright Sunday morning. We had dutifully hoisted up the yellow sick flag to announce our arrival and expectation of clearing. We waited for the officials. We waited a half hour, and then we waited an hour more. No familiar official port rowboat came near us. Finally, Pa, disgusted, said, "Come on, let's land anyway." Nana was having a relapse of her "mountain sickness," and Mother, concerned, decided to stay with her.

Pa and the five children landed on the stone dock. And there, sure enough, were our two types of welcoming committees, a group of attractive young English people examining the new arrivals from an open touring car, and the squalling, squabbling taxi drivers. But another representative, unexpected and unwanted, also awaited us on the dock. A large policeman in full uniform, pith helmet, white jacket, dark trousers, and his billy club in his right hand strode up to Pa, put him under arrest and started to march him off to jail. A great deal of noise bubbled up, mostly from Pa. Quita looked as if she would cry. John stood next to me and called after Pa as he was marched off, saying softly so Pa couldn't hear, "Remember, God created this world for us to enjoy. Don't let the Old Boy down." Just then, through the hubbub, I noted with distinct delight that a handsome young Englishman in white shorts had jumped from the open car at the end of the dock and was running to our rescue.

"Don't worry," he called to Pa, who was disappearing down the road, hauled on by the policeman, "We'll 'arrest' the children, take them into custody and keep them with us. You pay up the fine. We'll go swimming!"

Our prince charming took Quita by the hand, shepherding the rest of us to his car.

"It's illegal, you know, to land in this port on a Sunday. Stupid, of course, but so stands the law. They'll take your father to jail, and the governor will be hopping mad because he hates to have his Sunday services interrupted. He'll fine your father about $20, and then your father will be hopping mad. So we might just as well go along and be well out of it, I'd say. Here's my wife, Mrs. Aird, and here are two bankers, and this is Hettie, and that regal beast is my police dog. Call me Whiggs, and speak to me with respect, for I am the Sub-Inspector of the Police, and I hereby put you all under arrest. Jump in!"

Charmed and never giving a thought to that oft-heard parental warning, "Never drive off with strangers," we climbed into the car and drove far, far away to a beach of black stones and sand stretched in a curving cove. My belief, instilled by romantic movies of the '30s, that all English men were reticent, aloof types was quickly corrected. We were drawn right into a fierce, noisy game of water baseball using an old tennis ball and a waterlogged board. Eventually, however, the game deteriorated into pelting each other with the stinging wet ball.

We had left Willy crouching on the rocks. He couldn't swim because of the plaster cast on his arm, so Whiggs thoughtfully provided him with a sport of his own—catching eels. First, Will smashed snails on the rocks and dropped them into the black pools. Then he waited for the long eels to come out of their dark hiding places and slither toward the bait. Willy then pounced down on them with a pair of pliers and tried to squeeze their slippery shapes tight enough to throw them out on the sand.

Exhausted and stinging from our ball game, we joined Will. Whiggs went to the car and came back with screwdrivers, jack handles, pliers, sticks, and a hook. He handed them out, and we all went eel hunting. We shouted and laughed as we waded through the black water until an eel lashed up and twined around Whiggs's arm, throwing us into a screeching panic. The hunt ended when we finally caught a little eel. Whiggs flipped it over for the dog to tease back into the water. About that time, Whiggs decided we really should go and see how Pa and the Governor were getting along.

Pa was sputtering by the dock, but Whiggs cheered him up by inviting us all for an afternoon excursion to the other end of the island. This was as pleasant an interlude as our morning arrest. We drove off in three cars, having added a pretty, dark woman named Rosie to our party. Passing through miles and miles of lime orchards, we drove up into the mountains to a swift cold mountain stream. A high waterfall roared into a deep dark pool. We swam first in the pool, then crawled under the falls, letting the water crash on our heads and throw a crystal curtain before us. John found a cave in the wall behind the falls. Crawling in, he beckoned me to follow him. We pressed our bodies against the wet rocks. In this cool cavern we had all the delights of swimming underwater and being able to breathe at the same time. The noise of the falls before us kept away the sounds of the other people, and in this watery, womblike darkness we sat silent, immersed in our own inchoate lives. I did not dare look at John. I wanted to reach out and touch him, be Becky Thatcher again in the cave waiting to be rescued by Tom Sawyer, but again John did not get the message. We stayed still until the suspense of our silence grew overwhelming and shot out into the world again.

Inviting our new friends out for cocktails on the *Blue Dolphin*, we continued our bandying talk and teasing—laughing, happy, all of us. Whiggs had an impressive appetite, almost as good as Pa's. We gave them the rarest of the rare in the tropics: fresh apples brought from our Delaware orchard. And we shook hands heartily all around as they departed. Leaving the ship, they gave us a British "Hip . . . Hip . . . Hoorah!" and we waved back, sad to leave their friendly, shining island. Pa was right after all. The English were great.

Then we sailed off to France. We children stood in the bow as the *Blue Dolphin* tacked into Fort de France, the principle port of Martinique.

I knew right away I had made a sound choice when I'd elected to be captain of the *Zélé*, for riding at anchor was a three-masted French naval training ship. I belonged with them, of course, and stood tall on the bowsprit ready to give orders to the swarms of young men moving about the decks and rigging. They were wearing white berets with huge red pompoms. Al and John, of course, considered this ship just another of the defeated fleet that they, as the English, had dominated. Smitty dipped our flag as we passed, and several of the young men saluted us. I returned the salute with a broad grin of gratitude, trying not to hear Pa's ironic discourse on the failure of the French to pay attention to the Treaty of Versailles. Pa believed in treaties.

We landed in a gray drizzle and wandered slowly through the narrow, winding streets, admiring the balconies over our heads, exploring the delights of a French bookstore, trying to translate passages of the French version of *The Black Arrow*. We bought stamps for our collections and finally ended up, very hungry, at a sidewalk café, the sole occupants of the establishment. We scanned the French menu and selected "*filé haché à la Russe*" which turned out to be hamburger, plain and simple. The poor proprietor in his long white apron exhausted himself and his wife trying to keep us supplied with loaf after loaf of fresh French bread, served with sweet butter. He could not understand why we kept clamoring for water. He had brought us bottles of wine. What more did these Americans need?

In the afternoon, after a drive through the jungle, we became archeologists, walking over the ruins of a Caribbean Pompeii, the destroyed city of St. Pierre, smothered and solidified in 1902 in a rain and flood of burning lava from the still-active, still-muttering volcano, Mount Pelée, rising ominously 4,000 feet above us. The lava had trapped an instant forever, mocking time and the process of decay. Pa hinted that the extermination of the French in this disaster was one of nature's ways of correcting mistakes.

On our way back to the ship in the launch, we listened to Ted tell us about his shore leave. "I decided I'd pay my respects to the statues of Josephine," he shouted over the engine noise. "I remembered her from my last visit here. This time I was in a carriage and got stuck in the mud. The hubcaps were already going under when I gave up that visit and dropped in at a sidewalk café to drink to her health instead, along with some of those boys off that training ship. Nice guys. Right, Nina? Then I had some coffee. Wow! That stuff has the potency of triple-distilled nitroglycerine! I yelled, '*Il est fort!*' The manager just smiled at me." By now we were pulling alongside the ship, and Sims was coiling a rope to throw to Smitty, who was standing on deck holding a boat hook.

"Remind me to tell you about the old French woman who thought I was kidnapping her granddaughter," Ted said off-handedly to me as he caught hold of the landing stage, for us to file up the ladder.

Back on the *Blue Dolphin*, I found myself wondering how and why islands that looked so alike in their mountainous green jungle warmth could have people so different in language and looks and habits. I had no answer, of course, but Pa's history lessons were helping.

15

Return of the Rescued

W E CAME INTO St. Lucia on the fifth of December, Ma and Pa's six-
teenth wedding anniversary. Tall Pa stood behind little Ma on the
after deck, his hands on her shoulders, scanning the approach to the island. They had started this day with a certain amount of nostalgic
chitchat, but as we sailed into the harbor of Castries—where Ma and Pa
had landed in lifeboats after the fire on the *Vestris* while on their way to
South America in 1919—they became positively verbose. Up on the hill,
at the end of the elliptical harbor, stood the same barracks that had shel-
tered Mother and Al while they awaited rescue.

"Say, Mom," Al interrupted the stream of Ma and Pa's reminiscences.
"You said I celebrated my first birthday here. I don't remember hearing
you tell about giving me a birthday bash."

"Certainly not," she replied. "I was too busy keeping track of who had
borrowed my sterno stove and who had your potty chair."

Reference to his toilet training silenced Al, but not Ma and Pa, who
went on regaling us with details of the shipwreck and rescue. Clearly, they
were proud of each other in their respective roles in surviving this traumatic event.

We spent three leisurely days in this port, one of the best harbors in
the West Indies, a base of operations for English naval ships during times

of war throughout their history. The crew took advantage of these days to paint the topsides, the part of the hull that showed above the waterline. The rest of us visited the clean, crowded markets, remembering, in spite of the tropic heat, that there were only fifteen more shopping days until Christmas.

Our pet plaything in this harbor was a homemade miniature sloop that a small native boy sailed out around us one day. Only about four feet long, with sleek lines and sails sewn together from flour bags, she was a source of admiration for all. Finally, the young skipper, flattered by our praise and by nature generous, allowed us to take turns sailing his tiny craft. Quita and I squeezed in together and explored the harbor. John tried it and capsized in a gust of wind. He shot out of the water as if projected from underneath by a catapult, propelled by his dread of sharks and barracudas. Even huge Pa took a turn, almost sinking the stalwart little ship. The young boy stood by the rail with us clearly proud of his craft, laughing at our antics, comfortable in his role as the newest member of our family.

Pa had also brought a pile of up-to-date newspapers on board. So our siesta hours were spent catching up with the rest of the world. I liked reading newspapers then and still do. At home we subscribed to the daily *New York Times*, the *Philadelphia Bulletin*, and the Wilmington evening paper. I had become an avid newspaper reader around age six, starting first with the funny papers. Our chauffeur, Pete Riley, liked the funnies too and bought papers that had many more funnies than the *Bulletin* or the *Evening Journal*. All five of us children spent Sunday mornings over at Pete's apartment, lying on our stomachs on the floor, silently reading in the sour, leftover cooking smells of his place. When I was eight, however, I discovered you could learn surprising things from newspapers.

In the fall of my eighth year, I came home from school one day and went to pick up the newspapers for a quick read, but the newspapers were nowhere to be found. There wasn't a paper to be seen. No big deal, I simply paid a call on Pete and he, always obliging, produced his papers. I held up the front page of Pete's *Philadelphia Bulletin* and there was a bold-face headline about our Nana, my own grandmother. It announced that she was a millionairess and was being sued. I was astonished. I had come into a whole new world that had been there all the time, one I hadn't noticed or had sized up completely wrong. One stunning fact was that our family was considered rich. Another was that some clan doings seemed to be unmentionable inside our own voluble family.

The forbidden newspaper detailed the divorce of my mother's brother, Joe. Uncle Joe had married a pretty little chorus girl in Hawaii, whom I had met on a damp hot September afternoon in the grove at Dalhousie. She was steely sleek and, unlike Nana or Mother, was wearing lots of makeup. Clearly, I decided when I met her, there under the great trees, that she was ruining her outer self and proclaiming her superficiality. She couldn't possibly be nice, I thought. She wasn't. From the paper I learned that this made-up chorus girl, now my aunt, was suing Nana for a million dollars, charging her with "alienation of affection," whatever that meant. She and Uncle Joe had been married less than a year, and Nana was so indignant about this woman's unscrupulous greed that she refused to hire a lawyer to guide her through the trial. Nana knew she was right so she decided justice would automatically follow, only to learn, too late, that it is always best to have a lawyer by your side in a court trial. The chorus girl and her smart lawyer walked off with the loot, leaving a confused Uncle Joe and a hissing-cross Nana. For weeks, while the trial was going on, Ma and Pa pretended nothing special was happening, though they talked in whispers to each other and went on hiding the papers. I kept up with the daily courtroom doings off in Pete's quarters, and, of course, never spoke about it to them.

This business of coming from a rich family really had me baffled. How could it be? Mother, Quita, and I darned the family socks every night while Pa read aloud to us. Our family scrimped and saved and handed down clothes. Buying an Easter outfit was unheard of, a ridiculous and unnecessary expense, since Pa had as much respect for Easter as he did for Christmas. Mother never even had the windows washed. She said she found the rays of light filtered through dirt more intrinsically interesting than dazzling clarity.

When Uncle Joe's divorce was going on, we lived in an informal rambling household on a hill. Our neighbors, the duPonts, had much more land than we did and lived in chateaux. Besides, our chauffeur and maids never wore fancy uniforms like the duPonts' help did. Pete always smoked cigarettes when driving us, which was never done by the other chauffeurs. That had all added up in my mind to a single conclusion: We were poor. Now, after this new revelation, I was puzzled. If we were rich, did this mean we had to keep it a secret, or was it just Uncle Joe's misalliance that had to be secret? I studied the newspapers hoping for a clue. I did not dare ask anyone about what was clearly a ticklish issue.

Still, I liked reading newspapers to learn about the horrors of the Depression—breadlines, strikes, suicides, that sort of thing. Pa and his friends argued about the Depression all the time. To them, only politics would solve the problem. I had a hard time understanding the differences between the Republicans and the Democrats except for the general principle that Republicans were good and the Democrats evil. I read avidly about the private lives of our eminent men and women. My favorite was the international swindler, Ivar Kreuger. I read about him on the train coming home from the Friday afternoon concerts of the Philadelphia Orchestra.

Rattling though the gray wintry evening light, through the drab sooty city of Chester—when I wasn't watching for the sparkling lights that read "What Chester Makes, Makes Chester"—I read on about the life of Ivar Kreuger. I struggled to find out how one man could twine so many countries around his wicked finger just by making ordinary kitchen matches. The intricacies of his money manipulations were beyond me, but his evil character was not. When he committed suicide I was relieved. But suicide presented me with a problem. In Kreuger's case, it seemed justified: Good riddance. But friends of Pa's, fathers of schoolmates, they were committing suicide too. They had lost all their money, Pa explained, and could see no way of regaining control of their lives. In that case, I didn't understand how suicide solved much. Wouldn't the poor wife have to take care of everything whether she wanted to or not? And anyway, why would money control a life?

Pa, reading his papers in the quiet port of Castries, finally could contain himself no longer. He had come to the columns on Roosevelt. All newspapers in those days were sure to carry the latest on Roosevelt, and

Pa always reacted to our president's latest moves with vociferous objections. This time an article explained how the Public Works Administration was functioning. Pa objected.

"It's wrong to use citizens to do unnecessary projects." He spoke loudly enough so that we all had to stop what we were doing and listen. "States and local communities know what needs to be fixed. They should be setting up such programs. Roosevelt is interrupting the unconscious equilibrium of the forces of the market place. The invisible hand of the free market, man's instinct for acquisition, his profit motive, and his innate goodness, these drives will keep capitalism going. Doesn't *That Man* realize that business cycles are part of the evolutionary process? We shouldn't tamper with them. If you leave capitalism alone, both property and income will be equalized."

I often wondered, years later, how Pa would have felt if he could have read Al's Pulitzer Prize–winning book refuting this doctrine of Adam Smith's. "See here, he continued. "Owners of land, bridges, and roads have a moral obligation to keep them up. It is *not* the federal government's responsibility. How can decent, hard working individuals create new initiatives to get men working and money flowing if they are all tied up in government red tape. It's crazy. These Democrats will ruin us." Pa stopped only long enough for us to look up, hoping he was through, but no.

"From the dawn of history," he said, picking up a new theme, "to this very moment, politicians, whether in public affairs or private organizations like labor unions, as well as churchmen of all sorts, have had utter contempt for the depth of peoples' minds. They shout slogans and cite stereotypes. But we must go beyond these inferior people and look to the real movement of historical forces. We, like St. Paul, must add the ingredient of love. Good intentions will not be enough. Hell's paving stones are good intentions. We must combine our deep understanding with concrete action. In the long run, advertising without a quality product profiteth the stockholders nothing."

"Pa?" I interrupted. He was getting boring again. Besides, we had heard this speech many times over. "Was Ivar Kreuger pushed by the invisible hand to do what he did?"

"*Honi soi qui mal y pense,*" he replied, a phrase he was always using as a conversation stopper. He infuriated me. The French Ma was teaching me did not give me the skill to translate this one. I really wanted to know what he meant by that phrase and understand how Ivar Kreuger fitted into Pa's schemes, but Pa called an end to the lecture as abruptly as he had interrupted us minutes before to return to his reading.

When the tropic night fell with its always-unexpected suddenness, the strains of "The Old Irish Washerwoman" drew the children to the bow. Charlie and Ted, returning from shore leave, had come back on board with a battered old accordion. Charlie had seen it in a little shop and professing a talent with accordions, persuaded Ted, the only crew member with any spending money left, to buy the instrument, promising to pay him back on the installment plan. Charlie's dance tune grew louder, propelling Ted to the center of the seated circle of admiring listeners. He grabbed the cap off sedate Mr. Doyle's white head and danced around seeking contributions. "Peep! Peep!" he squeaked, pointing to the heavens as he pirouetted around us. Charlie shifted to a waltz, and the sad and sorrowful old Doyle rose and shuffled across the deck, swaying lugubriously from side to side. Ted whisked up to him. "May I have this dance?" The couple never joined. Instead a free-for-all ensued with Ted almost pushed overboard. They couldn't agree on who would be the female partner.

Our pleasure was interrupted by a call from the stern. We were being ordered below to clean up in the whisky water and dress up. Tonight, we'd be dining ashore at a hotel. As we lined up to climb into the launch, Pa muttered, "I suspect the good cheer in the bow has been helped by that free bottle of booze the ship chandler gave Charlie."

After dinner, returning to our ship, we stopped at the end of the dock and climbed the high, wide gangplank of the glistening white cruise ship, the *Lady Hawkins*, tied up there. A mate greeted us and introduced us to the purser. The purser, a young officer in starched white, high-collared uniform, showed us his ship, so huge and remote from our little craft.

The ladies on board were dressed in flimsy gauzy long dresses and sparkled with jewels. The officers looked more like Hollywood's idea of sailors than honest sailing men, the kind we knew. I took in this world of formal clothes, etiquette, supervised walks ashore, ballroom dancing, and bridge and contrasted it with our simple, salty life. I was glad to find how much closer to the sea we really were in all ways compared to these lofty visitors.

The *Lady Hawkins* sailed shortly after we'd returned to the *Blue Dolphin*, coming close around our bow, a blaze of lights, the band playing, propellers churning up the phosphorus in the quiet waters. Suddenly, I felt brave and solitary, leaning against the binnacle of our little ship, ready to continue our adventures. I was proud of our solid small family and our disheveled crew. Looking at the diminishing lights of the big ship, I said to myself, "Let them go their stylish ways. We are the true searchers."

Our own departure from St. Lucia was noisy. We put into the dock to take on oil and water. Just as we were about to cast off, Charlie came up through the forward hatch carrying two bushel baskets of apples, brown and mildewed, soft and running in rot.

"Here you are, dearie!" he called and heaved an apple at a tall girl walking down the dock. The effect was remarkable and instantaneous. Instead of being indignant, as I was, embarrassed by such bad manners, the girl seized what she could of the apple and shouted, "Thanks!" From nowhere came a swarm of people yelling, "More! More!" We all came to the bow, crew and children, and heaved the rotten apples to the mob. A screaming free-for-all was building up on the dock as the apples squashed on contact. Captain took control and ordered us out, but fast, and Charlie rubbed his sticky hands in satisfaction having got rid of some of that damned fresh foodstuff.

16

The Vast British Empire
in Two Short Stops

W<small>E HAD TWO</small> more English islands to visit, Barbados and Trinidad, before we would come to the great continent of South America. A heavy easterly wind drove us down to Barbados, and we were relieved to sail into the quiet of the big, busy port of Bridgetown. Coming into the harbor, we passed a working windmill with white sails, reminding us of the mill near our house in Nantucket. This time the welcoming committee came to us before we could even get ashore, bum boats and ships' chandlers, bumping alongside in their small crafts, waving their ads.

One chandler obligingly brought out our mail, a sack containing bundles of envelopes, magazines, newspapers, and cables, a real haul. With mail at hand, all other activity ceased. Disregarding the sun, the harbor activity and one another, we followed the delicate web of written words that led us gently homeward, entangling us once more in the world we had left and the people we loved.

Al chuckled deep in his chest. "Read this letter from Sophie," he said. "She's thanking me for saving her from drowning that time I pulled her out of the pond at Dalhousie. Remember?"

No one answered. His remarks were not sharp enough to break the thread of our concentration, but a shout up forward from Chief caught our attention. He was blowing his nose. Captain stepped forward and patted him on the back. The other men shook his hand awkwardly. His news was of the birth of his fifth child, a girl. Then the crew turned to Mr. Doyle, who was leaning against the foremast. He spoke briefly and disappeared below. His news was of his brother's death.

We had visited a lot of English ports, but this one was the grandest of them all, a true outpost of the Great Empire. We stayed there five days and spent most of our time in English clubs. We sipped lime squashes at the Yacht Club; swam at the Aquatic Club; lounged in stiff chairs along the walls of the Marine Club, watching the dancers in the dim night lights; and saw Wild West movies at still another club. We never did get used to the practice of the English playing "God Save The King" at the end of each feature. I didn't like this practice. I wanted to think about the film, extending the plot into the future and relishing the smashing victory of the hero. I resented being recalled so quickly to duty and Empire. After the crowds had filed out of the Club Room, Pa and I would sit together at an upright piano and thump out our favorites, "Lord Jeffrey Amherst," "Boola Boola," and a last triumphant "Fair Harvard." I figured out modulations in the bass as Pa played the melody in octaves in the treble, singing fortissimo and off-key as he went.

An amenable young bachelor, the manager of the Yacht Club, a proper Englishman, took a proprietary interest in us children. I wasn't sure why, but assumed it was because I was so charming—the eyes, you know, the look. I was too young and unsophisticated to suspect the obvious, that the manager was the product of English public schools with a yen for boys. He took Al and John off sightseeing the day we arrived and returned to take the rest of us to dance at his club. The next day he was about to drive off with Al and John again in his little English Austin when Quita, Willy, and I begged to come too. After a moment of hesitation, he let us squash into the tiny, open car and drove us over the green island. The rolling hills made us homesick for the hills of upper Delaware and we spent most of the afternoon at an old plantation. The house had been built in 1735 in the Palladian manner—classic, white, surrounded by formal gardens and notable outbuildings, in particular a tiny plantation chapel in stone. The manager gave us a running commentary on the slaves and their owners, while the monkeys in the woods behind us chattered and squealed. Once again, the sequence of time was interrupted and we were in 1735.

On our second day in port, a little yawl swung close to our stern and anchored behind us. We shouted out an invitation to the crew to join us for drinks. A redheaded Englishman of about twenty and his two young friends came on board and told us of their plans. They were sailing to the Pacific, to Cocos, hoping to find treasure. As this island was on our itinerary, we pricked up our ears. The three adventurers alternated between enthusiastically revealing their plans and withholding crucial information. They had extensive maps and charts but weren't about to divulge their clues as to the location of treasure. This didn't bother us too much. We figured we'd beat them to the island and get digging long before they got there—not that we had any clues as to where to dig. These boys were so immersed in the port club life that it looked as if their treasure hunt might be postponed indefinitely.

Mr. Henchal was the ship chandler we chose, mainly because we discovered that he had a family of many children and seemed to take a special interest in us, wanting us to have a good time in his port. Through his connection with the Hamburg American Line, he engineered a visit to a German ship anchored near us, the *Magdalena*, a huge passenger vessel on a southern cruise. The captain of the *Magdalena* was a special friend of Mr. Henchal's and to oblige him agreed to send his launch for us. Mother lined us up, smoothed our plaid gingham dresses, brushed Quita's and my hair for the third time, tweaked the boys' ties straight and said we were ready. She and Nana put on their best linen skirts and silk blouses, hats, and brown brogues while Pa delivered a brief lecture on the problems of Germany since the war. Germany, Russia, and Italy, he proclaimed, were corrupted by the tyranny of totalitarian state power, the loss of individual freedom. Why then, I wondered, did we get so gussied up for the baddies?

Captain Kolher stood at the head of the gangplank to meet us. From my novel and newspaper reading, he fitted my idea of how the German people should be represented. The stiffness of his white uniform controlled his fat flesh, although one or two little rolls escaped over the collar. His eyes were a cold blue, but his welcome was warm and genuine enough, spoken in a deep voice with a thick accent. I had to listen especially carefully; his words had a way of building into a guttural surge that left me behind. The ship was clean, orderly, and comfortable but so grand that one would have to search for intimacy.

Pa had told us to mind our manners. "Civil tensions can be eased by civil tongues," he said, so we were on our best behavior as Captain Kolher led us to the main salon. Orangeade was presented to the children and the grownups were served tall steins of dark brown beer. Even the children, allowed a sip of beer, could tell the difference between this and the 3.3 percent prohibition brew served at home. The captain took us from bilge to bridge, and then we dined in splendor. Al, John, and I sat at the first mate's table. I took in the elegance of this dining room and decided it deserved the name "salon," though I definitely could go on calling our eating chamber on the *Blue Dolphin* a saloon.

Ma and Pa belonged to the "Pay-Them-Back" school, so it was inevitable that Captain Kolher receive an invitation to dinner with us. The *Magdelena*, however, was about to sail, leaving Mother only able to offer a quick glass of rum. As Captain Kolher was leaving our ship, he teasingly tried to persuade Willy to return to the *Magdalena* with him and take over the job of co-captain. Willy firmly refused, standing at the door of our saloon with his legs apart, arms crossed over his chest, his chin flattened down on his neck, so the captain left him a memento instead, a hat band with "Magdalena" written across it and his address, in case Willy changed his mind. As the *Magdalena* sailed out of the harbor past our stern, she thrilled us with her salute, three blasts on her deep, vibrant foghorn, and the German flag at the stern was dipped for us. We returned the salute, Willy blowing on a giant conch shell to supplement the thin bleat of our foghorn. We waved and waved until the great ship was out of sight, happily unaware of the awful historical forces that would soon put Al, Will, and John in military uniforms fighting the Germans.

On the fourth morning in Barbados, as we awaited the repair of our jib and bowsprit, it rained and rained and rained, a cooling bath of gray water after days of tropic glare. Two Barbadian natives from the harbor police wearing dark capes came rowing around us in their white boat on a tour of inspection of the harbor. Pa leaned out from under the awning.

"When is this bad weather going to stop?" he shouted.

"This ain't weather, sir, this is only a haze," came their cheery answer.

Dampened, Pa drew back under the awning and continued reading aloud the last chapters of *Quentin Durward* while Mother behaved peculiarly. It must have been the cool, refreshing air that did something to her metabolism, the way spring affected the average housewife at home. She suddenly had an uncontrollable urge to rearrange furniture and clean. Since most of our furniture was bolted to the floor, Mother was at a disadvantage. We could hear her thumping and grumbling below. Pa seemed glad to be able to go on reading, distancing himself from her occasional imperious commands. She continued to redistribute clothes in closets and drawers, picking up discarded items from dark back corners, poking in recesses. She came on deck occasionally with a look of triumph as she threw debris overboard—all those rotten shells, dead crabs, fish skeletons, movie stubs, and the like that we had tucked into our bureau drawers, our precious collections. She watched with satisfaction as they sank slowly into the sea while Pa read louder and louder, not even asking if we wanted the next chapter, protecting Ma from what he could sense was our growing need to protest her peremptory behavior.

The next day was still overcast, but we swam at the Club with our new friend, the manager, and his tall, athletic pal. That night, these two men took us kids to see *Tarzan, the Ape Man*, with Johnny Weismuller playing Tarzan, and gave us lime squashes after the movie was over. They, of course, had to be paid back and entertained by us, so they came out for a farewell drink before our departure for Trinidad that afternoon. We saw them off the *Blue Dolphin* with a chorus of good-byes, only to realize we weren't going anywhere. Our anchor was afoul on an abandoned pipeline. Captain summoned a native diver who appeared for work clad only in a brief loincloth, no aqua-lungs or goggles or other impedimenta. His bronze body plummeted off the bow, and in a matter of seconds he burst to the surface announcing, laconically, that the anchor was freed.

So we sailed off to the south again, before the wind, our tackle creaking, our lines taut, and the gray-pink of the tropic sunset fading to the west. As soon as we left the harbor, we hit a choppy, murky sea. Our supper was remarkable in that the electricity went off, leaving us in darkness. A unanimous groan filled the void, then a burst of giggles, a scurrying, Charlie cursing over the hot stove, Chief growling, "Where the hell are my bill-nosed-pliers?" knowing perfectly well they were under Willy's pillow. Quita spilled lemonade. Ted found a flashlight and shone it on the generator while Chief's tools clinked away. The defect was soon corrected, and our lights flooded on again.

Led by a school of leaping porpoises, we sailed all the next day down past Tobago toward Trinidad. Pa started *Robinson Crusoe*, with his children lying around him on the deckhouse listening. Defoe was extolling the virtues of the middle class and the Common Man. I interrupted Pa to ask what class we belonged to, but I should have known better. All I did was launch Pa off on another lecture. Pa said we were part of the Common Man. The United States existed for the Common Man and capitalists would equalize us all to this one class. Then Al made things worse by suggesting that the Marxists had a different way of equalizing us all. That really started Pa off.

"I've always agreed with my grandfather, Henry Varnum Poor. When he was a reporter for the *New York Tribune*, along with Horace Greeley and others on the paper, he decided to pay Karl Marx to come to New York. Having read Marx's excellent articles on our Civil War, they wanted to talk with him, thinking they might hire him as a reporter for their newspaper. When I asked my grandfather to tell me about Marx, he answered, 'He was a very bright young man but sadly lacking in experience.' You have to live in the world and know it before you can reform it. Remember that. Now Marx, dear boy, was unreliable in his conclusions. And terribly dull. I don't see how he could enflame anybody, but he did. Marx saw the evils of his day just as Dickens and Thackeray did, but he hadn't really researched the problem. So this, combined with faulty theories of the early nineteenth century, distracted him from really seeing how much progress was being made. Marx's gods, the proletariat and the capitalists, are well drawn, I'll have to admit, and the story of their battle Homeric. That part of his writing does make great reading; reminds me of the spats between Athena and Poseidon in Greek myths, but they do not, and never have, in any age or place, represent reality."

"Read!" commanded Willy. "This is boring."

Muddied by the outflow of the river Orinoco, the water around us was no longer a sparkling greenish blue, but a brownish green, an unpropitious bilious color. The soil of South America was welcoming us. Then a halyard snapped and the fisherman's staysail crashed to the deck, which interrupted Pa's reading, but did not stop him. After supper John, Al, and I went to the bow to listen to Charlie play his accordion, while Nana read to Quita and Willy.

The next morning a huge wave took the ship and slapped it over to the next wave, almost succeeding in throwing me out of my bunk. I looked at the Big Ben rattling on the bureau and noted it was 6:00 A.M. The motor was shaking the ship with its mechanical jiggle, and I could hear the flapping sails jerking the sheets through the blocks. I dressed, climbed the companionway, and found green Trinidad before us. We were sailing through a churning riptide and approaching the Dragon's Mouth, a narrow passage between walls of rock, a fitting illustration of Robinson Crusoe country indeed! We passed crags and caves and even the bare, white bones of a wrecked schooner.

Once inside the calm of the long harbor of Port au Spain, we sailed leisurely along the coast, by green estates running down the slopes to the shore, symmetrical, cultivated. A fuss of small boats and a waving crowd on the starboard shore were gathered to watch an amphibious plane take off. Later we learned that this was Charles Lindbergh on his way to South America. Once in the inner harbor, we had the pleasure of recognizing our old friend, the *Lady Hawkins*, the cruise ship we had boarded in St. Lucia. I grabbed the binoculars and tried to pick out the figure of the handsome purser, with no luck.

Up until now, our English ports had been just that—England English. This port led us to the British Empire and India. We were now, in effect, in the Far East, where generations of Hindu immigrants had come to live. The streets were narrow and twisting. The place seemed to be an extended bazaar. Indian women in saris, with round dots on their foreheads, walked serenely through the crowds. Some were veiled and wore gleaming, tinkling gold and silver bracelets on their arms and ankles. Willy held my hand. This town was really foreign. It was scary.

We walked slowly along the main street under the awnings, through arcades, silent ourselves in the overpowering noise. A man ran up to us holding a placard covered with jingling bracelets and necklaces, shouting about his wares and shoving his glitter at our eyes. A quiet Indian woman held yards of fine lace, delicate in its black tracery, up to the sun for us to behold. From a music store nearby, a Victrola blared out a calypso song. A monkey store stood next to a parrot store, and their inmates added their cacophony to that of the street. When we came to a mosque, Pa instructed us to take off our shoes and line them up in pairs by the door while we went in to seek a little quiet. Once in the dusky stale-smelling space, we stood speechless, gazing at the intricate system of cusped horseshoe arches, the wild swirling of arabesques and geometric patterns of the mosaics that jangled our eyes, just as the noises of the street had jangled our ears.

We spent the afternoon at the botanical gardens, wandering through a bamboo forest and a grove of olive trees, then past a nutmeg and a clove and a bayberry. We rested a moment under the shade of a mahogany tree and we ended our visit with a game of tag around the Brazil nut trees with home base the monkey-pot tree.

When the *Blue Dolphin* sailed out through the Dragon's Mouth again, late in the afternoon, we hit the familiar riptide and ran through a series of rain squalls into the steady prevailing wind that would carry us through the night along the northern coast of South America. The next day Quita, Willy, and I, with time on our hands, sat down behind the forward ventilator and built a city out of the cardboard from Pa's laundered shirts. The houses in our city were shaded by groves of trees, Delaware trees, buttonwood and maple, blue spruce and gingko, and the hills had holly and the houses had boxwood and magnolias, and all the children had to catch the school bus every morning, disappearing into the world around the block.

That night Mother wrote home to Mary Morris, declaring that our run down the West Indies had been a "triumphant passage." She was readying herself for a joyous return to South America.

17

South America Revisited

I'D BEEN AWED by the mountains of Haiti but decided Haiti's mountains were mere hills compared to the ranges of South America that were now coming into view. This new, immense land mass emerging before us, climbing up into the clouds and turning to ice, was a sharp contrast to the succession of green dots of islands. We were sailing along Venezuela's rocky coast, aiming for La Guaira.

When we got there, we found the port had no land to enclose it, no natural harbor to welcome us. A ridiculously small man-made breakwater, running parallel to the shore, would be our only protection from the heavy, rolling seas. Spray from surf crashing against these rocks flew so high in the air that it seemed as if the little red-roofed houses, perched on crags and precipices above the port, would wash away.

We tacked back and forth, waiting for the pilot and port doctor. "Wow!" exclaimed John, as we children stood respectfully together watching three small fishing boats, flying Venezuelan flags, nearly capsize as they wallowed dangerously in the high seas that funneled through the narrow entry into the port. Once through the gauntlet ourselves, we tied up alongside the other ships in the little harbor behind the breakwater. We had to wait for a few passport difficulties to be resolved, doused all the while by the foamy spray of crashing waves, before we could go ashore.

Ma and Pa were in a sunny mood indeed as we climbed up onto the quay. St. Lucia had drawn them together with memories of their *Vestris* trip, and now they were positively exuberant, so glad to be returning to the South America they loved, where they had had such a fruitful time at the beginning of their marriage. Giving us each a hand as we jumped out of the long boat, they were carrying on together in their resurrected fluent Spanish, laughing, leaving us quiet and wondering what would happen next. Although Spanish had been my first language, I had long since forgotten it, as had my siblings, and we really didn't know what they were talking about. Annoying. I felt left out.

Pa, with a pat on Ma's shoulder, announced in English that he was off to hunt for railroad information to get us to Caracas, the capital of Venezuela, up in the mountains behind the port. Mother set out for a stroll, her children trailing her like so many ducklings. We were all renewing our acquaintance with our land legs when Ma stopped abruptly, staring at a signpost. "What's the matter?" asked Al, joining her at the post. Ma pointed to the sign. "That arrow leads to the local leper colony." We understood perfectly why she turned and ran, not walked, back to Pa who was standing at the ticket window of the train station.

"Ralf!" she declared, "You buy first-class tickets! Think germs, not budgets!"

"*Si, si, che,*" answered Pa, pleased but puzzled that for once she had overcome her usual penny pinching. He turned to the little man behind the iron grille, requested in his best Spanish, "Eight first-class tickets, *por favor, señor.*"

The ticket man said, "Excuse me," and ran to find his superior. The superior came and studied the problem. Unable to solve it, he called the central office in Caracas. The ticket man leaned toward Pa, shaking his head sorrowfully.

"Oh, *señor,* we are so sorry, but we cannot sell you first-class tickets. You will have to go third class."

"Please explain the difficulty, *señor*," said Pa with a touch of indignation.

"It's so simple, *señor*. We only have four first-class tickets in print. You are eight in your party."

The Spanish became tempestuous in its speed and tone. Huge Papa waved his arms in magnificent gestures. The little Spaniard waved back with alacrity. Finally, the officious man gave up and agreed to create four first-class tickets in his own spidery handwriting, which almost matched the four existing printed first-class tickets. We ran and jumped on board the only first-class car just as the electric train was pulling out of the station.

The car was small but elegant with seats for twelve. We were the only passengers present. The chairs and walls were pale blue with gold trim. Ornate gold-framed mirrors hung at the ends of the car. I felt as if I had walked into a European drawing room rather than into the prickly green plush Pennsylvania Railroad Pullman seats I'd expected.

Slowly the train moved out of the station and into the suburbs of La Guaira. We could see that heavy surf still pounding over the breakwater. As we looked down from the heights, red roofs and pink patios passed below us. We moved out over a trellis bridge

"Now, children," Pa announced, pausing, indicating the lesson of the day was about to begin. This time the miraculous engineering project that let the train run up the mountain so steeply was the topic; but when the train came to an abrupt halt, Pa had to cut his opening paragraph short "Oh, too bad," he said dejectedly. "The electricity has gone off." I looked dubiously at my father. Rather than confront him, I turned and pressed my nose against the window to stare at the dark jungle around us. A mountain stream leaped over the boulders in its path, leaving a trail of splashing diamonds in the slim sunrays that spiked the dank greenness. Pa visibly cheered when the train regained consciousness, and we moved into the sun to continue our tightrope act, running along a waving ribbon of track bed that paralleled a road.

"Boy! I'm glad I didn't have to build this road!" exclaimed Willy, gazing at a huge wooden cross on a nearby peak overlooking the road and the track. Pa had translated the plaque at the base of the cross for him. It read, "For those killed on active duty in building this highway." To Willy, the great size of the cross meant only one thing: a great number of humans had been sacrificed. As we ran alongside the road, we passed a succession of formidable blocks, a pile of rubble from a landslide, and a huge tree fallen across the white strip, tensing me up as I awaited similar blocks on our track and the consequent crash. Far below us, on the edge of the sea, we saw a maze of white walls in the sun that enclosed the condemned of the leper colony. I mused on what it must feel like to know for sure you were dying, rotting away. I shivered. "Mummy, where's my coat?" I asked, amazed at feeling cold after so many weeks of roasting sun. My long, fitted, powder blue wool coat matched the color of the car and felt odd against my skin. It was welcome, however, as we rose 12,000 feet above sea level into the rarefied atmosphere of the upper mountains.

Pa, always enthralled by engines, began reminiscing about his experiences in France during the war, and that led to further reminiscences on bringing railroads to Argentina and Chile. Somehow this bought us to the inevitable lecture on capitalism.

"There are two kinds of people in this world," he began, "givers and takers. Capitalists are givers; takers the parasites of society. A taker is anyone who fails to return to society an equal or greater amount of those things that he required or consumed in his daily existence." Pa charged us to be capitalists as he had been in South America. "We must make machinery and create new outlets for our products to keep pace with the growth of the wide world of customers. You must never make a profit and keep it for yourself or you'll turn into a taker. You must plow your rewards back into your community, so that it can continue to grow. Now Paul Robeson," he declared loudly trying to keep our attention, "and the painter, your mother's teacher, John Sloan, are givers."

Characteristically Mother was paying no attention to Pa's story; she never did. But this time, Pa did get her to look at him.

"Now the pioneers conquering the West," he continued, "were takers, because they razed the land as they went, exhausting the soil, never thinking of the people who would follow." The lecture ended as we came slowly into the station at Caracas.

We stepped off the train into a huge space planted in a baroque display of brilliant red, purple, and orange flowers. There were plashing fountains. Tropical birds with lurid plumage darted over us. We all crowded into a large taxi and headed into the hilly city. As the streets grew narrower, the crowds thinned out. Sidewalks often rose five or six feet above the street, coming down to street level at the corners with a flight of steps. The overhanging balconies shut out the sun. Simon Bolivar, the George Washington of this country, on or off a horse, was the central statue in every park and square. Pa was orating on the subject of South American politics, the course of recent revolutions and dictators and counter-revolutions and new dictators of this Spanish city.

Suddenly an explosion like a pistol shot sent the taxi careening and crashing into the high curb.

"Assassination!" yelled Alfie.

"Stop that!" shrieked Nana, indignant and frightened. Quita and I clutched each other. The explosion proved somewhat less exciting than the revolution we were sure we were in—just a tire blowout.

Pa decided we should see a bullfight, although Mother and Nana were not enthusiastic about the idea. We all marched off in the afternoon to a vast classical amphitheater at the edge of the city. We pretended we were Romans at the Coliseum as we climbed up the tiers to our perch near the top in the sun. In Dominica we had seen a Joe Penner movie poking fun at bullfights, painting a ridiculous picture with wide brushstrokes of slapstick, so we felt ready to scoff and remain aloof, strictly spectators. Two unthreatening local bulls stumbled into the arena, picked and poked and pursued by the diabolical little dancers. I tried to cover my growing horror with a cloak of sarcasm; but gradually, I was joining in the animal-like enthusiasm of the mob, spectator no more. I had become an active participant in the ritual.

Next came two imported Spanish bulls, projected out of the pen in succession, fierce and murderous. I leapt to my feet with the rest of my family and screamed with the crowd, hypnotized now by the ballet of the banderilleros with their scarlet capes and glittering daggers. They killed the first bull, sending us all into a crazed surge of screaming and whistling, men throwing hats in the air, women waving white handkerchiefs. A little boy in front of me threw up. Then a band played soothing music to calm our sadism. Two mules, bedecked in sumptuous cloth and jangling bells, dragged the dead bull through the dust, circling the arena twice. The final climax of the afternoon came with the introduction of the matador, Pepito Bienvenido, resplendent in purple, cerise, and pink silks, who was to be pitted against the last and fiercest of the imported bulls. Pandemonium. The police were powerless to stop the stampede that swirled around the hero after his triumphal kill. A howling mob rushed into the ring and lofted the tiny fighter on their shoulders, tossing him high to the sky, throwing him from person to person, finally bearing him triumphantly past the silk-decked box reserved for the official guests of the day, dark señoritas in mantillas and generals sporting arrays of medals. It was hard trying to return to being normal Americans after all this.

That evening, at the German Hotel where we were staying, we filed into the dining room for another large meal. For the past few days, Al and John had taken to teasing me mercilessly. I had been fending off their assaults in a heavy-handed way, enjoying the battle. But now, all of sudden, here was Al being a model of politeness, smiling graciously as I came to sit in a chair he held for me. I shouldn't have been surprised when, with a smirk at John, he pulled the chair out from under me as I sat down. I landed on the floor, hurt and momentarily indignant. I didn't have to say anything, though, as I stood and brushed myself off. Nana was bawling him out until he blushed. Maybe I was bruised in flesh, but as I gathered myself together, I knew I was learning how to deal with males who thought themselves superior. This, I was sure, would serve me in good stead as I continued to grow up, judging from the number of "superior" males that now seemed to surround me.

After a rather subdued dinner, we all retired to luxuriate in our first freshwater baths since San Juan. We slept that night under blankets, shivering in the clear, cold darkness. The next day we coasted down the mountain to La Guaira in our train and were back at our ship for lunch.

Our departure, as with our arrival, was delayed by passport difficulties. Pa went ashore to cut red tape while we bided our time on deck watching the port scene. By now we were used to the waves shattering against the breakwater and sending spray in shining rain over our heads.

The arrival of a tanker from Wilmington, Delaware, our hometown, sent us children into a fit of cheering the new arrivals, jumping up and down, waving and shouting, to their bewilderment. A Dutch gunboat followed the tanker, skidding along the waves into port. A twenty-one-gun salute from the fort on the hill welcomed her. The gunboat responded with the same number of shots. This, of course, inspired us to play out a South American revolution on shipboard that only had to stop when Pa showed up.

With all hands on board, we braved the heavy swells and sailed out to sea. That night the waves ran high. No one slept. Mother and Quita, now in the preferred upper bunk of our cabin, were drenched when we took a comber over the bow. Those portholes never stopped leaking. Nana and I compared notes at breakfast. We were both stiff from trying to hold ourselves in our bunks through the night. Roly-poly old Mr. Doyle reported that he fell out of his bunk twice. But the wind was a fair wind, and it drove us along to the island of Curaçao. We were ready for our last island in the European Grand Tour circuit.

18

Dutch Dichotomies

W E HAD BEEN to Holland before, when we'd stopped at Saba, just after our unhappy stay at Puerto Rico, but somehow it had not seemed properly Dutch. Now we were approaching the island of Curaçao where two wide-armed windmills, turning slowly in the wind, bought us much closer to Holland. Indeed, the flat, marshy land we were approaching almost demanded dikes.

Saba had been a tiny extinct volcano, a cone rising symmetrical and solitary out of the great, gray ocean. We couldn't even make our own landing but had to wait for burly Dutchmen to come and take us in to a narrow shale beach rising abruptly, steeply between huge boulders. We had held our breath, awed, as we approached the high surf. Our Dutchmen, in a long boat that reminded us of Nantucket whaleboats, swept us in with their oars, riding a tall wave up the angled shore. We had to jump out quickly before the next wave could catch us and pull us back into the undertow.

Donkeys waited for us there to carry us up the long flight of steps curving around the volcano to Bottom, the town at the top, tucked into the crater cavity. The donkeys amazed us. They really climbed. Some of the steps were four feet high. The donkeys, even the one with Pa on his back, put both forefeet on the top of the high step and hunched up their rears in a great heave. I stayed in the saddle by clinging to my donkey's neck. Once in the orderly town, with its immaculate Dutch-like houses, we felt as though we were in a proper Holland. The governor's wife, a buxom hausfrau in a cloud of chiffon, gave us a cool lemony drink with froth on top and let us play with her sad-eyed spaniel. The children of the town were eager to play with us and take us into their houses.

Remembering such eloquent hospitality, we were eagerly looking forward to our next Dutch port, the one we were now rapidly approaching. But I was still puzzled by the Dutch. They lived beneath water level in Holland, so why had they chosen such an elevated spot as Saba to colonize? And I thought they were daring. How did they know the volcano was truly extinct?

We waited a while, tacking off the shore of Curaçao, until a bridge the length of two city blocks, supported by fourteen pontoons, swung open to admit us to a wide canal leading into a landlocked harbor. To our delight we found this town built around an intricate system of canals, just as a Dutchman would have had it. We tied up right next to the street running along the main canal, stepped from the deck to the sidewalk and began to explore.

The houses seemed to be copies of Dutch paintings. They stood tall and narrow, crowded together, rising three stories high. The only condescension to the tropics was the color of the houses—some pink, some deep red. A bright blue house stood between two soft gray buildings. Around a bend in the canal, we spotted a tall orange house rising above the murky waters. But the sturdy brown oak doors kept northern European climates in mind. The timbers of the houses were exposed, outlining the frameworks of the stucco structures.

We found the town immaculately clean, the cobbles of the streets laid in symmetrical designs. "Very Dutch," said Nana, although she had never set foot in Holland. The main traffic of the town was carried on in the canals. Pristine side streets were only wide enough for pedestrian traffic. "Also Dutch," said Pa, who never had been to Holland either. The harbormaster befriended us and invited us to his club to meet his blond wife and their white-haired baby. He took us for a swim in a coral cove; and then, back at his club, treated the grownups to beer and us children to lime sodas. Unfortunately, Pa and Al were suddenly stricken with a mild ptomaine poisoning and had to run back to the boat and to bed.

After supper, conveniently tied up right there at the curb of the main street, Nana, Mother, John, Willy, and I jumped ship, quite literally, onto the cobbles and began wandering through the town in the bright moonlight. Nana and I were momentarily sidetracked when we simultaneously lost our hearts to four sailors from a Dutch navy battleship. We branched off from the rest of the family and silently followed the young men in their bright blue uniforms, instinctively imitating their long sea strides. When they entered a bar, however, Nana felt it necessary to pull me along with her back to our group. We found John entering a small, dark store run by a tall Indian in a white suit, and we all followed him single file into the incense-saturated bazaar whose shelves held exotic eastern goods. Mother and I found collections of wonderful miniature ivory animals. How I would have loved them a few years back when I spent hours with my china-animal families working out the drama of their lives down on the mossy banks of the brook below the pond at home. The trick boxes laminated in bright patterns with sliding sides absorbed the boys, particularly Willy. Sated with shopping, we walked again down the narrow streets along the canals, admiring the moon behind the rigging of the fishing fleet.

Ted hopped back on board just as the children were trying to postpone bedtime, begging Ma to let us listen to the sad strains of a three-piece band at the Café Suiza across the street from our berth. Ted was humming happily, twirling along the deck towards the forward companionway.

"Tra! La! And a hey-de-hey!" he sang as he waltzed past me.

"Were have you been?" I asked hopefully, loving his stories.

"Who me?" said Ted circling to a stop. "Wow! What a night! What a girl!"

"Oh, come on, tell!" I begged.

"Well, it's like this: Mr. Doyle and I went through all those Hindu bazaars, and we decided to drift into a café to enjoy the music and quaff a bit of German beer. It was real nice in there, smoky and dark, and some mighty good-looking girls. There was one in particular, a black-eyed Spanish queen I had my eye on, so I got up to ask her to dance."

I broke into his story, remembering some of mother's dictates on man-woman relationships. "Ted, I thought you told us you had a girl in Nantucket, the one who runs the sweet shop on Centre Street. Aren't you going to stick to her?"

"Yes, yes, I am, but sailors, well . . . you know about sailors." I didn't, but I was hoping to find out.

"To go on, before I was so rudely interrupted, there was this thug of a waiter. He got hold of my shoulder and made it clear: no dancing without a coat. Well, I studied the problem scientifically for a while and came up with a pretty good solution. I took the coat off the waiter's back, and me and my dark-eyed señorita had our dance. How I looked in that little white jacket that was far too small for me, I don't know, but I was too busy learning a Spanish tango to really care, and oh, what a lovely girl she was! Well, that's all for now. Good night. See you in the morning," and off he danced to his upper bunk.

We stayed three days in Curaçao and then sailed west for Panama in a rush to get there by Christmas. We held our noses passing Aruba, whose oil refineries reminded us of Marcus Hook, New Jersey. We had begun preparing ourselves for the Pacific, feeling an uneasy anticipation of truly new places, not British, not even European. We carved cakes of Ivory soap (99 and $\frac{44}{100}$ percent pure, guaranteed to float) into sculpted ships as we listened to *Robinson Crusoe* and marveled at the Sierra Nevada de Santa Maria, the snow-capped Andes rising in the distance. In the evening, accompanied by Charlie and his accordion, we sang Christmas carols. We were hunched tightly together close to the bowsprit, which was as far away from Pa as we could get. We didn't want him to start up on one of his anti-Christmas diatribes. Thanks to him we would be without candles or strings of colored lights to illuminate our Christmas season; but it really didn't matter, for we had, instead, wild waving curtains of phosphorescent light thrown up by the bow as it sliced through the waves and the brilliant mysteries of the southern constellations overhead.

One night we passed close to a freighter heading east. They signaled us in Morse Code. We stood mystified, none of us ordinary seamen able to interpret the message. But what we could not understand, we made up for in imagination and invented meanings for the flashes of light that jiggled across the sea to us.

"They are wishing us a merry Christmas," I said and pretended not to hear what seemed to be off-color translations coming from Ted and Sims. Anyway, the men were laughing in quick short roars.

19

Letters to Sophie: Panama

December 24, 1933
Hotel Tivoli
Panama City

Dear Sophie:
We have just arrived at Panama! The pilot who took us through the canal knew Frank Bourne's sister well. We followed a Japanese passenger boat through the canal. The canal reminded us of the Government Cut at Cat Island. On each side, the tropical undergrowth was terrific.

Going through the locks was marvelous. They are huge! As we came up, we could see the gigantic wall dividing the two sides. Men rushed around throwing ropes and shouting. Little donkey engines rushed up and down towing many, many boats, large and small, great steamers puffed and blew whistles; and when we went into the locks to go up hill, two enormous, gigantic, colossal, huge, unimaginable gates slowly closed behind us. It gave you the creeps, seeing no machinery or anything pushing them. The water comes rushing in, causing whirlpool after whirlpool, making the boat tug hard at the hawsers, and altogether it is most exciting.

We climbed three locks this way and went into Lake Gatun. We passed an enormous emergency dam and came out past a steamer and passed many tropical islands; these thrilled us all, especially Al who said he would come down here, clear away the thick undergrowth, build a house, get a sailboat and then proceed to have a good time. After a hurried lunch on deck (with the messiest spaghetti) we arrived at Gaillard Cut, where it has been cut through a mountain, showing strata's of earth and stone and occasional landslides.

We came to Pedro Miguel locks, and we wanted to get to Panama fast, so the man asked us how fast we could go. "Eighteen knots," was the answer. "Well, you'd better make twenty!" Since the Blue Dolphin has never done more than four knots under power, we didn't quite live up to our boast, but we hurried into the lock, all by ourselves. We went down very rapidly, the water rushing out below. Just before Miraflores locks our clutch went on the blink! We couldn't go into reverse, but it was soon fixed. Then when we got into the lock, we nearly ran into the wall, and the only thing that saved us were the tremendous Negros who were holding our hawsers. After coming out of the locks, we continued down a canal with great mud flats on each side. We could see a canal, which the French had attempted with all the old machinery lying around. We were soon in sight of Panama. All we could see were the docks and many airplanes. The town was behind a mountain. We anchored by a buoy. We were waiting for the launch to get fixed before we went in town, and Smitty walked by saying, "When she stops, you can't get her to go, and when she goes, you can't get her to stop!" We practically went into hysterics.

I know you are having lots of fun tonight, hanging stockings. Do you have a Christmas tree? We have many here. As we came down the street almost everybody's house had one. They even have one here at the Hotel.

Al and John have just been downtown and came back reporting that the streets were jammed mostly with drunk sailors, marines and soldiers.

Send my love to Mary, etc.

Love always,

Nina

* * *

December 27, 1933
On Board the Blue Dolphin

Dear Sophie:

How are you? I'm hot and sunburned and healthy, as a matter of fact, I'm about the healthiest child on board. Al has something wrong with his stomach.

John is recovering from fever. Quita won't eat. Willie has a broken arm—and me—well I'm fine!! But I miss my riding and piano terribly.

It's scorching here, the only place that is the tiny least bit warm or cool is under the awning. But when you start hiking those narrow streets crowded with people—pity us.

Tell Bill Phelps that I've been very faithful to his diary. Once I wrote 5 pages and One Half! Am I not vicious though? Really it's quite a job in this heat.

Daddy is meeting the Governor now. Mother is sorting laundry below. She is mad. It took Ted about ten trips up and down the stairs with his arms full to get it all below. In Haiti, Mother said we had the same amount of laundry done and it cost $6 and she just read the bill for this laundry and its for $50. Wow!

I miss you very much, but that will only mean that we'll like each other better when we see each other again. I doubt if I'll know you, you probably will have grown so much. I know you won't know us. We are tough looking; hard-bitten mariners, as a matter of fact, I think we have been bitten by all the things that bite in this countryside. But I guess we can endure it. I guess we'll have to!

How was my dog Boola when you last saw him? I hope he was alright. Send all my love to Mary, Bill, ect. ect. ect.

Loads of Love
as always,
Nina
THE END

No, wait a minute!!

You don't need to send it, save it for me though love, Nina

You draw so well and because I think you'd like to. Don't do it if you don't want to

Please do me a favor and draw me a picture of what you do in South Carolina because I'd like to know, and because

love, Nina

* * *

Dear Sophie:

How are you, I am fine, so is everybody else. We took Quita to see a doctor, to see if she had anything wrong with her, but she didn't.

This afternoon Daddy, Al, John, and I went all through the fortifications of the Panama Canal with Captain Gillan. He is very nice, and had been to Dalhousie several times when he was stationed at Fort duPont. We saw antiaircraft guns on a hill and then drove on a causeway that got covered up in the rainy season and got to an island fort. We walked in through a large building to a long tunnel, going half way through the mountain. It had curtains to be dropped down in case of an attack of gas. We all decided it would be an excellent place to spend the next war. We turned a corner and came to a large elevator. We went up and up and up. If we'd gone by stairs, I think there would have been 3,000. When we came to the top, we wound around many dark passages, and finally came to the top. There were some observation towers, and two Enormous 124 inch guns. We walked down to these and examined them. They only shoot 35 miles accurately!! The little ones only shoot 15! The 16 inch one was all wheels and nuts and bolts, almost too big to imagine. After much explaining and exclaiming, we started down the mountainside, and came to a camouflaged observation post. We came to three windows, covered, almost with rock, and a tree almost covering it. It certainly was well camouflaged. After going back across the causeway, we stopped at the balloon hanger, where there were trucks after trucks! Several of them had enormous searchlights, others reflectors!

Another nice man we met was Major Corvel, who came out to the boat yesterday for tea, and got drunk, because he had been with congressmen all day, and he asked Daddy to get him that way. He sang Willie the craziest songs. And Willie liked them very much. He was the one who took us all over the locks and let us all go into the place where they work it. He is very sweet.

Another one, who I haven't met yet, and who I'm going to tea with this afternoon, is Mr. Crane. He is, from Mother and Dad's point of view, very nice and looks like the older duPont boys. Nana, Mother, Daddy and I are the only ones going (I had a special invitation!)

We are having loads of fun. Last night Al, John, and I hired a coachee and went all over the town. It was more fun!! We saw many soldiers and sailors. You see most of them in the bars, which there are plenty of. We went past the President's Palace and watched the guards standing attention with long guns and bayonets on the end!

I'll bet you are having loads and loads of fun in South Carolina. I miss it and you very much.

We've all had a lovely Christmas and I enjoyed all my presents very much. I hope you do too.

We are leaving, or rather hope to leave tomorrow afternoon. It will be nice getting on the Pacific. It looks ever so cool and peaceful!

Please send my love to Mary and Bill and everybody else,

love as always,

Nina

P.S. Give this note to Mary, Please!

P.P.S. Please write me a letter.

* * *

December 29, 1933
Panama City, Panama

Dear Sophie;

I went to a lovely tea yesterday. We had lots of fun. We took Al, John, Nana, Mother, Daddy and I in one car, to a nice little pent house looking over the water. We roller skated on the flat terraced roof. Everybody was very funny. There were Mr. and Mrs. Robinson who are sailing to the Galapagos on a boat anchored near us, the Svapp and Mr. and Mrs. Crane.

They had a darling honey bear that looked like this:

He really isn't a honey bear, but that's what they call him. I have to go now, so:————

Love always,
Nina
P.S. Write me some letters
P.P.S. Send my love to the family.

20

Readying For Real Adventures

LIKE COLERIDGE'S ANCIENT MARINER, we sailed out into the Pacific as if "we were the first that ever burst into that silent sea." Until now we had been traveling on well-known shipping lanes and hopping from civilized island to civilized island, from culture to culture, finding somewhat expected scenarios; but, now, at last, we were the "painted ship upon a painted ocean," embarked upon a solitary search for adventure on uninhabited islands. The pirates' cave in Nassau, a tourist site, was a mere warm-up for this—the prospect of a true treasure hunt. The Atlantic and Caribbean had proved tumultuous, erratic, choppy. The Pacific, like its name, welcomed us with a soothing sea, lulling us in its long, low swells.

Because we would now have extended stretches at sea, Pa beefed up our schooling. He and I concentrated more than ever on algebra. I was beginning to get the gist, but was not sure of myself at all. I just kept nodding my head when Pa exclaimed, "You see? You can do anything you want if you just apply your will." I practiced will all right. Pa also recommended common sense when I began to panic about those letters going back and forth across the equal sign. Pa was all hope, waiting for glory. This left precious little room for failure. I often stared at him and wondered how his optimistic instructions would help me deal with the pain, terror, guilt, and shame that kept appearing in the novels I was reading;

I was, after all, beginning to get a taste of these bitter parts of life. Such feelings did not fit in Pa's pantheon of light. He believed, like Emerson, that man was a method, a force in selecting principles, attracting to himself his own types; and if you stayed optimistic, so would go the world. Pa wouldn't want me shilly-shallying around with doubters and cowards, but I had a feeling I might.

Pa was such a strong Unitarian that we had no day off or spiritual tasks to accomplish on Sunday. God, as Pa so often explained, had completed His job of ordering the universe. Running back to Him at this late date with supplications and regrets was futile. So we kept school on Sundays. Pa, however, gave special dispensation to John that first Sunday on the Pacific, because John was a Roman Catholic. Or maybe it was just because John was ahead in Latin. I couldn't be sure.

Pa's generosity towards John, the Roman Catholic, was surprising. Roman Catholics as employees were to be expected, but to have one living in our quarters—like a member of the family—that was remarkable. Pa's views on Catholicism were not to be discussed in genteel society; and Mother had made it plain to us that Catholics and Jews inhabited different worlds, which we would never know and need not know. But now here was John, and he was one of us. Or was he? We worked at our studies while he sat on the stern with his fishing line trolling the wake. I was introduced to the concept of Divine Justice on that first Sunday in the Pacific. John did not catch one fish.

We went below for our traditional formal Sunday noon dinner. God obviously wanted us to enjoy the fruits of the earth and celebrating His works with a Sunday feast was O.K. As soon as we were served, Pa began telling us about Cocos Island, our next port of call. Cocos is a speck of an island five hundred and fifty miles southwest of Panama, six miles in circumference, uninhabited and solitary in a great expanse of ocean. It was much like Robinson Crusoe's island, Juan Fernandez, further down the coast of South America, where Alexander Selkirk had been a castaway. He and the island became the models for Defoe's novel.

We knew Pa would not get to the point right away. We would have to be patient as he took us through the background material of the Incas of

Peru, with their extreme form of communistic government. They reminded Pa of Plato's theories. Plato, he said, would have approved of the
Incas. Pa did not. Then came the part about the genius of the Incas as engineers. They didn't use mortar; nor did they have writing or written literature. Their knowledge of mathematics and engineering impressed Pa,
but I was beginning to lose interest in Incas.

Sensing a growing lassitude in his students, Pa moved us up on deck
as he finally arrived at livelier materials. He began by describing the great
riches of the sun-worshipping Incas, of their gold and jewels, and how the
Spaniards conquered them and destroyed their culture. The Spaniards
then built their own rich kingdom, and all was stabilized until 1821
when Simon Bolivar, whom we saw immortalized in statues in Caracas,
came with his armies, sweeping down towards Peru to liberate the natives
from the Spaniards. The Spaniards, certain of pillage, fire, and destruction, collected and stored in the great cathedral at Lima their immense
treasure of Incan and Spanish art—jewels, silver, life-sized statues of solid
gold emblazoned with precious gems. It was a massive concentration of
wealth, and they prepared to defend it.

At this moment, said Pa, with Bolivar and his armies coming down
the mountain, an English brig out of Bristol, cozily called the *Mary Dear*
and captained by Edward Thompson, anchored in Callao harbor, the port
for Lima, to restock supplies and take on water. The frightened Spanish
priests, hearing cannons closer, held a council, and sent deputies to Captain Thompson. Would he take the treasure horde from storage in the
cathedral and sail it off the coast until Bolivar and his forces had done with
Lima and returned northward? An agreement was drawn. Thompson
would be well paid for his services, and a guard of Spanish soldiers would
go aboard to watch over the treasure until it could be safely returned to
Callao. The priests made an inventory on parchment to keep at the cathedral, which has been the guiding document ever since for treasure hunters.

Under the cover of night, and here Pa lowered his voice building up
the suspense, great wagons carried the loot from the cathedral down to
the *Mary Dear*. At dawn, Captain Thompson set to sea. Once clear of the
coast, he began organizing his crew. On a moonless night, the English-

men murdered the Spaniards, tossed their bodies to the sharks, and escaped with the treasure. From that time on this treasure's whereabouts are hard to trace. Evidence and clues make it seem likely that Thompson sailed directly to Cocos Island. The story, as it has been told and retold, says that it took twelve boatloads to get the treasure ashore at Cocos, and that it was buried in a cave in Chatham Bay. The bulk of this documented treasure has never turned up. Occasionally something on the parchment inventory is found on Cocos, a gold cross, or a single doubloon. Once a bejeweled crown turned up in the hut of a South Sea trader, who said it had come directly from Cocos. Some searchers say they have proof that the treasure was transferred to one of the Society islands, probably Christmas Island. Many an expedition has set out for Cocos to find this treasure, bearded cutthroats and highly organized scientific societies alike, to no avail.

Pa paused in his lecture. "You want to know an interesting legend? They say that the heartbroken Incan priests, who had been left at home, betrayed in their trust and powerless because of Bolivar's invasion, secretly traced the treasure to Cocos. They sent scouts there, who found it, but they couldn't transport it home, so they left a guard of honor on the island, high in the unexplored hills. This guard of Incan priests goes on generation after generation and is there now, waiting, guarding, mysterious, and I must add, just a little bit miraculous, but such is the role of the priest."

"Oh, Daddy, read some more," said Quita, "Don't stop. This is exciting!" When Quita said, "read," she wanted Pa to go on talking. Like Willy, Quita found Pa's spoken story and the stories he read much the same.

"There's not much more to tell, Quita," Pa replied, "except for one thing. Beware of bad luck if you try for the treasure! They say that once you let yourself become absorbed in hunting for it, you're fated to encounter tricks and tragedy. Bad luck will follow you as long as you persist in the search."

Sailing along in a spanking breeze, we covered a stretch of open ocean listening to Pa and Nana read aloud. I puzzled over the difference in Pa's and Nana's choices of novels. Pa was reading *The Fair Maid of Perth* by Sir

Walter Scott, whose style has always annoyed me—so much racing up and down hill and dale and describing every last leafy dell. I preferred fast plot development, but at least this novel starred a young girl and female adventures for a change.

Nana was actually a better reader than Pa. No one we knew ever surpassed this gentle woman's gusto in reading aloud, her intellect, her passion. Her voice rang with music, capable of modulating from whispers to shrieks, carrying the cadences of Uncle Remus's Gullah, the whimsy of George Jean Nathan or the delicacies of Maria Edgeworth. She gave each character its own voice. Her reading was magic. She cast a spell.*

And now Nana was embarking on Herman Melville's *Moby Dick*. There she sat on deck, little Nana, in her striped canvas chair, up to windward, close by the wheel, reading to us. The wind caught at her silky white hair, blowing it against her deeply browned cheeks. Her lilting voice ran a treble line against the long, rolling song of the sea.

The contrast between Scott and Melville had me baffled as I oscillated between their messages. Scott's novel and Pa were romantic and long-winded. They went in for goodness, truth, and beauty in lush vegetation. Scott's opening sentence was 124 words long, including nine commas and words like "lucubrations." After being involved in wars, feuds, murders, and suicide, the beautiful maiden heroine, who tends to faint at the sight of blood, marries her true love and lives happily ever after. It all seemed very far away in the long ago, proper but distant. British.

---

*Nana's grandchildren were not the only ones who benefited from her reading. Not long ago, a cousin was out clipping the hedge under the living room windows of Nana's summer house on Nantucket. A man came up to my cousin and said, "This hedge is very important to me, do take good care of it. I am a native. I grew up here. One summer day, I was walking by those windows above your head. They were open. I was just a kid. I heard a woman reading aloud and snuck in behind the hedge and listened. I was so taken by the story that I came back every day for one solid month from one to three in the afternoon, hiding behind the hedge, spellbound by that woman's voice and the way she read and the story itself. She sparked a desire in me to go on with my education. Most of us boys didn't leave the island after school, but I went on to college and ended up a lawyer. I've never forgotten that voice. I think she kept me going."

On the other hand, the first sentence of *Moby Dick*, "Call me Ishmael," bulleted me to attention. From then on came dread, evil, obsession, and massive drownings in the inscrutable sea. And all this starting from Nantucket. Every sentence was in my immediate time, pushing me into urgent rearrangements of my mind. The heroine in Scott's novel had a female companion known as the "glee maiden." Ishmael had a savage for a companion. If Scott wrote from the point of view of a young woman, Melville disregarded women altogether.

So what was going on here? Why did Nana choose to read about the dark world of driven men, while Pa romped on the moors of Scotland with a bevy of dewy-eyed women? Why did Pa choose to inform us about light and duty, and Nana darkness and fate? Which told about the real world that I could expect to grow up in? I was definitely leaning towards Melville, Nana's reading being so persuasive.

After her initial chapters, Nana laid the book down on her lap and said, "Promise me you boys," meaning us girls, too, of course, "will read this book again when you grow up. I can tell you like it, since it describes life at sea so well—and it does have that Nantucket connection—but there is much more to this book than a sea adventure. You're too young to understand it all now, so promise me, please, that you will read it again when you grow up." We promised, and so she went on, halting every now and then to show us the Rockwell Kent woodcuts. I was grateful for her advice; and when I grew up, I read not only *Moby Dick*, but all of Melville's novels in succession. Many years after that literary orgy, I married a Melville scholar who was astounded when I told him of Nana's reading *Moby Dick* to me on the high seas when I was thirteen. "Impossible!" he declared. "Women never read Melville."

On our third day at sea, with Nana reading in the afternoon sunlight, John poked me and pointed to a dark object rolling in the water about a hundred feet away. As Nana completed her sentence, I stood up and gestured to the gang, bringing their attention to this odd object. It looked like a tree, about twelve feet long, with a branch rising out of the middle.

"Interesting," said Pa, "I wonder what currents could bring that log way out to this point in the Pacific?"

As we gazed and pondered, our log picked up its rear end and dove. Al and John leapt to their feet, raced below for guns, and reappeared on deck in seconds. Quita and I jumped up and down on the deckhouse in gleeful suspense. Willy ran forward to alert the crew to a break in routine. The "log" surfaced again, closer this time. Al and John peppered the water around him with shot. Enraged, the startled and unidentified marine monster turned suddenly to charge the ship in a torpedolike swath through the sea, aimed directly amidships. Quita, Nana, Mother, and I screamed in unison, trampling each other on our way to the far rail.

"Moby Dick!" I yelled, delirious with joy at the climax to our afternoon. "We'll sink!"

"Oh, hush, child of wrath and indignation!" scolded Nana, her voice shaking.

The shark, perhaps a whale, or a very large fish, dove just before colliding with our black hull. John dropped his gun and hastily threw his heavy deep-sea fishing line over, but his hands trembled so that the coils tangled. He gave up his project with a loud, "Oh damn!"

"All right, children, come along," said Nana. "Let's go on. Nina, for heaven's sake, calm down and sit still. You're scaring Quita."

Captain, bemused, stood by the wheel, chuckling between his leeward spits, sighing a little at his lively charges. A modicum of quiet was restored when our adversary surfaced again off the stern. Like Ahab, we children rose as one, shouting at our symbolic foe.

"Shoot! Shoot, Alfie!" I screamed. "Get him! Kill him!"

"Nope," answered Al, succinctly. "Can't. He's out of range. Honest, Nina. No sense wasting bullets."

"Oh phooey!' I said, dropping back on a cushion, resigned, waiting for Nana to start reading again. She'd read only six sentences when two hissing spouts of water rose to starboard, about three hundred feet away.

"Whales," said square, stolid Smitty, matter of factly, as he walked by to take a turn on the mainsheet. We were all on our feet again, eager to see real whales for the first time in our lives, whales we knew so well from all our rainy-day visits to the Whaling Museum at Nantucket, and now from *Moby Dick*. We tiptoed and jumped, Nana behind us, trying to get a close look at the mammoth beasts of the sea. Suddenly Nana let out a piercing cry and sucked in her breath in a gasp. We pivoted around just in time to glimpse a fifteen-foot fish fall back into the sea after a graceful leap toward the sun. Our soothing Pacific sail was tending toward the chaotic. Was this a new trend? Was it true, after all, that portents of doom were appearing to us since we dared to covet the Incan treasure? Were these warnings? I assumed with delicious certainty that they were, and that we were heading for trouble.

Pa scanned his startled family and demanded quiet. "Hush up. All of you," he said. "Listen to your grandmother." Nana read on through the change of watch at four, when Mr. Doyle took over the helm. The first mate stood in his white shirt and white officer's cap, behind the wheel, rocking on his semicircles and humming. He stopped abruptly, for his attention had been caught by a motion just under the stern.

"Say!" he interrupted, "you ought to see this."

We ran to look down at a huge, long sea snake writhing by the stern.

'O Christ!
That ever this should be!
Yea, slimy things did crawl with legs
Upon the slimy sea,'

quoth Pa, reciting Coleridge, "I think its time we ate."

On the last night of 1933, we sat around the supper table trying to offer up our New Year's resolutions but only stumbling and stuttering. At home, we never had trouble shouting out plans and hopes and corrective actions for the next year. But here, sailing alone across this vast and rolling deep, with deserted islands shrouded in mystery ahead and dangerous beasts around us, who was to say what might be good, or nice, or even close to useful for the future.

We adjourned, unresolved, to the deck to watch a full moon turn in under a quilt of cloud. Then we shifted to the detached world of games, which had no past, present, or future. Willy begged Mother for six pieces of hard candy. The four older children sat on the leather sofas, while Willy hid the candies on deck like jellybeans on Easter morning. After a scramble, we found all but two and shifted to hide-and-seek. This game was made easier because the person who was "It" could find his prey by sniff-ing. In spite of the toughening layers of tan acquired in the Atlantic, and in spite of the shadowy protection from the sail for most of the day, we were getting deeply burned by the sun. Mother anointed us all with a thick layer of heavy, yellow Unguentine, "The First Thought in Burns," so we moved about in its characteristic medicinal aroma. Nana was always after me, ordering me to stop basking in the sun. "You'll disappear in flames," she pronounced.

I ran to hide in my favorite secret spot, the tiny slicker locker, know-ing the dank, reeky room would put up a strong-smelling curtain of rub-ber, dried salt, and perspiration over the telltale Unguentine. I wrapped myself in Pa's huge poncho. John was "It." I could hear him slowly open the shuttered door, muttering to himself. He poked in the darkness. "I'll bet you're in here, Nina, I'll bet you are . . ." Suspenseful silence. I could feel myself turning red from holding my breath for so long, eagerly antic-ipating his closing in on me.

"O.K., Nina, I'll bet you're in here. . . ." With a twinge of panic bought on by the darkness, he struck out at the mysterious shape before him. His palm caught me across the side of my face.

"Owwwwww!" I wailed, rising volcanically from under the coat. John beat a noisy retreat to the goal, the saloon table, yelling, "Dracula! Dracula!"

The grownups had had it. They ordered us to bed.

Just as we were waking up on New Year's morning, Sims stuck his oval head down the companionway and shouted, "Hey! Get up here on deck! And happy New Year to you, too!"

"Oh, for pity's sake," muttered a sleepy Al, but we did slowly assem-ble on deck to view an amazing scene. Hundreds if not thousands of por-poises were all about us. They rose with curving leaps towards the sun, falling and whitening the water in the silvery dawn. I could recognize the rulers of the sea and their attendants, but Sims didn't. Where I saw gods and demigods dancing in the dawn to greet the New Year, Sims could only comment, "Never saw so many porpoises in all my life. Must be some feeding ground."

Ted joined us. "Amazing how concentrated they are on whatever it is they're doing. They're such curious mammals. They usually come right over to a ship and dance around the bow, teasing for speed, sort of directing your path, but they're not paying any attention to us at all."

Now they were reaching a frenzy, leaping higher and higher in long lines of glistening blue, splashing sparkles of salt spray, oblivious of our presence. Finally, they danced and leapt and dove out of sight, and we descended for breakfast.

"Well," said Ted, one hand on his hip and the other holding the pitcher that filled our glasses with frothy Klim (milk spelled backwards, a white powder with water added, which we unanimously hated). "How many of you heard the foghorn go off last night at midnight? Cap set it off to celebrate the New Year. You hear it?"

We looked sheepishly at one another. Not one of us heard a thing. Even Nana, famous now for her sleeping problems, looked surprised at the news.

"You should have seen Charlie and me," continued Ted, "Boy! We really hit that deck on the double! Figured we were colliding with another ship. All I could do to sleep again after that scare."

New Year's Day, however, was no holiday. School kept on as usual. After lunch, Nana continued reading Melville on deck as we sat encircling her. Quita and I finished darning our sock pile and took up our own sewing projects. Quita was working on a pillow cover in a cross stitch that she had designed herself, a scene of the *Blue Dolphin* under full sail with a pale blue sky in the background and a palm tree at the edge to lead your eye in and hold your attention—all through dynamic symmetry, of course.

I was letting down the hem of my gingham dress when the seventh wave came, higher than the others, and rolled our ship further to leeward than usual, catching me off balance. I grabbed for support, but clutching only my straw sewing basket, I rolled off the deckhouse and onto the deck with a thud, cracking my head on the rail. My sewing basket sailed out of my hand and flew into the sea. I sat up, rubbed my head, and with desolation watched my precious basket, its spools of brightly colored threads, my blue and green—painted darning egg drift out of sight, bobbing about as they withstood the nibbling of the waves. An insignificant jostle from the sea had abruptly thrown me from my comfortable cushion of domestic security and nearly separated me from safety. The sea had transformed into the giant again. He was always biding his time, lurking, spying, and waiting for me to fall into his maw.

The kind captain, noting my dismay and pain, called me to him. "Nina, come on back here to the wheel and let me show you how to splice rope." I went gladly and spent the rest of the afternoon there at his knees, kneading the prickly hemp, working the strands into short splices and eye splices, roughing up the skin on my fingers and thumbs. I practiced other knots. Then John joined me and we raced in tying half-hitches and bowlines.

Going below to get ready for supper, I stopped by the bureau that Quita and I shared. In Panama we all had received money to buy ourselves presents. Al, in his manhood, had spent a lot of time trying on linen suits, finally choosing just what he wanted for $5.00. Quita had found a miniature Chinese tea set for the Chinese doll Mother had bought her in Curaçao. Willy had bought a complete fishing outfit—spoon, wire leader, and line—not a toy but the real thing. And I had rebelled. I bought the forbidden: a rayon bra, silk stockings, powder, and lipstick.

Nana had looked at my purchases and snorted, "Female fripperies! They give me the heebie jeebies!"

Mother was adamant. "Don't you ever dare to put that rayon next to your skin. Don't you know that your skin can't 'breathe' in that stuff! You must wear cotton. Only cotton."

They both took a dim view of my new female shape, figuring correctly that I had a long way to go before I needed a bra. Neither one of them had ever worn a bra, so they carried on about that, too. As for the makeup, Pa joined the women in denouncing it. Nana and Mother had been born with exquisite skin, never a blemish, always smooth and radiant. They never bought oils or creams to soften their skin. They never even allowed soap to defile their faces and preferred washing with spring water fresh from the ground than regular treated spigot water. I had wide-open pores, oily skin, and pimples. Why couldn't they see this with their ordinary eyes? Pa was always saying I should take my own initiative, so I had. So why was he sneering at me? He and Emerson said to insist on yourself. I had. So there, I said to myself, as I opened the drawer and peeked at my new forbidden purchases. Of course, I had yet to find the courage to put on any of these articles, but I was getting ready.

After supper, we were quiet for once and played twenty questions as we watched the moon rise, an ocherous ball lighting a sheeny path across the black, undulating waste. Mother said it was my turn for a tub bath that night. I lapsed into dreamlike serenity as I climbed up the stairs and telescoped myself into the tub under the dark phosphorescent water, dimly lit by the one bulb hanging over the basin. I was almost asleep before I could get back to my upper bunk, where the gurgling of the water by my ear sent me quietly into oblivion.

21

Ben Gun Revisited

J OHN SIGHTED COCOS the next afternoon at 1:30. The wind was light and
erratic, so Captain ordered the motor to be started. His impatient charges
were excited with the prospect of landing, and he knew they didn't want
to wallow on an airless ocean. Mr. Doyle and Sims challenged the children
to a knot-tying contest, anything to quiet down the rising pitch of our
voices. We concentrated on making Turk's Heads out of marlin. John
made the best one, a tiny one, fit for a ring finger. When no one was looking, he turned and presented it to me.

John gave me this astonishing symbol without comment. He was not
much on commenting. He and Al had proved such close friends that I had
come to think of John as another brother. I'd long since despaired of moving along any decent romantic plot line as far as John, the hero, and I, the
heroine, were concerned. The five children were now one family. We
shared and directed our public and private adventures together. Yet, this
ring gave me a flicker of hope that I was not permanently embedded in
his mind as a sister. My quivering tendril of love might be allowed to
grow after all. I, too, dared no comment but went below instead. I placed
a kiss on George's dark, brooding forehead and turned and slipped into
Quita's and my cabin.

I found my doll, Sophie, tucked in under the sheet of my well-made bunk. I picked her up—my flat, gray Sophie, my constant childhood companion—and pressed her damp linen frock with my palm against the bureau top. The precious ring would replace her. Slipping the ring under the pillow, I thought back to that boy-hero-adventurer I'd been trying to develop since the beginning of the trip. No, I wouldn't be like that. Nor would I fall into the trap of being like one of Scott's heroines. Not like Nana and Mother, either, so old-fashioned, permanently out of date. Maybe I ought to go for something like those flexible lovers in *Anthony Adverse*, only I couldn't imagine how I'd do that. I opened the top bureau drawer and gently placed Sophie in it, nestling her head on a pair of white socks and covering her with a cotton undershirt. And there she stayed for the rest of the trip. I kept the ring on my finger at night, but the rest of the time it lay safe, hidden away under the pillow.

At the end of the day, as the sun set, the twin peaks and high rock cliffs of Cocos rose silhouetted against the bright bands of orange, pink, and yellow of the sky. A school of porpoises led us toward land. The wide, spreading wings of soaring man-o'-war birds glided by our masts and frigate birds flew alongside us, inspecting our craft. We were entwined by eddies of land air, the faint scent of flowers, and hot green jungle growth. A whale spouted us a farewell from the outer deeps.

The children sat astride the bowsprit, eagerly reviewing the lore of the Incas and the story of their mysterious treasure. While the crew was busy furling the foresail, Chief was below nursing his thumping engine along. Captain was at the wheel with Pa beside him, Mother and Nana in canvas deck chairs in the stern. The last reflections from the sun were disappearing as we chugged along in a faint anticipation of light from the moon not yet over the horizon.

We clung to the coast, heading east to the best harbor, Chatham Bay, where Captain Thompson had supposedly buried his treasure. Two conical rocks stood sentinel at the entrance to the bay. One of them, Nuez Island, hid the cove from our view as we approached. It was completely dark now, so we turned on our running lights—the red and green port and starboard lights, and the lights on the bow and mast. As we came quietly around Nuez Island, we burst into shouts of astonishment. A tall sweep of flames burned high on the mountaintop. This fire was abruptly extinguished the minute we rounded the point and our lights were visible from the hill. All was darkness again.

A stampede from the bow to the stern resulted from this manifestation. Quita threw her arms around Nana. Al and John fell in with Sims and Smitty, who were as awed as we were. I jumped up and down before Pa. Willy jumped randomly.

"It's the Inca priests!" I cried, already sure of treasure and fame. We cast our anchor in the deep, spark-splashing water. Suddenly our eyes picked up a bobbing light near the edge of the cove. Captain looked through the glasses but could not distinguish anything unusual. We all tried the glasses, but the darkness was dense. When the fat, slouching moon rose out of the sea, its glow enlightened us, showing us the line of the beach, the shape of the rising hill, and there, where the light had been, a small schooner riding at anchor.

As soon as our ship was secured for the night, Ted, Charlie, and Sims tossed a dory over and rowed across the bay to the schooner. We could see it rolling gently in the swell, a dim light bleeding from the porthole of the squat cabin. As our men laid in their oars, the skipper of the schooner stuck his head up the hatch and greeted the men with a hoarse growl. He had obviously been watching their approach.

"What d'ya want?" he demanded.

Ted, our perpetual diplomat, tried to ease some information from this surly man but succeeded only in being grilled himself on the purpose and nature of our crew. The man sneered, "Yeah, sure," when Ted told him the *Blue Dolphin* carried a bunch of kids on a family lark. Our men were not invited aboard, which would have been the usual port procedure, so they rowed back to us even more curious than when they'd set forth.

John, Willy, and I could not wait for Ted's reveille and "Rise and shine!" We were dressed and on deck before six o'clock, viewing with excitement the prospects before us. The cove was banded by a semicircle of white sand, with large boulders holding the ends of the beach in place.

Palm trees bent over the sand, swaying with simple dignity in the trade winds. The jungle of ferns, six feet tall, snakelike vines, tangled undergrowth, and a riot of prickly palmettos rose abruptly from the sand, climbing two thousand feet up the hill. Red and yellow flashes from jungle flowers accented the massive spread of green. The trees toward the top of the hill were short, six to ten feet high, with umbrella tops. Dramatically dropping in a flashing fall over these verdant precipices were three cascading waterfalls, spraying out over boulders and falling finally into the blue salt sea. The naked black rocks, Conical and Nuez, astern of us, marked the passage to the ocean. Roosting birds covered their crags, each rock supporting its own specialized colony. Nuez was home to man-o'war birds, and fat, white, stupid-looking boobies covered Conical. Already a line of boobies teetered on the spring stay between our two masts, peering down at the activity on the deck below and fighting off marauding frigate birds. Ted walked by just then, contemplating the whitewashing we were in for and muttered, "Lucky thing whales don't fly."

"Say," blurted John, "What's that? A gray tent or sail, or something? Over there, back into the jungle on the left under that tallish clump of palms. See it?"

I took the glasses from him and examined the strange patch of color in the jungle and then turned the glasses to the hill. "Boy, somebody was sure ambitious. Take a look at that zigzag path up the hill. And hey, look, it ends in a huge old hole up there with heaped-up, dried-up old earth all around it. Do you think those people ever got anything out of that hole?"

"Well," added John, politely pulling the glasses out of my hands, "there's one thing I don't really understand. Every book on this place says the jungle is impenetrable, but that hill sure isn't. You know what I think? I think that whole side of the hill was burned off. There isn't a single tree on that stretch, just that old long brown grass."

The early morning chill made me shiver, so I slipped a coat over my shoulders. Right after breakfast, Sims and Smitty were ready to ferry in the first load of passengers, Pa having sensibly dispensed with school that morning. I'd put on my L. L. Bean hunting boots, rubber-soled and leather-topped. I was ready for a jungle adventure. The children were to go in first.

The sun warmed the cove, strengthening the sweet scent of the damp jungle. Twenty-eight fathoms below us, the sandy bottom showed clearly. We held tightly to the thwarts as the men chose the best comber to ride in on. The boat went shooting up the beach in a rush of white froth. Jumping out quickly, we helped push the dory out during a lull in the surf. Sims and Smitty, with a surge of energy, rowed back to pick up Ma and Pa and Nana.

We children turned from the surf to survey our El Dorado, bunched together under the glaring tropical sun. Before we could move, however, before we'd even discussed our plan of attack, a rattling in the under-growth congealed us as if we'd been frozen in a game of statues. A strange figure was emerging from the undergrowth, a small unshaven man of about thirty, gaunt and brown, wearing a tattered, once-white, linen suit. Quita and I, unsure of jungle etiquette, reverted to dancing-class manners and slipped him modified curtsies. Brave Alfred stepped forward and said, "How do you do, sir. I am Alfred Chandler and these are my brother and sisters, and my friend, John Hurlburd. We are from Wilmington, Delaware."

The shrunken, dark man, shaggy and disheveled, drew near, limping in a jerky thrust forward. His eyes frightened me. His glance kept darting over us, scrutinizing. He was unsmiling. As he drew closer, we could see that he was shaking all over, palsied, rippling with uncontrollable tremors.

"So . . . " he said, slowly. "Well, I'm George Cooknell, from Coventry, England. Howchydo." He stepped forward, apparently to shake hands, but changed his mind and twirled off in a cartwheel instead. Conversation came to a standstill. George Cooknell, I decided, was as startled at finding five children on his beach as we were at meeting a modern Ben Gun. How wonderful, I said to myself, he has a proper English accent just like every-one must have had in *Treasure Island*.

"Say", said John, at last, trying to ease the tension, "is that your little schooner out there?"

"Oh, no," Mr. Cooknell replied. "No. No. That belongs to Mr. Valentine, from America. Mr. Valentine is out here with his friend, Mr. Stanley Lewis. He says . . . ," here Mr. Cooknell, for emphasis, stood on his hands, "he says he is looking for scientific evidence that Cocos was once connected with the mainland, but I don't think so because every time I go up to the top of the hill where he's digging, he shoots at me."

"Oh," said John, looking to see how Ma and Pa were coming along.

"Valentine came out here with his father, but his father was discouraged after a month and went back to New York. The father writes books. His son has a wooden leg. There was another man here, too, a deserter from a fishing ship, but he got discouraged and hitchhiked back to Panama. That's how I got out here, bummed a ride out on a ship that was passing this way." His voice dropped, his shaking stilled. "It's a long trip from England."

"I guess," said John, "that if Mr. Valentine is digging at the top of the hill, it was his fire we saw burning last night, the one that went out so quickly when our running lights came into view."

"Fire?" questioned Mr. Cooknell. "Valentine doesn't have fires."

"Mr. Cooknell, sir," I said, smiling submissively, head tilted down, "we've read that the Incas guard their treasure on the mountain top. When we saw that fire, we sort of thought that maybe it was the Incas."

"Of course," said Mr. Cooknell with no hesitation, and did another cartwheel, "of course. It's a mystery all right. Place is full of mystery. Valentine thought he heard a man sneaking around his tent the other night and shot four times at the prowler, but he didn't get anything. But then he never does, even when he's potting at me. I've heard dogs barking up there. Now how did dogs get there? And Valentine sees cats with long, pointy ears creeping through the undergrowth. I say, here's someone new."

We turned to find Pa gallantly handing Mother and Nana onto the beach. The ladies were dressed as if about to go off to tea with old friends on Delaware Avenue, freshly clad in linen blouses buttoned down the front, coarse linen skirts, straw bonnets, their ever-faithful sensible brown lisle stockings and brown leather brogues.

Pa took over the conversation with Mr. Cooknell, who continued his gyrations, shaking and flinging himself into cartwheels and handstands. We children were getting used to him, but Nana looked alarmed. Coming to rest, Mr. Cooknell admitted rather grudgingly to Pa that he was searching for treasure, but beyond that, he refused to go. He was not ready to divulge any information.

"Like to have a whack at going up into the interior?" asked Mr. Cooknell. "Be glad to show you some of the problems involved here."

We accepted with pleasure and lined up single file behind him. He led us to his tent, a gray mildewed sail flung over a fallen palm tree trunk. A shed made of driftwood stood next to it. John and I nodded to each other, remembering this from our morning study of the cove. Here Mr. Cooknell picked up his machete and off we marched into the jungle.

"See here," said an indignant Nana, "why aren't we going up that perfectly good zigzag path through the tall grass down there along the beach? Do we have to struggle through this tangle?"

Mr. Cooknell turned disdainfully and said, "That's Mr. Valentine's path. He shoots if you get too close. Follow me."

The warm, saturated air—a rotting jungle miasma—settled over us. We moved slowly. Vines caught at our arms and feet, tiger grass sawed at our legs, sticky, hot leaves slapped our faces. I began to sweat and itch. The overlapping green-leaf roof shut out the sun. We went about a hundred feet in silence. It had taken almost half an hour. Our interest in George's problems was beginning to dissolve in the heat.

"How long before we get there?" whined Willy with the classical opening of impending childhood revolt.

"Now you just keep right on marching," commanded Mother, anxious to nip that threat. Alfred, however, had more success with her (he always did), wheedling with rational exactness, persuading her that a swim would be beneficial for all at that exact moment. So we came about face and began to march back to the beach. Pa stayed on so as not to hurt Mr. Cooknell's feelings.

By the time we reached the beach we were hopping and shouting in pain. In our enthusiastic acceptance of Mr. Cooknell's exploring project, we'd forgotten the strong warning given us by sailors who had been to Cocos. Beware the red ants, they said, and we never thought of them again. Too late, we realized the cause of our suffering. Armies of tiny red ants were the scourge of Cocos. They lived under the leaves and vines, and had crawled onto us as we struggled through the jungle. They worked their way deep under our skin and settled down to bite. The bites felt like bee stings, but bee stings can be plastered with mud, the pain relieved. Nothing could be done for these bites. They were in too deep to treat externally. The pain did not ease off, either, but went on at its original intensity for about an hour.

We ran crazed to a cool brook flowing across the beach. Mother and Nana moved to a waterfall farther down the strand. Peeling down to our bathing suits, we waded into the fresh water, following the stream up into the jungle, the leaves high above our heads keeping out the sun. We reached a deep, cool pool fed by a high waterfall. There we sat, under the falls, curtained in a translucent shimmer, letting the cool water soothe our pain.

I remembered Al's Wrinklebelly story about the Giant Ants. Surely, these vicious little red devils must be miniaturized versions of the scary ones that invaded New York and ate humans. I let the water run over me, contemplating bugs, my bathing suit, and my mother. My bathing suit was a heavy green wool body-gripper with a high neck-line, sensible wide straps over the shoulders, and a thick skirt over the longish underpants that chafed my crotch. Mother bought it in Panama. This bathing suit, I decided, was ridiculous. I remembered the printed cotton bathing suit I'd tried on; it had a halter strap and a low back. I thought of how cool and suave it would have been to wear at the beach. But Mother would not even look at it. Now why had she insisted on this woolen variation of a mini Mother Hubbard? Indignation slowly ran off down the stream as I figured out the problem. I glanced at her and wondered how she could keep her hard-held assumptions clear of counteracting statistical evidence. Querulousness turned to anger as I leaned against a rock. I took to pulverizing pieces of coral. Soon calm, I made dribble castles of the remaining coral detritus at the stream's edge.

Mother kept her sanity, I decided, by maintaining set formulas. She had been taught, and had lived long enough to know, that ocean water is cold; that the body of a child cannot resist cold; that sudden changes of body temperature lead to pneumonia; and therefore, a child should be dressed warmly when going to swim in an ocean. Logical enough, but she forgot to adjust for tropical waters. I sighed and accepted this limited view. At least she was safe. She was cushioned and propped by comfortable clusters of the notions she had inherited and learned. Remove a cluster and she would be flustered and probably cross. Leave her alone, I advised myself. I also advised myself to move ahead on my own and on my next birthday buy a new bathing suit with tiny straps, a bare back, and extremely low frontage. It would be silky and smooth in red and white stripes.

"I'm s-s-scared," announced Quita. "Come on, Nina, let's g-g-go find Mummy. It's so dark in here!" We slowly filed down the stream, ducking overhanging branches, and came again into the glare of the white beach. Sims and Smitty had landed and were ready to begin the shuttle back to the *Blue Dolphin*. Pa didn't want to end his conversation with Mr. Cooknell, so Pa invited him out to lunch. When the dory drew alongside our ship, we climbed up the rope ladder and made a swift dash to Nana's airy after-cabin where Nana anointed us with her scented Larkspur and Cologne, cooling our still-stinging ant bites while we awaited the announcement of lunch.

Seated at a proper table, with a glass of Pa's amber corn liquor readying him for a four-course meal, George Cooknell surveyed his sympathetic audience and decided to talk. Experiencing amenities after weeks of privation sloughed off his normal British reticence. Little by little, in waves of self-justification and concern, he told us his story.

George said he was an Oxford graduate and had been living with his bedridden, aged mother. He'd never married and had no other family. He'd been worried more and more by his mother's failing health and needed money to give her adequate care. He discussed this problem with his old friend, a seafaring man, Captain Lucy. Over long afternoon teas, George and Captain Lucy devised a way of making a quick fortune to relieve the aged parent. Captain Lucy would sell George a precious map he had inherited from his grandfather, who was also a seafaring man, or to be more precise, a pirate seafaring man. This map, with an "X" to mark the spot, revealed the exact whereabouts of a fabulous pirate treasure buried on Cocos Island. George set off at once, leaving his mother to make out as best she could until he could get back with the loot.

We children leaned forward with new alertness for we realized George was talking about other treasures, not the Inca one, but about the pirates in the Caribbean in the late seventeenth century. He was explaining how their trade in the Caribbean had become overextended, overcrowded, forcing hundreds of pirates to move to the Pacific, crossing the Panama Isthmus to set up shop in borrowed or commandeered ships.

George was turning out to be as good a storyteller as Pa. He had us attending in excitement as he shifted to the adventures of a few pirate hardies who had spurned the walk across the Isthmus and sailed, instead, around the Horn. One of these was Captain John Cook, commanding an English pirate ship, with Edward Davis signed on as quartermaster. With their fellow pirate crew, they'd captured a thirty-six gun Danish frigate in the Caribbean and rechristened her, appropriately, *The Bachelor's Delight*. They chose this ship to get them around the Horn and into the Pacific.

The Bachelor's Delight sailed into the Gulf of Nicoya in New Spain, now Costa Rica, where Cook died. The crew then elected Edward Davis as Captain. Davis proved an excellent leader, a kind and gentle soul for a pirate. He was soon in command of a fleet of pirate ships manned by over a thousand English and Frenchmen. They systematically raided towns along Central and South America coasts, climaxing their efforts in a planned attack on the Spanish fleet.

The colonial Spanish administrators of the Philippines and South America, pirates themselves, George pointed out, sent an annual levy back to the King of Spain—a huge collection of gold, silver, and precious stones. The treasure was collected at Panama and sent by mule back across the Isthmus; and from there, through the pirate fleet to Spain. The Viceroy of Peru, organizing the annual shipment, and wary of repeated pirate seizures, sent a fleet of warships to ensure his treasure's safe landing in Panama.

As George spoke of this Spanish fleet's approach, he was clearly getting excited, twitching more than usual "It was on the seventh of June, 1684, that Davis's fleet of ten ships set out to capture the Spanish fleet of fourteen ships. But those smart Spaniards outwitted Davis. They went to an unexpected port hidden by a thick fog, unloaded their treasure, and sailed back to Peru. The pirates caught up to them, but when they learned they were too late, the crews mutinied. Davis was too much a gentleman," George said, "much too decorous in his treatment of captured crews and cities, and, besides, he'd just lost the big haul. So the pirates broke up to plunder in smaller groups, or to sail boldly alone."

George went on to explain how Davis took *The Bachelor's Delight* and started sacking cities, deciding after a few months to return to the east coast. But before he sailed back around the Horn, he went to Cocos to take on water and bury his loot for later use, a sort of old-age pension fund. George's map had descended from one of Davis's crew.

George's trembling lessened as he finally got to the point. "This is the treasure I'm looking for, the gold of Edward Davis. Captain Lucy's map shows where it is." George stopped again and looked at us carefully. He leaned forward and lowered his cultivated English voice.

"I have tried to reach this spot. It's a cave between Flathead Island and Sugar Loaf Island around the west side of the island, but I can't reach it. The jungle route is impassable, impossible; well, you saw for yourselves this morning what it's like. Would you consider taking me to that cave in your longboat? I should share the treasure with you if you would."

A moment of suspenseful silence followed as Pa made up his mind.

"But of course!" he exclaimed. "We'll split the moola sixteen ways, one part for you and one part for everyone else on board, but before we divide the treasure, all expenses of this cruise must be paid for." He stood up. George stood up. They shook hands.

Mother miraculously let us skip naptime. With our lunch barely digested, we were off to find our gold. Our first impression on heading out of the harbor was of the sinister number and size of the sharks that swung their fins by our longboat. Their primary interest, until we came along, had been the downy white baby boobies that were accidentally toppling off their roosts on Conical Island. These sharks, some longer than our boat, and judging from their eager attachment to us, still unsatiated, swam along with us. They moved with deceptive ease for such great fish, suddenly streaking forward ahead of us or tailing us in our oily outboard-motor wake.

The beauty of the island, however, soon made us unmindful of the lurking danger. Cliffs rose abruptly from the sea, washed over by green waves of jungle vines. Crystal waterfalls cascaded over all this, making the island shimmer and dance in the bright equatorial sunshine. We'd stopped talking because of the roar of the outboard and were huddled against each other, cringing as each wave bought a new soaking of spray. The wind had kicked up a choppy surface sea. We were well out of sight of Chatham Bay now, alone in a very small boat in the full Pacific swell. Pa was in the bow, the children, Ma, and Nana amidships, and George, Sims, and Smitty in the stern.

Our reverie was broken by a scream of agony from Pa, who had leapt to his feet, arms outstretched, yelling, "Jesus Christ!" Pa never yelled and seldom swore in front of his children, yet there he stood, ashen, immobilized, having done both. In a torrent of seconds, we all realized why. Just under the bottom of the boat, a gray, leathery monster, about fifteen feet wide, undulated slowly beneath us. Before we could react, the great beast slid clear of us to the stern, rising up out of the water sixteen feet into the air, falling back and hitting the surface with a resounding smack, a ton-and-a-half of giant manta ray.

"Oh, my God!" gasped Pa, now collapsed and deflated in the bow. We children burst into an explosion of shouts, describing to each other in detail just how we would have gone to our certain death had the ray decided to flip while under us. John remembered reading about the sounds of a shark biting off a man's leg—the man's screams and the loud crack as the shark bit through the bone. Al said the blood of one of us would attract hundreds of other sharks. I was trying to dig up a fitting horror when

Mother looked at Quita's face and told us to be quiet. Willy could not contain himself.

"Suppose he'd flipped *after* he cleared our boat but had fallen back *into* our boat. Wow!" We stared into the dark waters in deep meditation. Again, no one talked. It never occurred to any of us, however, to turn back. We were determined to get that treasure and too preoccupied with the demands of the search to remember the curse on treasure hunters that Pa had warned us about.

Almost as startling to me as the manta ray's appearance had been Pa's behavior. He was like the rest of us after all. He did get scared. Life isn't all a big bowl of cherries when you come face to face with a manta ray in a tiny boat surrounded by sharks with no possibility of rescue. Will and sensibility weren't going to save you. How did this episode, the terrible storm the first week at sea, the accidents and illnesses of Puerto Rico, fit into the Heavenly Machinery? What mechanical parts had God and Pa missed? Maybe Melville had a better grasp on life than Pa. Malevolence shadowed us. Beware.

About twenty minutes later, we came in sight of three or four caves. George sat huddled in the stern, shielding his unrolled map from spray with a borrowed slicker. Suddenly, he stood up and pointed.

"There it is!" he cried, and sure enough, just where X marked the spot on the map, there was a gaping, jagged-edged hole in the cliff, with a long ledge running toward it. Sims turned the boat in toward the rock cliff. But Pa and Sims, and even George, soon realized that the seas were too high to approach the cliff. We would have to wait for a calmer day to bring home our boatloads of loot.

"Calm down, kids. We'll be back," Pa said, trying to soothe his disappointed crew.

22

Treasure Lost, Treasure Found

A S WE CLIMBED back on board our mother ship, we found the men just back from a shore trip of their own. Ted leaned against the rail and puffed at his pipe, waiting for us to calm down from telling about our meeting with the giant manta ray.

"Most of the sharks out there were after you fat kiddies, so we felt we were safe to swim in the surf. We hung our clothes on the nearest hickory limb and jumped in. Felt real good, too, even though I didn't dare go out too far. Then, feeling sprightly, we rowed around to Wafer Bay. It's off there," said Ted, pointing to the east. "It's a rocky coast, but let me tell you, when we came into Wafer Bay, it was worth all these blisters on my hands from rowing. I would have given my right arm to have a movie camera with me. Don't think I've ever seen a lovelier tropical scene. We passed our tobacco and matches to Chief to put in his hat, then jumped overboard and pulled Chief and the boat in through the breakers. We had a project, you know.

"I'd heard tell of an experiment some seafaring man had tried here. He'd brought chickens to Wafer Bay, and I thought I might pick up some fresh eggs for your mother. You know how she is about fresh eggs. Well, I guess the wild hogs got them or the chickens headed for the hills, 'cause I found no trace of chickens or eggs. Lots of old shacks, though, and one had a heaped-up pile of old beer cans right at the door. Makes you stop and wonder. Who on earth lived there, how did he get all those cans, and what a powerful thirst he must have had, and with all this good water around him too!

"Well, we were strolling along, picking flowers, when we decided to bring down some coconuts. We heaved stones up at them, and Sims used a boat hook, and when those nuts fell on the tin roofs of the shacks, it sounded like cannonballs. We began to think we were at war. I was leaning down to pick up a piece of coral to throw, and, just by luck, I turned it over in my hand. There, staring at me . . ." here Ted, infuriatingly, stopped to tamp down a new load of tobacco and relight his pipe, ". . . I saw a human face giving me the eye. No kidding, kids, there he was. This coral was shaped like a head with two holes for eyes and one for a mouth, and someone, years ago, had painted a face on the coral. I call it "Coco," and he's going to be my mascot from now on."

Charlie called Ted to the galley, so we wandered to the stern and took up shark fishing, waiting for supper to be served. I shuddered, even safe on deck, as I watched sharks attack our twirling hooks in vicious, swift swipes. When a sudden tropical downpour darkened the sky, I began to pull in my line, looking forward to the drier comforts of the saloon; but a four-foot shark had hooked himself on my line.

"Oh, O.K., O.K. I'll haul you in, cut you off at the hook and you can swim away, free at last," but at that moment, a five-foot shark bit off half the body of my four-foot shark, which inspired me to cut the line then and there. As I turned with disgust from this bloody scene, I saw the crew grouped around the bow, watching the water with more than usual interest. I wandered through the rain to the bow and looked over the side. Not comforting. The men had caught two sharks of almost equal size, tied their tails together with Manila rope, and thrown the unfortunate fish back into the sea. As I watched, the men shouted bets back and forth, cheering for their favorite, as the ill-fated sharks tugged against each other. The free sharks, quick to realize the disadvantage of the tied sharks, attacked them from the sides and under their bellies. I looked at the expression on the men's faces as they reveled in making a life-and-death battle into a wagering sport and recognized the brutality I had known at the bullfight in Caracas. Not wanting to get caught up in that hysteria again, I headed to the stern to find Pa, hoping to absorb a little of his unswerving faith that man's soul can transcend matter. I was feeling evil just watching those men.

"Score one for Melville," I was saying to myself, when a yelp from Willy made me run to the stern. For the last half-hour, Willy had been sitting cross-legged under the awning out of the downpour, rigging up a gigantic hook to catch a monster shark. Like most of his inventions, this one was a smashing success. By the time we had all run to him, he was fighting to stay on deck. Sims grabbed the line away from Will, and the men started taking turns playing in the monster. Al and John ran for their guns and peppered the catch. Finally the men dragged a ten-foot shark up to the side of the ship.

Mother, surveying her small son's afternoon catch, announced that she would take a picture of the triumph, and would the men please string up the shark on a launch davit while the family ate their evening meal? And that they did. But by the time we finished supper, it was too dark for photography, so we postponed recording the catch until morning. By morning, unfortunately, the entrails had dropped disgustingly out of his open mouth into the sea. Mother took her picture, with Willy beaming beside his catch, and then Sims cut the shark down. The tenacity in holding onto life and the power of reflex in this terrible fish were soon apparent. He had fought the hook, been peppered with shot, had been dangled out of water for twelve hours and his guts were gone. Yet, when he hit the water, he swam off weakly toward the bottom of the sea.

We were all leaning over the rail watching this spectacle when Ted, who was next to me, whispered, "Hey," drawing me closer to him, "remember my telling you about Coco, my new mascot that I found on the beach yesterday? Well, last night, up in the fo'c's'le, each man had a terrible nightmare. One by one, they turned and twisted in their berths, moaning and carrying on. This morning at breakfast each man recited his terrors and suddenly they all turned on me. Sims pointed a finger at me and said, 'That face! That's what done it. That rock you brought back with you. It's got a curse on it!' Smitty right then and there kidnapped Coco, right out of my berth, and he was all set to heave him overboard, but I wrassled with him a bit and got Coco back. Don't tell the men." And here Ted's voice was barely audible: "I've hidden Coco in the bottom of my ditty bag." Ready to mark my hands with blood and swear that never, never, ever would I expose the secrets of the brotherhood, I went off to breakfast on tiptoe.

As soon as breakfast was over, we were on deck in a circle around Pa and the captain standing at the stern contemplating the day. "We can't get into that cave today, I guess," Pa said sadly. "The wind is still too high. It'll be blowing too much of a sea up against the cliff. And remember the admonition on George's map that says, 'Approach at high tide.' Right now, the tide is low. With luck, we may be able to get at the cave tomorrow. Now don't look so disappointed, children. Thank God you are alive and healthy. That is quite sufficient for us all. I'll cheer you up a little by saying that we won't have school. We'll have an exploring expedition instead. Ready the launch, please, Chief, we will be taking off right away."

After a brief run getting fresh fish for Ma's supper, Pa decided we would visit George Cooknell again. George spotted us coming in, waited for us on the beach, and gave us a hand hauling the longboat out of the surf. We had a picnic lunch together and then came the required quiet hour. Pa, having grown vigorously all these years with no nap, proving that he didn't need one, went off with George to shovel in the pit beside the tent. George had an experimental dig going there. The rest of us had to sit in the shade under Mother's watchful eye.

Naptime came to its long-awaited end when Sims, Smitty, and Ted joined us, and Pa and George emerged from the jungle. George, now surrounded by his appreciative and enduring audience, began to tell us more about treasure hunting. As I listened, I let his upper-class English accent make his theories sound plausible, conservative, and wholly sane.

"I have here, look now, a willow wand. If I hold this willow wand so, loosely in my palms, and walk slowly and think about my treasure, the wand will jump to the site of gold. Mr. Chandler, perhaps you would be interested in burying your gold watch and fob for a minute while I demonstrate? Thank you. Thank you so much. Now, one of you children, please, if you don't mind, take that watch and bury it. I'll turn around and close my eyes, and then you'll witness my true divining powers. Ready?"

Al took the watch and fob, looking closely to be sure George wasn't peeking, or Pa peeving, and walked off down the beach and buried it. With a serene smile, a lessening of compulsive tremors, George began to use his magic powers. He held his willow wand loosely, closed his eyes halfway, and following the tug of the wand, staggered off in a trance, leaving his audience open-mouthed in suspense. He wove unevenly down the beach; and when he came to the X-marks-the-spot, the willow wand leapt from his hand and landed on the newly turned sand. George was instantly on his knees, scrabbling the sand and triumphantly presenting the watch and fob to Pa.

"Oh! Let me try!" begged Willy, but he didn't have the divining gift. We lined up, each awaiting our turn, and buried and reburied Pa's watch and fob, with no response until we got to John. John had the power, knew the sensation, and let the willow wand pull him to the gold. George grabbed John by the elbow.

"Come boy, come with me! You can provide a check on my findings. The wand jumps for me every time up there where I'm digging. Let's see what happens to you. Oh! I say! This *is* an important clue!"

Pa, Al, John, Willy, and an eager Sims, Smitty, and Ted all hustled up the jungle path led by a machete-waving George. Mother, Nana, Quita, and I were temporarily more interested in avoiding red ants than finding gold. We stayed behind to play on the beach but could hear the excited voices of the men through the trees and vines. Sure enough, the mysterious willow wand pulled John, blindfolded, right to George's pit where the wand jumped from John's hands. We heard the shout. For the first time on the trip, Pa told us later, Smitty lost his cool. He grabbed the shovel away from George, jumped into the hole and set to digging with feverish determination. We heard a louder shout when Smitty's shovel struck a hard object, but Smitty regained his composure and his usual taciturn manner when his treasure chest turned out to be the rotting root of a long-decayed coffee tree.

When Al and John persuaded Smitty to take them fishing, I begged to come tag along. We jumped into the dory and headed out beyond Nuez. I had the feeling that we were traveling in heavy crowds as Al and John rapidly hauled in long shiny yellowtails, blue-fin jacks, and fat groupers. The man-'o-war birds came in swooping flocks, curious and hungry, diving at the lures, beating their long wings about our heads. Then a black rainsquall caught us and drenched us. A tuna, heavier than four men could fight, snapped John's line and swam away. Al, too, lost a big fish. I was soaked through with rain and salt spray. Fish scales covered my hands. Cold fish slapped against my bare feet, but all of this I easily endured because Smitty, under a blue gob hat turned down against the rain, smiled at me silently, and I knew he was glad that I was there and that I could keep silent too.

The next day before breakfast, Pa and Captain had a conference on the after deck to decide on the time and tide for our attack on the treasure cave. They were met with glee when they declared the wind light, the tide right, and our departure immediate. After a rushed breakfast, Mr. Doyle joined the family in the longboat while Sims and Smitty rowed the dory in to pick up George. They met us at Conical Island, where we tied the dory behind our longboat and started on our quest, surrounded by the now familiar entourage: porpoises by the bow, sharks off the stern and swarms of frigate birds, man-o'-war birds, and boobies overhead. I assumed the giant ray was also out there, somewhere, waiting for us to scratch his back.

In twenty minutes we had found our cave again and were ready for the great revelation. Mr. Doyle rowed George and Sims in the dory toward the cave, while we waited in the longboat, motor off, rocking in the swell, watching the dory bob up and down on its way toward the face of the cliff. The only break in the surface of the wall was a narrow ledge leading up and into the mouth of the cave, which explained why the map specified high tide as necessary for getting into the cave. Only at high tide could you reach that ledge—the road to treasure, fame, and fortune.

The Chandler children before departure. *Back row, from left:* Alfred, Nina, Quita, Willy. *Front:* Sophie.

Now experienced sailors. *From left:* Nina, Al, Quita, Willy (in cast), Ma.

Quita and Captain, with parrotfish. Jamaica Bay/Acklin Island, Bahamas.

Nina, on donkey, en route to the Citadel, Haiti.

Nana, in center, with Pa and friend in Panama.

Willy and his shark. Cocos.

The *Blue Dolphin* at sail.

Crossing the Equator.
Back row from left:
Sims, Ted, Mr. Doyle,
Smitty. *Front row:*
Chief, Willy, John.

John and Al at Cocos.

The Baroness and Philippson at Hacienda Paradiso. Galapagos.

From left: Philippson, Chief, Mr. Doyle, and Captain leaving Hacienda Paradiso.

From left: Smitty, Sims, and Charlie with turtle eggs. Galapagos.

Willy and the seals of South Seymour Island. Galapagos.

Captain's navigation lessons. *From left:* Nina, Quita, Captain, Willy.

Lessons over—time to cool off on deck. *From left:* Al, John, Nina, Quita.

Lucky for us, the sea this morning was calm and unruffled. The great depth of the sea here meant that the waves would not break and crash against the cliff; they just rhythmically and slowly rose and fell against the face of the rock. Mr. Doyle backed the dory up to the cliff. Sims and George, crouched in the stern, waited for three waves to rise and fall, gauging the distance between the top of the wave and the ledge. With a great deal of courage—but after all, a great deal of incentive—and with the dory rising like an elevator, they jumped onto the ledge before the dory dropped twenty feet below them. Flattening their bodies against the cliff, they slowly worked their way to the cave's entrance and disappeared inside.

I was quietly contemplating how my photograph would look in the brown rotogravure section of the Sunday *New York Times*, sitting nonchalantly on a bulging chest of fabulous historical and monetary value, when George reappeared. One look at his despairing gesture, George's hands spread out empty before him, his palms open to the heavens as his witness, let us know, each one of us, that the cave was empty.

Back in the launch, George hunched over on the middle thwart and moaned. "Someone's beat me to it. They've taken all my gold away, all my treasure . . . oh, poor mater, poor mater . . ."

Sims was more sanguine. "Don't give up yet, Mr. Cooknell. We really couldn't get the lay of the land. You see, Mr. Chandler, the high tide made the surf break in and flood the cave, so we really couldn't explore it. Maybe when the tide is low, we could get in there in the dory to the back of the cave and find the stuff. I'm sure it's still there." So was each of the five children.

A silence closed in on us, but, as always, Pa came up optimistic. "What a lovely chance to explore the whole coast of this beautiful island!" We agreed begrudgingly and picked up our spirits, which had lain like the jellyfishes around us in the bilge. Off we went, towards Cape Dampier, the northernmost tip of the island. The project was short-lived.

Our motor began to chortle and choke and, finally, it resigned altogether. For a whole hour, Smitty toiled over the plugs and magneto flywheel, the cylinders and carburetor while we sat, smelling the oily, greasy machine and watching the shark fins rotating around and around our boat. Al told us, once again, the story of the Nantucket whaler, the *Essex*, which in 1820 was rammed and sunk by a whale, and how the men in a longboat just like ours were at sea for ninety-one days and ate each other up. This inspired Mr. Doyle and Sims to get out the oars and row in nervous jerks in the direction of the *Blue Dolphin*. At last, the motor started with splutters and spasms and we made it to our ship. We were to sail out of Cocos that night.

"Don't leave yet," Ma commanded Pa. "Wait until we get our laundry done. The water is so lovely here. Let Alfred, John, and Nina take this basket in to that nice pool over by the edge of the beach there and scrub these things out. Children, rinse and wring the clothes out well and spread them over the stones in the sun. The bleach will do them good and think how fresh they'll smell. Now, hurry along!"

Sims and Smitty rowed us in, and Pa came along to have one last probe in George's pit. Al, John, and I set to work in the pool, copying the women by the stream we'd passed as we rode our donkeys up to the Citadel in Haiti. Like them, we took heavy rocks and beat them on our hapless clothes against the boulders, assuming that thumping drove out dirt. We were soon very hot from our exertions in the equatorial sun and unanimously decided we were entitled to a cooling swim. Having not brought bathing suits, we parted company, Al and John going east, and me heading westward. I wandered out along the tidal basins on the ledges of rock until I was out of sight of the boys.

I undressed in the hot sun, the tiny coral-colored land crabs my only voyeurs, with the jungle protectively close behind me. On a coconut tree trunk, a little lizard stopped in his scramble, frightened, and blew his neck out into a big red ball to scare me. I lay for a while, warming my bare body on the hot black rocks, poking at inquisitive coral crabs with a worn-smooth piece of white driftwood. I couldn't see the harbor: a pile of black boulders shut off my view. I did see the top of the masts of the *Blue Dolphin*. She looked as if she were dressed for a fête, the illusion of flying pennants created by the row of boobies on the spring stay.

As I lay there, I saw "Elbe, 1836" scratched on a boulder. A hundred years ago, two hundred years ago, even as far back as the fifteen hundreds, men found this island, inscribed their names, and rested and refreshed themselves just as I was doing; but surely, I must be the first thirteen-year-old girl to lie on this very rock. I smiled and looked down on my body, finding pleasure in contemplating my uniqueness. I remembered that when I was about seven, a younger male cousin proudly displayed his nakedness to me. I was struck at the time by the inconvenience of being male, with limp appendages hanging unprotected. The female form seemed eminently more sensible; all sensitive parts neatly encased and out of sight within symmetrical lips. I was glad, I decided, basking on that rock, that I would grow up to be a woman. Now, these many years later, I congratulate myself again on having had the luck to be born female.

Slowly, in the setting sun and warmth of the stone, I realized that, for the first time in many months, I was actually alone, really alone, but sure, too, that this blissful moment could not last. I slipped then into the shallow rock pool and washed away remnants of the past. I lay still, baptizing myself into the faith of Eve, the Eve who would be forced from Paradise, alone, unrelated, free—free to will, free to choose, free to err. Tenuously, I was meeting myself, my pure true self, for the first time. I was delighted to make the acquaintance in this paradise and ready to be ejected into the real world.

Climbing out on the boulder to dry in the sun, a chambered nautilus in a cranny caught my attention. I picked it up and turned it in my hand. This, too, was a wondrous shape, a finely balanced spiral. I thought of Mother, a closed circle, and of Pa, he of the straight line going onward and upward forever. Such an expanding spiral as the one I held in my hand could limn my life, circling on itself, never complete, sliding into the next rising turn, accreting new facts and foibles, creating new shapes and changing, yet following a true path. But to where?

John shouted from the distance and I knew the first rule: my nakedness must be covered. I quickly slapped off drops of water and got stickily into my clothes. We said goodbye to George and wished him luck with his willow wand. He stood on his hands in a farewell salute as we took off through the surf. Then we met with an accident, confirming my doubts about no straight lines to proper ends. The pounding ride through the surf had driven the plug out of the bottom of the dory and we were sinking. John, Al, and I held the freshly mashed and bleached laundry high out of reach of the greedy sea as Sims and Pa struggled to get the plug back in and bail the water out. We heaved the laundry up to Ted and safety as we drew alongside.

We sailed off at dusk, just as we had come. When we arrived at Cocos, we were excited by the prospects of treasure. I had no idea, then, of course, that I would find something so rare and so different from pirate's loot. I had this tiny newborn something of a self. I was smugly pleased to have found it, and I attended to its arrival in silence.

At supper, Pa said, "George showed me his diary. I guess we pass inspection. He wrote a lot about our visit. His last sentence was, 'I like these Chandlers. They have no side.'"

23

Ghosting Across
the Line

WE WERE AT sea again with no land in sight, renewing the ancient ritual of watches and waiting. Lying on deck one morning, I thought back to that tiny yellow warbler that had landed, exhausted, on the companionway sill beside me during the hurricane in the Atlantic those first days of our trip. I remembered my amazement when he flew back into the raging storm. He could have stayed on the safe ship resting; but instead he was off and lost in the briny spume. He knew what he had to do. I was becoming surer and surer that greater forces than I could know were driving me, too, and that I, like the bird, could not hide or retreat once I had committed myself to life and its strange struggles. My baptismal bath at Cocos confirmed me in life, but I was still puzzled as to where, exactly, life was taking me.

We were sailing south in searing sun and light, fluky winds, ghosting along, headed towards the Galapagos. I stretched out on the deckhouse and scanned Al and John standing watch at the wheel. Boys might not be as sensibly built as girls, I thought, but they sure had a better time. I had long since known this. At home, I had to fight hard to be included in Al's gang. The boys roamed the countryside shooting crows or disappeared into the barn to the lofts of baled hay where they fought BB-gun and dart wars. With much pressure from Ma on Al, this boy's gang had finally let me into their inner sanctum sanctorum, the fort in the hayloft. Allowed only to be the nurse, I was always at the bottom of the heap, literally, deep down under the stacked bales, snuffling and sneezing, occasionally being honored by a dart in the cheek or a sting of BB bullets, waiting for the injured who never came.

I shifted my gaze to my mother and father, seated next to each other in the canvas chairs, reading. They certainly had changed since the beginning of the trip, I decided. Back then, all I could remember was arguments and bickering, their constant criticisms of one another. Expansive Pa versus stingy Ma. Exuberant Pa versus reclusive Ma. I remembered wanting to move away from both of them then.

Yet, as I watched them now, I could see they were alike in many ways, and this had been the glue that kept them together during hard times. They had always been rooted in a genuine fondness for each other, calling each other "Dearest," even when they fought. They wore identical bloodstone rings on their ring fingers. Ma had given Pa her father's bloodstone ring, and Pa then had a duplicate made for Mother. Bloodstones were meant to bring them good luck. Pa always said he would never kiss anyone but Ma. As far as I could tell he never did, not even us, his daughters. (Except in that moment of extreme crisis during the hurricane. Was he trying to say goodbye to us then?) And he probably never kissed that woman in New York. Women friends would come to our house and Pa would greet them with pumping strong handshakes. Ma would kiss them, brushing cheeks with the new arrivals. Ma wasn't exactly cuddly either, preoccupied as she was with her art and accomplishing her lists.

So they had always had common ground to keep their closeness, but I decided there in the sweltering sun, that the hardships of the Depression must have been what forced them apart. Pa losing his job had made it necessary to move in with Nana, so Ma lost a lot of the independence that she treasured, and Pa had a job he did not cherish. And then there was that tear-making "other woman" to be straightened out. Maybe they had just been bored with each other.

I went over in my mind how they had changed over these months, how many events had been pulling them back together since we started our trip. First had been organizing the trip itself, a lot of work they had to do in a coordinated way under pressure; then came surviving the storm, one family all together fighting for their lives. Pa must have been able to explain away his friend in New York, for I never heard Ma allude to her again. And I remembered them holding hands in the hotel in San Juan as they worked their way through those medical crises. Coming back to St. Lucia gave them back their memories of the *Vestris*, and then Caracas and South America surrounded them both in the warmth of thick happiness. It was as if they were back in Buenos Aires and ready to try their life as a true couple all over again.

They hadn't changed in their differences, however, and still had continued grounds for disagreement—and they often did, indeed, fight. Yet their differences seemed to complement each other now, rather than divide their territories into walled camps. The fights now eased pressures enough to let us all relax, and were forgotten by Ma and Pa as hurt that could be used in retaliation.

But what made them go in such opposite directions? I thought of Pa, quoting Emerson, as he loved to do. Emerson said, "A foolish consistency is the hobgoblin of little minds, adored by little statesmen and philosophers and divines." Pa certainly loved to rove zestfully into new territories. He was an inventor, creating practical machines like his gearless motor, which would conserve gasoline to help us all when the world ran out of oil. As a capitalist giver, he felt he must rescue others before they found themselves in dire straits.

Ma was always consistent. She was cautious, not bland but quiet and persistent, and above all practical, distributing her care and concern with great firmness and precision. She understood reality. Romanticism was not part of her being. She had studied with the "Ash Can" school of painters in New York who painted harsh reality, slums, and factories. This made her see the world differently from the rest of us. At Nantucket, she took painting lessons in a class with a Mr. Chase. Teacher and pupils went down to the docks and set up easels. Everyone faced the harbor and painted the quaint sailboats and seagulls, but not Mother. She turned her back to the water and painted the clumps of huge gas tanks behind the wharves.

And then there was the problem of trying to put away the labels that Nana and Ma used for Quita and me. Nana called us "boys," and Ma thought of us as only "little girls." Surely, there must be more options to follow.

"Nina! Nina! Where are you? C-c-come quick!" I jumped up and ran to the companionway to Quita's side. Another bird had come to us, a little land sparrow, dressed in drab brown. Like the flashing yellow-green bird in the Atlantic, this sparrow was exhausted. His soft breast vibrated rapidly, marking off in staccato time the energy he was using. He, too, was quite unafraid. Quita and I scootched near him. Quita, with her gentle, hesitating voice, soothed him, promising care and protection. As night came on, she slid a piece of cardboard under him, careful not to touch him, and carried him wobbling and fluttering to the chartroom for the night. We put some crumbs of bread and a saucer of water next to him. We all spoke to him and wished him a good night's sleep.

He was dead in the morning. We moved tenuously to the edge of wonder and fear at the closeness of death and quickly moved back to safety. We had a funeral. We placed the dead bird, feet stiff in the air, on the litter of cardboard he had died on. Remembering the undertakers at home, who shifted their Cadillacs from ambulances to hearses with a quick change of curtains, we covered him on his former bed with a paper American flag that Quita colored for him and weighted his feet with lead from one of our fishing lines. We stood at attention at the rail, saluting our dead bird as he plummeted into the ocean to be instantly consumed by the fishes and transformed once more into energy. At least that's what Pa said.

We were approaching the equator and beginning our preparations for the visitation of King Neptune. Most of us had crossed the equator before, but Willy, John, and Chief had not, and they had to face up to the initiation rites that would make them card-holding members of the brotherhood of the sea. The evening before we crossed the line, King Neptune came over the bow and ordered us to halt at the Equator to present the novitiates to his Court. On the ninth day of January at latitude 0°00'00'', longitude 91°40' West, in sight of the Galapagos, the ship's foghorn blew twelve times, the motors turned off, and Neptune and his Court came up over the bow. Willy, John, and Chief had been sent below while King Neptune, Queen Amphitrite, the Barber, and the Policeman grouped on the forward deck. Not even Pa, our classical scholar, remarked on the merging of Greek and Roman mythology here.

Neptune—Mr. Doyle transformed in an impressive long green slicker—stood as if just emerged from the sea (dripping from a bucket of water dumped over his head). He wore a full beard of unraveled Manila hemp that looked more like a grass skirt than a beard. A drooping green so'wester hat came down to the edge of his steel-rimmed glasses. In his hand he held a tall, cardboard trident. Nana said gods liked to be praised, but I couldn't make myself cozy up to Mr. Doyle, disguised or not. His temper and imperious manner towards Smitty kept me at a distance.

Ted's red mustache and coating of freckles didn't detract too much from the tall figure of Amphitrite. Amphitrite stayed close by Neptune's side, fluttering and simpering. She wore my plaid gingham dress, definitely too short and too tight for such a regal queen, and had long, golden, curly hair of hemp kept in place by Charlie's knobbly knitted red beret with a pink pompom on top, crowned by a newly created eight-point silver cardboard diadem. He carried a Spanish fan that Nana had bought in Caracas. Amphitrite left the King's side and sidled over to Pa, swaying her tremendous shoulders.

"Ralf," she drawled in her best Mae West voice, "C'mon up and see me some tahm and talk about mah last operation." The policeman, Smitty, prodded her back into her position in the Court. He carried a large club and wore a navy pea jacket cinched with a Sam Brown belt, and large white gloves, a dark so'wester and a natural-grown bushy black beard. He wore on his chest a five-pointed star of impressive proportions cut out of an S. S. Pierce can. Smitty would always look more the pirate than policeman. Close behind him stood Sims, the Barber, wearing a straw-colored, stubbly stiff rope beard and a wet slicker.

The Policeman went below and fetched Willy on deck. Putting his hands on the little boy's shoulders, he pushed him up to Father Neptune at the bow. He ordered Willy to bend low in obeisance and then whacked him on the behind. Then he pushed him over to an upside-down orange crate, made him sit on it, and told him to brace himself for his shave. The Barber stepped forward brandishing a large shaving brush—a length of rope frayed out at the end—and a quantity of mixed flour and water for shaving cream. He proceeded to lather up Willy and scrape his face with a long wooden razor. The Policeman finished the job by dumping a bucket of cold Humboldt Current water over him. Before the Barber shaved John and Chief, however, he added black stove polish to the flour-and-water slop. Amphitrite felt waves of compassion as she watched the novitiates' sufferings, cooing over them, holding their hands, and touching their shoulders solicitously with her fan.

Then came the branding. Charlie, in his white undershirt and stained white apron tied around his equally stained white pants, rose ghost-like up out of the galley hatch, making a lot of noise, sucking in his breath, whistling, bearing a red-hot soldering iron. John and Chief, now up on deck, had to turn their backs on the group, but not until they had seen Willy being stretched out on his back on deck. He was held down by the large feet of the Policeman and the Barber. While Charlie was "adjusting" the red-hot iron, he leaned down to Willy and whispered, "Scream like hell, boy, and give those men some idea of the burning fires that are coming to them." He rose and tuned to the Barber and presented him with the iron. The Barber reached into a can that Charlie was carrying in his other hand and took out a jagged piece of ice and applied it to Willy's bared stomach. Willy's high piercing shriek made goose pimples rise on my arms, and Amphitrite looked as if she would faint. John and Chief cringed and contemplated the sea. They, too, were branded by the ice iron, and then stood blackened, soaked, and finally triumphant as King Neptune bestowed their diplomas and pronounced them once and for all time true shellbacks.

I was proud when they received their diplomas; I had spent hours in the hot saloon drawing them and writing up the inscription with Ted leaning over my shoulder offering advice. He had crossed the equator many times and knew what the wording should be. I printed the diplomas very carefully on Mother's pastel paper. They read: *"Be it known that _____ has been tried before my Royal Court and has been found worthy to be called a true brother of the Ancient Order of the Shellback.*" This was followed by small print on their tests and privileges, complete with marginal drawings and a blob of melted wax for a seal.

The Court of Neptune slid back into the sea. Captain ordered the motor turned on, swore and spat at the fluky winds and currents, and started us in toward the shores of Albemarle Island. We were coming to strange and mysterious islands, and were well prepared for our landing.

As we slowly drifted down towards the Galapagos, Pa had been quickly covering the background history we needed to appreciate these enigmatic islands. He began with Charles Darwin, telling us how he left England on the *Beagle*, a ship the size of ours but carrying a hundred and twenty souls. "Impossible!" we exclaimed. We were only fifteen on board and bumped and elbowed each other at every point above and below decks. I had learned to enforce my own private sense of aloneness in an outer, limited, cramped, and crowded space. Pa explained.

"The ships had several stories then, upper, lower, middle decks, not to mention the bilge. They layered the people, but even so, it must have been very close quarters because those men not only lived together for five years, but they had several major collections to take back to England."

Pa sensibly began by telling us more of the history of the islands than about Darwin's scientific theories on evolution. He did read us Darwin's descriptions of the islands, but also those of the buccaneers and whalers who had come here, including our old friends, the pirate Edward Davis and the Nantucket whale men. Darwin told of landing on James Island with the ship's surgeon from the *Beagle* and finding Spaniards drying fish and tortoise meat. Darwin learned that these Spaniards had mutinied and murdered their captain, whose skull lay in the bushes. Darwin put a thermometer in the sand at that site. It registered 137 degrees.

As Pa went on, I wondered why on earth he'd put these islands on our itinerary. Darwin spoke of them as a black lava land, parched, with stunted trees. He said even the bushes smelled unpleasant and called the islands "Cyclopean." He was making me long for the green tropic lushness of Cocos, the paradisiacal island—never mind the red ants.

After a few days, we took to Nana's cabin. For one thing, a cold rain poured down at night, leaking into the cabins, forcing Ma to put out clothes and blankets to dry where we usually sat. For another, I was ill from the sun. My lips had swollen to twice their size, puffed up in ugly blisters. Glances in the mirror convinced me that my new self was definitely never going to be glamorous. I gave up practicing my low-slung eyelid look to entice John and ate my meals in my bunk. Mother brought the food to me, pushing up furrows between her dark eyebrows, that tall questioning curve rising over her left eye as she studied this worrisome abnormality—me.

In Nana's cabin, I could forget my painful face and listen with awe as Pa went on with the history of the Galapagos. The story began with the arrival at these bleak islands of our old friends, the Incas. Before Columbus sailed the seas, an Inca king, Tupac Yupanqui, set out with his men on inflated sealskin rafts tied together to find the western islands. He related his first island discoveries and how he had named them Hahua-chumbi and Nina-chumbi, which means "islands of fire." My mind wandered from Pa's tale as I toyed with adapting the name of Nina-chumbi and presenting myself as the Argentine volcano. Then I realized the boys would call me Nina-chubby so I abandoned the idea.

Pa went on to the discovery of the islands in 1535 by Fray Tomas de Berlanga, third Bishop of Panama. The Spanish king, Charles V, had sent Fray Tomas out to South America to investigate and report on the rule of Pizarro, the Spanish conqueror of Peru. Fray Tomas sailed from Panama in a square-rigger with many men and a few horses. The freakish, twisting currents and the lack of a driving wind drew the ship into the archipelago, just as it was doing to us. The men on board were jubilant upon arrival. They desperately needed food and water, but their hopes were shattered. After exploring three islands and attempting to dig a well, they ended with water ". . . as bitter as the sea." Through necessity, they learned what many other voyagers after them were to learn: chewing the fruit of cactus and sucking the water-filled stalks gave some relief. They celebrated Mass, and the bishop planted a rude Christian cross on the volcanic coast. After prolonged attempts at escape and continued vicissitudes, they finally did get away and reached South America to tell their tale. The bishop sent a record of the journey to his king and described the Galapagos. "It looked as though God had caused it to rain stones." Like Darwin, centuries later, the bishop was astonished by the tameness of the birds ". . . which did not fly from us but allowed themselves to be taken." Like many a well-bred Spaniard of his time, the bishop had a propensity for seeing treasure where there was none. The beaches, he wrote, had small stones that glittered and were probably diamonds and yellow stones that might be amber. "O blessed compensation for thirst and starvation!" remarked Pa.

The next Spaniards, a group of rebels escaping a civil war against Pizarro, came twelve years later. Also arriving thirsty and lost, they too were awed by the desolation and silence of the islands. The story of these Spanish soldiers, as Pa read it, made me think that Spaniards were born cruel, something I had suspected when we attended the bullfight in Caracas. Their boat in a flat calm, these soldiers converted their spurs into fishhooks and were concentrating on pulling in food from the sea, hot in the equatorial sun, when a sea turtle floated nearby. They threw a young boy overboard and yelled at him to swim out and catch the beast. Just then a breeze blew up, and the men sailed off, leaving the boy to be ". . . devoured by sea creatures."

So far the islands had no names, but Spaniards came often, usually unwillingly, and gradually the islands became known as Las Islas Encantatas, the Enchanted Isles. The connotation was of evil enchantment, not the nice fairy-tale kind, and was certainly appropriate for these black, primordial islands. Poorly charted, islands could appear where, on the map, there were none and disappear just as quickly. Strong currents driving up from the Antarctic took over the helms of the ships from the men and mysteriously redirected them. Mists shrouded the islands, sometimes making them seem as if they were moving.

After the Spanish came a long line of interesting and successful pirates, John Coxon, Richard Hawkins, William Dampier, Basil Ringrose, Ambrose Cowley, John Watling, and Bartholomew Sharp, as well as our now-favorite pirate, the old familiar, Edward Davis.

Nana had found another account of *The Bachelors' Delight* and read it to us. The ship had sailed around the Horn and was close to the Galapagos when these pirates made their first Pacific capture. They raided three Spanish ships and their haul consisted of eight tons of quince marmalade, ten tons of flour, ". . . a stately mule sent to the President [of Panama], and a very large image of the Virgin Mary in wood . . . sent from Lima by the viceroy." All of the loot was buried on the Galapagos. Flour? Why bury flour, I wondered? Who needs that much marmalade? Where was the treasure? This didn't match up to my definition of treasure. One of their crew, Ambrose Cowley, made quite good charts of the area, and from then on, the Galapagos became a haven for all pirates. They careened their ships here, buried their treasures, and lived in caves.

Next came the whalers with Nantucket names. During the whaling era, the long elliptical cove called Port Rendezvous, later Tagus, became the meeting place for the great ships. The harbor was well protected on three sides by high cliffs. Opposite the mouth of the cove was the island of Narborough, holding off long Pacific swells. On the cliff sides of the cove, the whalers painted their ships' names and the dates of their arrival to memorialize and to notify fellow travelers of their passage.

Then came the settlers, a series of misfits, derelicts, and crazies, beginning with an Irishman, Patrick Watkins, who deserted his English ship to become a drunken robber with an impressed black slave—it was a version of Robinson Crusoe with no redeeming features.

No matter what story we were told, all seemed to be ill-fated and harrowing. Captain David Porter sailed here during the War of 1812 on the U.S. Frigate, *Essex.* He not only dealt with Patrick Watkins but also won a major naval battle against the English whaling fleet. The English had been harassing the American whaling fleet, and Porter, with the help of the American whaler *Barclay*, captured the entire English fleet, valued at two and a half million dollars. Porter was extremely short of men to man the English fleet, so he put a twelve-year-old midshipman in command of one ship, a boy named David Farragut. Porter's victory was prodigious, his efforts heroic and ingenious. Yet the only recognition he received was a cursory rebuke from Congress. Porter had exceeded his orders by sailing around the Horn, so anything he accomplished after that was off limits, not to be condoned, no matter how great the victory.

"Bureaucracy!" Pa snorted. "If that doesn't take the cake! Just another example. I keep telling you, governments just won't allow independent thought and creativity. If Little Rosie keeps inventing new bureaucracies, you can kiss progress goodbye."

Nana paid no attention to Pa and moved on to tell the tale of Captain Benjamin Morrell, from Stamford, Connecticut. Morrell anchored his ship in Tagus Cove on February 14, 1823, just where we were heading. That night a volcano erupted on Narborough Island, ten miles away from the ship. His men rushed on deck in panic to see flames shooting out of Narborough. Morrell wrote that the ocean boiled and roared and bellowed. At three o'clock, an hour after the initial eruption, Morrell put a Fahrenheit thermometer in the water and found the temperature to be 61 degrees and the air, 71 degrees. By eleven the next morning, the water was 100 degrees and the air 113 degrees. The pitch melted in the ship's seams, tar dripped from the rigging, and no air was stirring so they were unable to sail away. By afternoon, the water was 105 degrees and the air 123. With his men near fainting, Morrell picked up a bit of wind and pulled up anchor. To tack out of range, they were forced to sail within four miles of the rivers of flaming lava. By now the temperature of the water had soared to 150 degrees and the air, 147 degrees. Several of the men collapsed. By eleven that night, they were safely anchored fifteen miles south of Narborough. Your basic Galapagos story, I decided. Fire and brimstone all the way.

John announced. "Narborough volcanoes are still active, you know." Aware of a general atmosphere of fright in the cabin, Nana admonishingly shook her finger at him, but then went on with yet another horror story. This one concerned the man who was sent to fetch the king and queen of the Sandwich Islands (now Hawaii, she explained) for a visit to England. His name was Byron, a descendant of Lord Byron, the poet. He and his entourage stopped at the Galapagos on his return to England, and the wicked enchantment fell on them, too. The king and queen died there of measles. Talking of Lord Byron made me long for the green hills and damp fog of England and also left me troubled that anyone could die of measles. You "had" measles. You didn't die of them, much less in the Galapagos.

We were now closing in on Albemarle and Narborough Islands with our motor running to keep us on course in the treacherous currents. The islands lay low and dull before us—a haunted land under a cover of gray mackerel clouds. We shivered in the cold. The ghosts of the islands wrapped round us. Quita and I crawled out on the bowsprit as we drew near the corroded shores. We had been on deck, but the vibrations from the motor annoyed us, and we liked curling our bare toes around the netting under the sprit. John joined us.

"That's Rock Rodondo over there," he said, pointing. "It used to be mistaken for a sailing ship because it's covered with white bird droppings." I blushed at the mention of excrement and hated myself. I blushed so easily. I was always blushing. I never could hide my feelings. I turned my head as if I was seeing something in the other direction, squeezing my hands tightly together, hoping that that would drain the blood out of my face to my fingers. John went on, oblivious, of course.

"Just behind the rock you can see Albemarle. I've been talking to Captain. He showed me our course. We'll go in between Albemarle and Narborough into Tagus Cove, just like the whalers used to do to have their gams."

The dried brown uninhabited slopes of the islands were now clearly visible. The land had been singed and cauterized by its fiery volcanoes. It looked leaden, the only contrast in color here were streams of black lava running over older fields of brown lava; the only movement, the line of lava swirls that, flowing into the sea, had been frozen in timeless patterns. We began to be able to distinguish trees, gray and bare, twisted sticklers for immutability.

John leaned forward, his feet in the net, his arms over the furled jib. He continued confidently.

"Do you know what it says on the chart? Captain just showed me, right there down on the chart room table. It's written out at the right-hand corner of the chart. It says, 'NOTE' and that's written in capital letters. 'NOTE,' it says, 'Caution should be used throughout the archipel-ago, as it is probable that geographic positions are in error.' So, gosh, even now in modern times, islands shift, and we can get wrecked up just like they used to do in the olden days. Even the U.S. Government says so."

He knew I would love the drama and he looked right at me as he told me this gem of information. He had forgotten Quita's sensitivities. He went right on, looking at me all the while, holding me tight to his story.

"We're going in right next to Narborough, the place that nearly cooked Benjamin Morrell. Ted told me Narborough blew up six months ago, so, as I've said before, it's still active." He smiled at me. I was charmed.

Quita made no comment, but crouched still, her brown toes curling around the swinging net, her tanned arms tucked into the bleached white sail. I could tell by the way her mouth straightened out, with the muscles pulling down the edges of her lips that she was unhappy.

Pa came along just then and told us for the tenth time about his grandfather's gardener. "Let me tell you about my grandfather's gar-dener," he began. "He told me wild tales as he goofed off in our vegetable patch in Brookline. I was only a child, but I loved his stories. He told me he was shipwrecked on these very islands. He always called them the 'Gallup the Goose Islands.'" Quita smiled at him, grateful to be returned to stories she knew.

24

A Gam at Tagus

THE SQUARE-RIGGED brigantine, the *Yankee*, rode at anchor in the cove. The *Yankee* had shared a berth with us at Gloucester as we both prepared for our voyages. And here we were again, side by side, weathered, our ships streaked with rust, our crews tanner and tougher. Captain Irving Johnson skippered the *Yankee* with his wife, Electra, known familiarly as Exy. They were spending a year and a half circumnavigating the globe with a crew of eleven young men, most of them just out of college, two young women, a fledgling doctor, and the only paid hand, the cook. How appropriate, I thought happily to myself: We, too, will have a whaler's gam.

Lying quietly in the landlocked harbor, protected from sea winds by high sheltering cliffs, we began an exchange of visits with the *Yankee* crew. The prospects made me giddy as we rowed to the ladder of the big, white ship and were handed over the rail by a welcoming group of rugged, tanned youths, dressed only in very short white shorts. For all my thirteen years, and my new self, I didn't feel the least bit confident that I was making an impressive entry. I was, simply, a mess: lips bloated and blistered, hair frizzled and bushy, my salty slacks unironed. But I did attract attention. The young doctor took one look at me, hurried below, and emerged on deck bringing me a healing salve. At least someone felt sorry for me. That had to be better than total neglect.

Conversation was easy. We had so much to show and tell. We started with the preliminary rituals of "And where are you from?" and "Oh, do you know . . . ?" We did find mutual friends, and with formalities accomplished the *Yankee* crew began telling us of their most recent adventure, their Nantucket Sleigh Ride. They had harpooned a whale from their lifeboat, and at one point in the five-hour chase, the whale pulled the lifeboat over the horizon out of sight of the *Yankee*. Before too long, the *Yankee* caught up with them and their dead whale. They hauled the whale back to Wreck Bay, on nearby Chatham Island, and hoisted it on the yardarm for photographs. They failed to tell us how they disposed of the whale, however, and certainly no trace of it was apparent. These bronzed young gods seemed too adventurous for my presently timid, shocked soul. Perhaps I really preferred being sickly in the conservative Board of Directors' saloon of the *Blue Dolphin* after all.

Two of the boys took Quita and me on a tour. I was instantly struck by the brilliance and cleanliness of the interior, especially the main cabin that was lined with upper and lower bunks. Their saloon was painted a shiny white. Each bunk had its own pair of curtains, the material patterned in tiny flowers on a white ground. This was in stark contrast to our dark, mahogany-paneled saloon with its stiff brown creaky smelly leather seats and black Franklin stove. I longed to shift ships and do my subsequent cruising in this Dutch interior, taking my icon George along, of course.

Our guides led Quita and me to the bow to see their ten enormous sea turtles penned aft of the bowsprit: Like seafaring men of old, they had stocked their larder with fresh turtle meat for the long sail across the Pacific. We met their pets, Lorita, a noisy green parrot in a cage made of wooden crates painted aluminum, and Innocence, a baby Galapagos turtle, only six inches long. Lorita and cage had fallen overboard on the run out to the Galapagos, but the *Yankee* had come about, no small chore for a brigantine under full sail, and rescued her.

As we talked under the white canvas awning draped over the boom, several of the *Yankee* crew were over in our galley eating homemade blueberry pie and fresh-baked bread. Mother and Exy talked about housekeeping at sea, Exy bewailing their cook Fritz's ignorance of baking and Mother bragging, for once, about Charlie and his use of dry yeast. But her compliments quickly faded when she got on the subject of fresh foods.

"Tell me," said Mother. "Does your man, Fritz, cook the fresh fish you catch?" Exy looked stunned at such a question.

"But of course! We absolutely depend on fresh fish for protein and just plain bulk. Goodness! I'll list all the different fish we've had since we've been in the archipelago and, oh! They are so good! Why, Mrs. Chandler, these are the great fishing grounds of the world. Men come for thousands of miles to catch fish here and take them back for sale in California, South America, Japan. All over."

"There!" exclaimed Mother vindictively. "I knew it! Ralf, just listen to that." She began her litany again. "I had to fight that devil Charlie at Cocos. The children caught such an array of wonderful fresh fish. Charlie was adamant. He said all fish are poisonous in these waters. He wants to go on and on serving corned-beef hash and salty chipped beef. He's just plain lazy. He does it on purpose. I'm sure of that." (Charlie must have had a "told-you-so" moment a few years later when news came that the crew of the *Yankee*, on their next trip around the world, nearly all died from eating poisoned fish caught off Pitcairn Island.)

As this back-porch conversation became strident, activity on the board the *Yankee* increased. She was to sail that afternoon for Pitcairn, three thousand miles away. We said goodbye to the Johnsons and their crew, taking with us several last-minute letters they wanted mailed at Panama, a book that Captain Johnson had written, lots of information on sailing around the Galapagos and rowed back to the *Blue Dolphin*. The oars lapped us along while John absentmindedly read off the painted names of ships that had anchored there: "*Columbus, Glory of the Seas, Chicken of the Sea, Viekoll, Sao Juan, Hussar, Cressida.* Look at that Japanese name. Anyone for pronunciation? The *Nourmehal*'s been here three times. *Flying Cloud, Cyprus, Santa Maria, Alva, Zacka.*"

"This must be the Forty-Second Street and Fifth Avenue of the Pacific," commented Pa. Al laughed just then, pointing to a sign on the crest of rising wall of rock. "Los Angeles City Limits."

"Seems like the *Social Register* to me," Mother said with satisfaction as she climbed back on board the *Blue Dolphin*.

We stayed on deck to watch the *Yankee* weigh anchor and unfurl her great square sail and raffee and move slowly by us. Suddenly a commotion on our forward deck demanded our attention. Ted had stuck his head up the forward companionway and had seen the *Yankee* moving by. He leaned down the hatch and yelled, "Hey, you there below! Your ship's heading out!" Three of the *Yankee* crew, below eating blueberry pie, projected themselves out of the hatch, rushed to the starboard side, jumped into their little dinghy tucked under our bow, and bent oars in a frantic race to their ship before she was off beyond recall.

That night, tucked tight under two blankets in my bunk, I closed my eyes and imagined a scenario. I was shipwrecked on a Galapagos crater and wandered into a camp of Spanish desperadoes, convicts, and buccaneers. Just when I gave up all hope of rescue, the *Yankee* came sailing into the cindery, sulfurous harbor, manned by the brave, bronzed, nearly naked youths I had just met. The pure white schooner with the pure white interior sailed me off from a fate worse than death. It was never too clear to me what fate was worse than death, but I took it for granted I would find out when the time came. With the rescue accomplished, I fell asleep.

Evolution would be the central theme of the rest of our visit in Tagus. On our sail down from Cocos, Nana had been our teacher on Darwin and evolution. One night she had interrupted herself in one lesson.

"Darwin," said Nana, looking over her glasses at us as we sat in the early evening light close to the binnacle, "was only twenty-two when he signed onto the *Beagle*. That's only six years older than you," she said, pointing admonishingly at Al and John as if they must be aware of the tight schedule they were under to accomplish great things. "And seven years younger than you" she said, turning to Ted who was at the wheel. Ted obligingly smiled at her and continued to keep his course. Now we were going to set our feet on the volcanic soil and meet the wildlife of these islands, imitating Darwin as much as we could.

In the morning, we divided into two groups. Al, John, and I went fishing with Smitty. We set off in the launch and trolled the cove, promptly catching fourteen big fat black groupers. I was happy being with the boys again and enjoyed anticipating the fight that would soon occur between Charlie and Mother about cooking those fish. But what I really liked best was going in close to the lava cliffs, the stratified layers of clinkers, and seeing fat, brown seals basking in the sun on long ledges, watching us with their great sad eyes and twitching their whiskers in curiosity.

When we returned to the ship with our catch, the crew, busy hauling in gold-spotted mackerel, hand over hand, belittled our triumph. They already had thirty. Ted was taking a picture of Mr. Doyle holding one of the fish to show unbelievers at home that northern mackerel were bountiful in tropic waters too. Charlie was busy salting down half the catch, cleaning the rest, and stuffing them in the refrigerator. Now, why, I wondered, did Charlie suddenly decide the poisons had left the local feeding grounds? Maybe he'd felt safe with familiar New England fish and could cook them without qualm.

Just then, the others returned to the ship. They had been exploring the shores of Narborough in the dory. Even Quita had overcome her distaste for the threatening island and talked in her excited stutter about a tiny vermilion flycatcher, a yellow canary, and a bird with a scarlet head and breast, and sandpipers and snipe. She marveled at how tame they all were.

"Oh, it was yummy," Willy exclaimed. "All that old brown lava rock running down to the water. It looks just like swirly old molasses anyway. And you know what happened, Nina? Some excitement! We'd paddled into this little cove, and we were just going along quietly, and suddenly we saw a huge pelican asleep on a rock. So we went right up to the rock, and I jumped off the bow right next to the pelican. I started to go up to him. He looked so tame. I was only a couple of feet from him, right next to him really, and just when I could have reached out and touched him, he opened one old eye and looked at me, and I looked at that big, old beak with that crusty horn-pointed thing at the end, and I just decided I'd get to know him some other time, thanks a lot, and jumped back into the boat. It was exciting, honest, really exciting!"

And Mother broke in to say, "There were seals, and they were so tame. They came out of the water next us, but made so much noise breathing through their watery noses, I was a little scared of them, but Nana wasn't and she called to them and talked to them and they stayed and looked and listened."

Nana interrupted, exclaiming over the great mother pelican, five feet from tip to tip of her wings, who dove, "Bang!" cried Nana, jamming her fist into the flat palm of her other hand. "She dove into the water and caught fish. She'd hold them for a while in her mouth and then take them over to feed her young in the nest. There were thousands of these pelicans, boys," looking at me. "Imagine! Just sitting on their nests. Thousands."

But the creature that thrilled them the most and won their hearts was the penguin. A cacophony of sound arose as all of them tried to describe the bird at once.

"Just darling," said Nana.

"He looked like a preacher!" said Pa.

"Like a duck when he swims!" said Mother

"Let's c-catch one for a pet," pleaded Quita

"I was in the South Pole!" shouted Willy.

"Lunch!" announced Ted, and we were summarily silenced.

After lunch and nap, we set off exploring again. Pa took John, Al, and me to find a cove that Captain had remembered. It was on the western end of Albemarle. We chugged along in the dory, out of Tagus and out of sight of the masts of the *Blue Dolphin*, down the brown, jagged coast, until we found a cove with a lovely beach and a natural breakwater. The beach startled me; it appeared to be black, sprinkled with diamonds, rich and sparking in the sunlight, and unlike Fray Tomas, I wasn't even starving or thirsty when I made this observation. So the monk wasn't so crazy after all, I thought, when he wrote his king. The mica in the sand was dazzling as we came in through the surf. We just missed bumping into a weighty sea lion asleep on the luxurious velvety beach, but he stirred as we swept by and waddled with ponderous dignity off into the water.

Since the swamp behind the beach was green and a forest lay behind the swamp, Al convinced Pa that they could find water and led him off to find it, which left John and me in charge of the dory. In one of the books we'd read, a New York taxi driver and some other men had been washed up on these islands. They had abandoned their lifeboat in a frantic rush for water, only to return from their futile search to find their boat smashed by breakers, thus ending all hope of escape. This admonitory tale, still emblazoned in our minds, led John and me to pull the dory high up on the beach before we went exploring. I had accepted his proposal with alacrity and an unnecessary giggle, so delighted was I to be wandering in the wilderness alone with him. I had almost forgot about my burned lips and my ugliness. He didn't seem to notice anyway, or maybe he was just used to me. We climbed over one lava field, fascinated by the many strange birds, and came to another beach with the usual slumbering sea lion. I stopped watching birds and concentrated on the sand. Countless shells had caught my eye, exquisite, delicate shells, and before I knew it, I was collecting again, keeping close to John.

"Hey! Look!" I cried out. "Look what I found." John crouched down beside me. We examined a long, white bone together. Undoubtedly human, I said, thereby knitting ourselves a tale that I would unravel that night in my bunk, still cherishing the feel of John's proximity.

We met Pa and Al back by the dory. Al had found water, but it was brackish. We returned to the ship in time for supper, but our day's exploring was not yet done. We set off right after supper in long pants, sweaters, and sneakers to find the lake inside a crater that we knew was behind the cliffs at the end of the cove. Just the children, "the boys," went on this trip, leaving the grownups to enjoy their quiet time alone. They sent our bearded buccaneer, Sims, along to keep an eye on us. Since no beach or landing stage existed in Tagus, we just rowed into the nearest cliff and scrambled off on the slippery rocks. Al, John, and Sims had guns in case we came across ducks, convicts, murderers, or just plain pirates.

From the deck of the *Blue Dolphin* our plan had appeared to be a simple evening's stroll. It turned out to be no such thing. The first obstacle was the crumbling lava cliff. I would place my foot carefully on a step of what seemed secure lava and get ready to heave upward. The step would prove to be a loose clinker, however, and I would slide down the steep cliff, throwing up a dry cloud of dust, filling my sneakers with scratchy lava stones. As I slid downward, I grabbed at passing shrubs that turned out to be thorny. By the time we had struggled to the top of the cliff, Quita and I did not care to go much farther. Scratched and scuffed, we sat down on the hot, charred stones and surveyed the view.

The *Blue Dolphin* lay below us. Down the other side of the conquered ridge was the round crater filled with dark water. We watched the boys and Sims slowly descending the slope through the dry dust. We could hear them cursing as they stumbled and slipped, holding their guns up over their heads. A curious phenomenon caught my eye. The rocks at the crater's edge appeared to be orange-red, a novel hue in this land of browns and blacks. As soon as the boys drew close to the water, and rocks began rolling down into the crater lake, this orange color disappeared. Tiny red crabs had completely covered the rocks, only to scurry away at the first hint of danger.

Darkness was rapidly covering the black mountains inland. Cool air crept into the crevasses and pushed out the stale heat. The boys climbed back up to us and sat down to rest. Sims amused us by starting landslides down the slopes, rolling big rocks over the loose ash heap, down to the water of the cove. We were absorbed with this play and forgot the abruptness of equatorial nightfall. Suddenly, horizons and perspective gone, we jumped up, feeling lost. Sims found a dried-up stream that we followed until we reached a seal highway, a path made by the big animals dragging themselves on their flippers down to the sea. When we came to a branch in the path, there was no doubt in my mind which way we would go, for blocking the alternative route were the luminous, ghostly skeletons of two seals. As we slid down the cliff to the water, we found Smitty waiting for us, sent out by Pa to fetch us home.

The uninhabited, still erupting island of Narborough, Albemarle's adjacent island, was to be our next day's destination. The family left the ship in clear, cool air, shouting goodbye to the crew who had resumed pulling in mackerel. We headed out the choppy channel in the launch,

Sims at the helm, toward the lava fields of Narborough. For once Pa left English history behind and led us back through time to an antediluvian age. Nana quoted Darwin, who said these islands brought him nearer ". . . both in space and time . . . to the great fact—that mystery of mysteries— the first appearance of new beings on the earth." And here we were, approaching the primal comet, the cooling sphere, on the lookout for dinosaurs, stegosaurus lizards, and hooded reptiles that must be wandering over the approaching volcanic tuff.

We puttered in and out of little lava lagoons until we found a long point and enclosed pool to study. We left Sims in the launch standing off shore, while Pa rowed us to land in the dory we had towed behind us. Silence was all pervading. We heard no sound of wind in leaves or trees, no babbling brooks, only the rhythmic splash of oars in water and the sound of drops falling from lifted blades. The short, stunted arms of the bare, white trees reached out to catch us and trap us for eternity. Long spiky cactus with tops like cattails grew out of cracks and crevasses of black lava, swaying a little, scolding us on our trespass. A peculiar smell, like a hot dirty oven or newly burned paint, lay over the land. Incongruously, the first bird we saw on this black burnt point was a fluffy pure-white baby booby with pale blue-webbed feet.

"Looks like some of those Long Island girls at the Yacht Club," I said to Al, remembering our gang in Nantucket. We girl sailors, with wet, bedraggled clothes, dirty torn sneakers, and unruly salt-sprayed hair, looked down on the tennis crowd in their pure white clothes. These girls had perfect page-boy bobs done in beauty parlors and talked in tidbits over vanilla sodas. The sailing girls swore, talked tactics, and discussed the laws of the sea as we approached protest meetings. We snitched cinnamon toast from tea tables as we walked by the tidy, sedentary girls.

The white fluff of a bird remained immobile, perishingly pretty with big black eyes looking nowhere. Then the ground around it suddenly came alive and scurried away. Quita and I squealed. Hundreds of marine iguanas, the lava lizards, about three feet long, had been lying still on the rocks, black as the rocks themselves, encrustations on the edge of Hell. Aroused by our arrival, they humped up their spiky backs, slapped their dragon tails and slithered off, into the crackling undergrowth and the sea. The swimmers tucked their legs under their stomachs and glided off, propelled by their strong tails.

We landed quickly and jumped out to catch one to study closely. Pa grabbed an iguana by the tail shouting, "Look!" We laughed as the miniature stegosaurus twisted itself around with its iron muscles, opened its hideous mouth, and spat at Pa. Disgusted by this display of bad manners, Pa held it out over the water and disdainfully dropped it into the sea.

At first the iguanas that stayed on the rocks seemed unafraid of us. They stared at us with unblinking, hostile glares, humorless and cold. We came on them slowly, and slowly they rose, hissed, and spat. Their breath seemed to smell of sulfur. I waited for them to blow rings of fire and smoke from their nostrils. John and I chased some, but they ran with such speed into the snaggled roots of the twisted trees that we never caught one. John and Willy finally trapped one in a crevasse. They grabbed it by the tail to pull it out, but it blew itself up and they couldn't unwedge it.

We gave up our "scientific study" of marine iguanas and turned to look around us. We had an audience. Two baby seals held their sleek heads up out of the water, watching us with their huge brown innocent eyes. Tame birds, an unknown tiny vermilion one, and a row of baby blue herons eyed us from the branches of the trees. Snipe and sandpipers skittered in a nervous dance on the fringes of the sea. Lording it over them all were the fat pelicans, like a species of prehistoric pterosaurs, shaking their drooping, leathery pouches, ponderously shifting their great weight from one foot to the other.

We jumped back into the dory to continue our exploration of the lagoons and came to an island covered with blue-footed boobies and marine iguanas, and a new phenomenon, the flightless cormorants, the most forlorn of species. They were awkward, mangy-looking birds with dark black-brown feathers, long snakelike necks, and large heads out of proportion to their bodies. Their feet were widespread and webbed, their wings only vestiges—short, stubby bent bones with fretted feathers, atrophied members. In our natural history book, we had seen a drawing of a prehistoric monster called a hesperornis, a diving bird of great size that lived in the age of reptiles, a hundred and fifty million years ago. No huge prehistoric bird could fly, and this silly little bird standing before us seemed a miniature model. As we rowed slowly by, the flightless cormorants began fighting each other, rushing at each other gawkily, trying to keep their balance by holding what wings they had stretched out like an aerialist's parasol. They pecked at one another crossly. One disdained the slow-motion battle and hopped up to the top of a rock to stand still, a figurehead looking out to sea, holding up his useless wings, a frozen challenge to change, an underachieved Winged Victory of Thamothrace.

On the next island, a penguin appeared, looking like a fat old man with a touch of arthritis.

"Yikes!" shouted Willy as one of the famous Galapagos sea turtles swam under our boat. "He's ENORMOUS!" A herd of seals joined us.

"Nature's own circus," commented Pa as we finally turned back to Tagus Cove.

Ma, studying the striated layers of lava of Narboroughs's shores, said, "It looks as if a giant had cut through the land to get himself a wedge of layer cake."

"Gall-and-wormwood cake," retorted Nana, "a bitter taste, indeed. Only fit for giants, goblins, or trolls, I'd say."

Pa sat in the bow, looking like Noah with his family gathered around him, saying goodbye to the evil old world and heading for the ark.

That afternoon John and I requested Charlie's permission to use the galley to make butterscotch. We were longing for domesticity and the hearth after our exposure to primal creation, God's wrath, and man's return. John said it was my fault the butterscotch was so runny because I'd overloaded the pot with butter, but I assured him he was to blame. I'd seen him sneak in that whole extra cup of sugar. We were still arguing as the five of us licked the last sticky remnants out of the pan and retrieved the three butter knives that had sunk to the bottom.

Fortified by the gummy butterscotch, Al and John went off duck hunting at the crater lake. Willy begged to go with them but Mother wouldn't let him. He puckered up his face and with smoldering rage, grasped Chief's bill-nosed pliers tighter and marched down to his berth to sulk. So, I thought, older boys enjoy freedoms that are denied to little boys *and* to "little girls." Not fair, just not fair.

Suppertime came but no sign of the boys. Mother raised her left, tented eyebrow. She was not concerned for their safety. She had an amazing confidence in her children. She knew they would not only thrive but also excel—although she wasn't much interested in what. She was annoyed now at the interruption of her daily routine. They were late for supper.

We went ahead without them, and when we had finished our food, there was still no sign of them. Finally Pa organized a search party. Willy was still lying surly in his berth, but Quita and I were allowed to go to hold the flashlights. We rowed in with Ted, Chief, and Sims. We were halfway up the awful crumbling cliff when the boys appeared. Al's shirt was torn. John's pants were shredded, but they did hold up one duck. They slid down to tell of their adventure.

They had found ducks on the crater lake all right, but the ducks kept moving out of range, leading the boys around the crater, over precipices, through brush. They'd bagged one duck but readily gave up hunting to try swimming instead. To their surprise, the density of salt in the water was so great, they could not sink or dive. They laughed telling us how the ducks came close to them, curious, now, about the intruders, well in range, quacking, as they glided in and out of the swimmers' path, quite safe, of course. The boys couldn't agree on the cause of the saltiness of the water. John claimed that an underground river came in from the sea, keeping the water level constant. Al claimed any such river would be tidal and would keep a uniform saltiness with the sea. I listened with respect. They threw so many variables at each other, juggling them all at once, that I felt muddled.

As the darkness and great stillness deepened that night, the bright lights of a diesel-powered fishing boat came about the point into the cove, starboard green, port red, and a wide beam from the masthead. She anchored beside us. Mother, in the unimaginative way of mothers, felt we'd had enough excitement for one day and sent the children off to their bunks, but Charlie took off his blue felt carpet slippers, for once, and put on his formal sneakers. With Sims, he rowed over to pay a call on the newcomers, who turned out to be from San Diego, California.

Our loquacious friend, Sims, regaled us with the details the next morning.

"Charlie sure was impressed with the cleanliness of that boat," he began, "and he sure had something to say about that great big galley. Those fishermen had it good. They were mostly Portuguese. They had real roomy quarters. Didn't seem a bit like those dirty, smelly fishing boats I've seen go out of Gloucester. Chief should have seen their radio set-up. We could have called any old ham, if we'd thought of anything to say. But kids, you know what I thought was the best of all? Well, it was the shrine they had in the main cabin, a real little chapel, with candles burning all the time before the feet of the Virgin. Imagine that!"

I could imagine that easily and thought for a moment of installing a votive light at the chin of George, but Pa wouldn't approve. It would set him off on a lecture on the evils of papists. Anyway, I like having my secret, my George, all to myself.

We never had a chance to see this ship, however. We sailed out of Tagus Cove at four A.M. bound for Villamiel on the same Albemarle Island, off around the southeast coast. I didn't get out of my bunk in the early dawn to watch our departure, but I could hear the men on deck grumbling under the command of Mr. Doyle.

"Forty-fathom Dan, the deep-sea man," Ted exclaimed, "you've earned your name this morning!" Mr. Doyle had paid out so much anchor chain that it took a half hour of hauling to get it all back on board. Smitty must have been out of hearing of the mate, because I heard him say, "Unnecessary. Damned unnecessary. Just a damned fool."

25

We Learn Manners
From the Convicts

"CHILDREN," ANNOUNCED PA at breakfast, "we have a job to do today, a dangerous assignment. Listen and attend. I shall tell you my plans. We're going to Villamiel, the convict colony. Villamiel means "honeytown" in Spanish. That's what I call the last word in poetic optimism. This island of Albemarle has quite a history. In about 1830, General Jose Villamiel, a leader in the Ecuadorian revolution against Spain, formally claimed these islands for colonization under Ecuadorian title, and they are still Ecuadorian. The first settlers were eighty soldiers who had been sentenced to death for the role they played in the rebellion. Their sentences were commuted, providing they spent their remaining days on the Galapagos. This was the group that Darwin encountered. The convicts had massacred their leader, a Mr. Williams, because of his cruelty, and it was probably Williams's skull that Darwin saw in the bushes. Ever since, Villamiel has been a convict settlement for Ecuador.

"Before we left on this trip," Pa continued, "I had several conversations with Dr. Townsend of the New York Aquarium, who works in that round building at the Battery on the end of Manhattan, and with our old friend, Houston Gaddis. You remember Mr. Gaddis, Nina, and his pleasant home in Virginia, with that great tank of tropical fish in his dining room? Well, these two men were out here on a scientific expedition for the New York Aquarium. They tried to land at Villamiel, having left their large ship in a small lifeboat, but couldn't find the entrance through the barrier reef. They capsized and washed up on the reef, clinging to it for dear life in these shark-filled waters, until along came a certain Mr. Gil from Villamiel to rescue them. They stayed with Mr. Gil for several days, took many photographs, and made quite a study of the flora, fauna, and fish. When they left, they promised to send Mr. Gil copies of their photos and reports of his island. Now I have been chosen to deliver these to Mr. Gil."

At this point, no one even asked for the sugar, as we listened to the tale unfold.

"Very well and good so far, but now comes the interesting part," said Pa, pushing back his chair and crossing his arms over his ample chest. "Dr. Townsend and Mr. Gaddis gave me two very urgent warnings. They were quite emphatic about them. Number one: Beware the barrier reef at the entrance to the harbor. Well, they could certainly wax warmly about that, since they nearly met their end on it. The second warning is more interesting. Number two: Beware of Mr. Gil and his men. Mr. Gil is a convict and he leads a convict crew. Never for an instant are we to let down our guard. Our friends say that these convicts are destitute and desperate. They have few supplies. Water is scarce and bad. They wouldn't think anything of cutting our throats and sailing away in our schooner. Mr. Gaddis said that the only reason Mr. Gil had been kind to them was because an Ecuadorian Government ship lay at the mouth of the harbor all during their visit, so the gang on shore felt it a good policy to lie low. Dr. Townsend urges extreme caution. If a boat comes out from Villamiel, we are to be very careful and let only one man on board at a time, and we must be prepared at all times for an armed attack."

Pa paused and gazed appreciatively at his open-eyed, open-mouthed audience and then pushed his chair back a little more.

"Now," he said, "hurry up and make your bunks, and we'll get on with our Latin."

But Latin didn't flow easily that morning; our minds were busy shaping prospects for our proposed afternoon visit as our bodies stiffened, battling with the elements. We were under full sail, running through a strong wind squall and were freezing. We were wearing heavy coats and scarves, and were huddled together, chilled on the tipping deckhouse.

"Pa, I can't think straight. Declensions and conjugations just don't stick. It's too cold."

"Nonsense, Nina. Can you stop? Ixnay. Keep at it."

So I did, unsure whether I, too, could substitute a little shorthand pig Latin for the long lines that needed parsing.

About lunchtime, we rounded Essex Point, following the same route as Morrell on his flight from the seething seas of Narborough. We rounded the southern tip of Albemarle and confronted the high bluffs and numerous volcanic cones that ran along the central ridge of the island. Although the familiar clouds hung around the tops of the mountains, the upper slopes and plateaus were a refreshing green. So far, Albemarle's coast had been in the lee of Narborough, but now that we were well below the shielding island, we could see great rolling seas crashing in against the black jagged lava cliffs and throwing ribbons of white foam into the sky. Behind the flying spray, we saw clumps of low-growing green mangroves holding their ground.

At four o'clock, running a close reach, we stood two miles off the scattered houses that made up the town of Villamiel. Captain called all hands to bring the ship into this dangerous region. Sims stood on the spreaders, high up the mast, on lookout for reefs. We shortened sail while Smitty stood at the port side heaving the lead line over for soundings.

"One hundred eighty fathoms," he called back to Captain at the wheel, coiling the dripping rope ready to heave it over again. "Seventy-one fathoms . . . twenty-nine fathoms . . ."

Charlie paced the bow in his torn carpet slippers. Uneasy, wanting to help in these dangerous maneuvers, he crawled out to the fisherman's pulpit on the end of the bowsprit. He had stood there only a minute, scrutinizing the waters below, when he turned and yelled to Captain.

"Reef! Dead ahead!"

Captain spun the wheel hard over. Ted, Chief, and the boys uncleated the sheets and paid out line feverishly. Blocks rattled as the lines ran through them. The ship groaned, but we were safe. We hove to, then, and surveyed our position. Captain and Pa, by the wheel, discussed our landing.

"Captain Johnson was inside that barrier reef with his *Yankee* just this past week," said Pa, "so I know we can get in there. We'll have to find the channel. The *Yankee* draws twelve feet, so we'll get through all right if we can find it."

"Yes, sir," replied Captain. "But it's a chancy business, Mr. Chandler, and I just don't like to take chances, not now, out here with all these ladies aboard." Captain heaved up his rounded shoulders in a gesture of concern over his responsibilities. There we were again, the ladies, the spoilers.

"Well, I'll tell you what we'll do," continued Pa. "I'll go in toward shore in the dory with the outboard and see what we find at close range. You keep working back and forth here and I'll report back to you."

"Yes, sir." replied Captain, and the dory was lowered forthwith.

Sims had already jumped into it and was holding her off from the black-painted hull when Pa called. "Come on, boys. Al and John, you come with us." Pa, unlike Nana, meant boys when he said it. I knew once again that Quita and I would have short shrift, and Willy, as usual, was in his separate category—"little boy"—and wouldn't be included.

We kept a close watch on them with our powerful glasses. As they drew near the main barrier reef, shoals cropped up all around them, and Sims would suddenly change his course, the little boat rolling in the great swells. We were imagining the suspense the boys were feeling when we noticed three men rowing out from shore to greet them. The two boats drew together. Pa tossed the welcoming craft a line and turned and towed them out to where we were tacking back and forth. Quita, Willy, and I leaned far over the guardrail, waiting for our first glimpse of Galapagos desperadoes in the flesh. Two dark young men were at the oars, and a heavy-set, fine-looking older man sat in the stern under a wide-brimmed hat that shaded his sunburned face. He wore a poncho cape over his hulking frame. Soon we saw his large black eyes and a fine set of big, white teeth that seemed to shimmer when he smiled.

"This is Mr. Gil," Pa shouted as he heaved a line to Smitty. "Get ready for boarding." Now, Pa had loaded our pistols before he took off with the boys, believing, as he did, all the dire warnings, and Smitty had a pistol tucked under his faded blue middy blouse. As an extra precaution Pa insisted that only Señor Gil be allowed on board. The two oarsmen, who turned out to be Señor Gil's sons, stayed in their rowboat tied alongside with Smitty standing over them. Pa was obviously unhappy curbing his natural hospitality. But Señor Gil and his sons behaved with gracious politeness. Pa led the alleged convict to the stern and, with formality quite foreign to his nature, introduced him to Ma, Nana, and the rest of the family. If there were any hurt feelings on the part of the sons and the father, they never let them show.

The terrible convict shook our hands and bowed low and held his hat over his heart. We were charmed. The conversation continued in Spanish. Ted swung up the after companionway with a tray loaded with highballs. It seemed to me that this social hour under the awning was more like the Nantucket Yacht Club race week than a meeting of adventurers and outlaws. Señor Gil told us about his ranch, half the size of the state of Delaware, with 40,000 head of cattle and a coffee plantation. His main problem, he said, was getting transportation for his goods back to Ecuador, as no ship stopped at Villamiel on a regular basis. Señor Gil turned suddenly to take Pa's arm.

"You must all come, your whole family, and visit me at my ranch. I have two places to welcome you, here by the sea, or at the hacienda on the slopes. Come for dinner and spend some time. We should be delighted and honored."

Pa began to accept enthusiastically, having regained his ebullient faith in mankind and losing the unnaturalness of precaution on the way. After an icy glare from Mother, he allowed that he and his boys would love to drop in for a minute, but that the ladies would not be able to make it. So Pa set off again with Sims and the boys, loaded pistols concealed, towing Señor Gil and his sons, who guided them into the harbor, arms waving. Again we covered their progress with our glasses, but once they landed we lost sight of them. The only moving forms we saw were flocks of pink flamingoes, stalking the marshes.

Quita and I were allowed to stay up late to welcome our men back to safety. I was curious about the novel way my father behaved when he was rowed alongside. It was uncharacteristic of him to want to get right to his stateroom without telling us every detail of his adventures. Nor was it like him to stagger crossing the deck to descend the companionway. And why, I wondered, was his speech slurred? Sims, securing the dory, smiled a wise smile and winked at me mysteriously. Al and John were no help.

"Oh, we just sat around," Al said annoyingly.

Mother also puzzled me. She scrutinized her husband's perilous descent below and spent a few minutes in silent thought. Then she quietly set aside her practiced feminine accouterments—her unobtrusiveness, her indirect approach, her statement of wish in the form of a question—and displayed her more familiar government-by-centralized-control look, marching back to Captain at the wheel.

"Captain Boutilier, sail this ship away from this island immediately. Those are my orders." All was silent then, but for the men on watch, following out the lady's command to move on.

The next morning, I dressed quickly, and hurried to the breakfast table where, happily, I found Pa. He was sitting alone at his customary place, drinking his third cup of coffee. For once, I had enough sense to ask no questions, waiting for everyone to gather. With his full audience before him, and "Just one more cup; thanks, Ted, it's delicious," Pa was happy to tell all:

> Once we were through the barrier reef we found the water very calm. We landed on a fine, hard beach where we were instantly surrounded by a very friendly group of men mixed up with tame flamingoes and donkeys. Our boys wandered about after we landed, and I muttered to Sims to stay right by the dory and not let anyone get near it. I went up with Gil to his house, a rather sketchy affair, and sat on his front veranda and talked. As we talked, tall rose-colored flamingoes walked about among the bushes by the house. They looked for all the world as if they

had stepped out of Alice in Wonderland, *and we would have a game of croquet using the little turtles for balls. I'd spotted the turtles in a pen by the house. Many fine young men came and went. They were all introduced to me as Gil's sons. Finally, I was too curious and had to ask my host a question: Where did all those sons come from? He gave me a lengthy reply.*

"You see, Mr. Chandler," he said, "I once held a rather high position in the Ecuadorian Government, but a reform movement started and some certified public accountants arrived. The stupid police were waiting for me at the ferry opposite Guayaquil, so I dodged them by rowing out to my schooner and sailing out here. That was thirty years ago. While I was still in office, I had purchased this half of Albemarle from the Government and had a decree handed down that no duties or taxes would be levied here for some sixty years. But it was difficult to get people to settle here, so I arranged to have some political prisoners sent out. Very nice people they were, too, but accustomed to a more refined life than was then possible here at poor Villamil. Hence, nearly all went back to Ecuador. There was only one thing left to do. I went to Guayaquil, quietly, so as not to be noticed by the police or my enemies, and purchased ten white women. Since then I've been populating my estate with contented citizens who wish for no other life, as here is their home. Therefore—all my sons!"

Well, I wondered quietly to myself, where were the daughters? Were they sold back to people in Ecuador? Didn't he need women, too? Pa stirred in his chair with a chuckle deep and rumbling. Pa produced a few hints.

I wanted to ask him if under his purchase contract he could return a woman who failed to produce, but not being sure of local etiquette on this point, I said nothing. He didn't introduce me to any of the women. But he did introduce me to some little glasses filled with a deep amber-colored liquid, which he proudly said he invented and made on his place. On sipping mine, I was most agreeably surprised.

"Señor Gil," I said, "If good fortune should ever bring you to my mother-in-law's rice plantation near Georgetown, South Carolina, I

shall be able to give you this same drink. There the natives call it 'corn likker,' or, when drunk before it ripens, 'white mule.' It's got some kick."
Now as you can easily see, it was not long before a very cordial relationship had been established between us two.

"Señor Gil," I continued, "there has been some bad mistake, and I must apologize to you and all the good people here. At home in the States, people write and say that you are all very tough here, muy bruto.'

"I, tough?" exclaimed my friend, "why that's impossible, my dear Mr. Chandler. Do you find us tough? Crude and poor, perhaps, yes, but tough never!"

"Is it true," I asked, "that you shot the hats off that scientific expedition that landed here two years ago?"

"Ah yes," he said. "I recall now that you mention it. Yes, yes. We did shoot the hats off those men. Oh, Mr. Chandler, you would have laughed so to have seen the surprise on their faces," and he roared at the memory of it."

"And did you throw that young student from Columbia University who said he was an interpreter for another scientific expedition down the well here?"

"Ah, yes. Yes, indeed, and how surprised he seemed to be, too." And again Señor Gil laughed.

"And when do you begin on me?"

"Oh, Mr. Chandler, you are my friend. You like my liquor. My estate is yours." He smiled. "But I see you need an explanation. Here are some highlights. Back about 1900, I was employed in our consulate in New York. The city wearied me, so on Sundays I would take the Central or the New Haven, getting off at stations in Westchester or Connecticut. I would take long walks through that lovely country. When I wanted to cross a large estate, I always asked permission from the owner to walk over the land, and it was always most courteously given. Often I was shown some special garden or grand view and many times I was asked to · stay for a meal, even though I was a stranger and foreigner, hardly speaking their language. Now, if I had walked rudely onto these places and started to pull up the flowers and kicked the dogs and, if when the *gardener had remonstrated with me, I'd said, 'Get the hell out of my way. I am a scientist!' they would have called the police. Here, Mr. Chandler, we have no police."*

"Well, tell me about the hat-shooting affair." I said. My host seemed eager to oblige and talked on.

"One morning, we sighted a great white yacht lying about where your schooner is now. So some of my boys rowed out to her and guided back a party. What fine clothes they wore, those men! Purchased at New York's best outfitters! They made us poor citizens of Villamiel feel very inferior, I can tell you. These men spoke no Spanish and my English was rusty for lack of practice; but as I was the only one who knew any, I welcomed them to our humble establishment and asked of what service I could be. But they did not ask favors. They demanded, as scientists, some of the 'extinct' Galapagos tortoises that were said to be here. Think of it! On my own ground and in front of my own house, being commanded by strangers to furnish extinct tortoises! So, thought I, these tortoises have great value to these men! I had several big ones tied under this very house. Their meat is excellent, and we must keep them alive to have it fresh— and there were others in the bushes. If they saw how many I had, I could not ask as high a price. So I consulted with my sons. 'Father,' suggested Ramon, 'If we shoot off these men's hats, they'll run back to their yacht. Then we can hide our tortoises before we trade with them.'

"So Ramon and his brothers shot off the men's hats, and it fell out just as they had predicted. Those visitors returned quickly to their yacht! As they stumbled over themselves in their hurry to get into their small boat, it was very hard for me to keep from laughing, I can tell you. Later, I rowed out to the great yacht and met its owner and the other well-dressed men. I came, I said, to apologize for the exuberance of youth displayed by my children and again offered my services and those of my estate to these distinguished gentlemen. Again they demanded tortoises, big ones, if possible.

"'Ah,' I said, 'that would be difficult. They are extinct, you see. But my sons, in riding high on the upper ranges of the mountain after wandering cattle, have seen tortoise tracks and might be able to locate a

specimen. Yet, of course, we are all so busy just now. It's too bad!' Finally, we agreed to equip an expedition for the search of these ancient animals, at so much a man and at so much a horse and at so much a mule per day. The next day we started off with four of the scientists and a lot of equipment. To make sure they would find the tortoises in the end, we strapped some half-dozen of them on mules and sent them to an appointed place high up in the lava flows. For four days Ramon led that party here and there over lava rock so hard to walk over. It began to look hopeless. Tracks they did see, but no tortoises. The scientists were for giving up the hunt, but Ramon urged them to continue just a little longer. As they approached the appointed spot, some of the boys rode on ahead and put the great tortoises in attractive positions among the rocks. And it was hard work, I can tell you, for those animals weigh many, many pounds. Then the boys concealed their mules and led their guests to their game.

"Oh, Mr. Chandler, the joy of those scientists when they saw the tortoises! It paid us for all the hard work we had been put to. They enthusiastically photographed the spot and the animals. Then came the problem of taking the tortoises down. How simple is the mind of the scientist. They never thought to ask how mules and rope could suddenly appear but our boys cheerfully helped to tie the tortoises on the same mules that had brought the tortoises up and joyfully escorted their trophies back to the beach. They were nice people too. They wrote a pamphlet about their discovery and sent me a copy."

I wanted to ask about the Columbia student, but by this time my host was showing some admixture of Nordic blood by taking just a little too much corn. A true South American, children, is never drunk. And feeling perhaps our mutual condition might accidentally cause a break in our present perfect friendship, I parted after many farewells. From then on I don't remember very much.

He turned to Mother and reached over and patted her hand. "I see your mother had things under control, and that we are at this moment on our way to Charles Island. This landfall, I know, will bring us adventure galore. The lady here, they say, wears black lace underwear and wields a pearl-handled revolver when she holds up any visitors that have the nerve to land on her shore. She seems to like kidnapping men. Now, how far did we get with *Fabulae Facile?* Nina, you're on *Ulysses*, aren't you? I think today you'd better do the chapter on the Lotus-Eaters."

26

The Baroness
and Her Lovers

A T LAST, in the second week of January 1934, I would set foot on
Charles Island, a port awaited with keen anticipation. A melodrama
was unfolding there, and maybe I could get a part in the production. The
leading lady was Baroness Eloise Bosquet deWagner Wehrborn, the pas-
sionate kidnapper with the black lace underwear and pearl-handled revolver. The story as we knew it up to our landing went something like
this: A doctor who was also a dentist, named Ritter, lived with his wife in
Berlin. He had begun an affair with a woman, Frau Dore Straugh, who became his disciple; together they were ardent followers of Nietzsche. They
were both nudists, both dissatisfied with Berlin and humans in general,
and four years before our arrival, had decided to run off together. For reasons that only a malevolent travel agent could untangle, they chose to flee
to Charles Island. Here they planned to reinstate their version of the Garden of Eden, living in the nude, eating only vegetables and fruit, expecting
to live to 140. Dr. Ritter—familiar with the pain teeth caused and consid-
ering them a source of evil—had all his teeth pulled and supplanted with a
set of stainless steel chompers. These had to be shared when, finally settled
on the island, Frau Dore's teeth rotted and Ritter had to pull them all out
without anesthesia. Once on Charles Island, they moved, with Herculean
efforts, huge boulders to clear the soil for a garden and built a small shack.

They were hacking out a meager existence. Birds ate their seed and fruit. Water from one of the rare springs on the island was scant. Mosquitoes and prickly pears raised havoc with their nudist program, but being Adam and Eve in a modern Eden, they had to persevere.

The year before we landed, another German family had moved to Charles, putting the Ritter ménage on guard. Mr. Wittmer was about forty-five and had been acting as secretary to Dr. Adenauer, then Ober-burgermeister of Cologne. Mrs. Wittmer was twenty-five, and with them was a nearly blind son of twelve by Mr. Wittmer's previous marriage. They settled in a pirate's cave quite far from the Ritters. Wittmer had been shell-shocked when he was an officer in the German Army during World War I and wanted to escape from the scenes of his youth to provide a new kind of life for his son. He spoke no English. The Wittmer's first child, Rolf, was born in the cave just before our arrival.

And then there was the Baroness. The Baroness was Austrian. Her father had been a celebrated railroad engineer and during World War I, while building the Baghdad Extension, his daughter had lived with him. They had moved on to Europe, North Africa, and Asia Minor. She spoke fluent German, Italian, Spanish, English, Dutch, Persian, and a smatter-ing of Arabic. She married a Frenchman, and they settled in Palestine, and then moved on to Paris, where she and her husband lived for ten years. She did some professional singing and kept a dress shop. During those years she became romantically involved with a tall, blonde Nordic Neitzchean type, a young German, with the English-sounding name of Robert Philippson. She decided to leave her husband and Paris. A friend of Philippson in the Ecuadorian Consulate in Paris persuaded the couple to settle in the Galapagos and helped them ready the expedition. How he thought this grand Parisian lady, who flew into a rage if society editors did not describe exactly what she was wearing when she dined at Longchamps, would live on this isolated, desolate pile of clinkers was an-other mystery to solve.

Just before leaving Europe, the Baroness decided to take along Alfred Rudolph Lorenz, also a lover, the flaxen-haired apprentice from her dress shop. When the three sailed for Ecuador, en route to the Galapagos, the

Baroness was forty-two, Philippson, twenty-eight, and Lorenz about thirty-one years old. The Baroness masterminded the project. At the Ecuadorian port of Guayaquil, she chartered a ship, sailed out to Charles Island, and landed one hundred ninety-eight packing boxes and twenty-four pieces of luggage. The threesome lived on the beach until they found water in the hills. Then they dragged all their gear up the volcanic slopes to build their new home.

Most of this information on the Baroness came from the tabloid press. I never thought of my Puritan father as a tabloid reader, but apparently his scope was wider than I'd expected. He had picked up several papers in Boston, just before we sailed, with a series of articles on the inhabitants of Charles Island. These he shared with us now.

The tabloids described the Baroness as a beauty with flashing dark eyes, a baroness of Vienna, a denizen of Parisian society, and a granddaughter of Richard Wagner. Reports from Guayaquil stated that the Baroness set the town humming with her appearance and her grandiose plans. She said she was going to build a big hotel on the Galapagos and arrange with the Grace Line to make her island one of their regular ports of call. Next came the news of the Baroness's arrival on Charles, now referred to as the "Island of Love" in honor of the doctor-dentist and his mistress. Adam and Eve were outraged by the newest uninvited guests at their garden party, these intruders who had had the gall to announce that they, too, would be living in paradise.

I studied the pictures in the tabloids. The Baroness was certainly seductive. Her hair hung long and loose over her shoulders. Palm trees waved in the background. Palm trees? On the Galapagos? The tabloids gave vivid details of the daily routines of the islanders and made it clear that the Baroness was adept at abduction as well as seduction. She greeted visitors to the island with that oft-mentioned pearl-handled revolver of hers, dressing herself in a black lace bra and panties. She drove her kidnapped prisoners (always male) back to her house to be her slaves and lovers, and kept them in line with a long bullwhip. One man, so abducted, had found eighteen notches in the post at the bottom of her bed, one notch for each lover, the last notch freshly cut. Another slave had peeked into twenty-four cases in the back room and found them filled with monogrammed French lingerie. The press did note, however, that the Baroness could be extremely pleasant with visiting yachtsmen, for visiting yachtsmen could be nice to her, supplying her with much-needed equipment and the intellectual stimulation she sorely missed.

One report told of a Dane from another island who landed on Charles to hunt cattle. The Baroness held him up and told him to work for her. He fled, but not without a bullet in his stomach. He recovered and reached civilization to send out a warning against her. Next, Pablo Rolando and his bride, Blanca Rosa, honeymooning in the islands, were shipwrecked on Charles (again question marks rose in my mind. Why would anyone go to the Galapagos on a honeymoon?). The Baroness captured them but found she hated having another woman on her hands, so she put the couple in a small open boat and set them adrift in the dangerous currents. Miraculously, a fishing boat saw the little craft and rescued the otherwise-doomed couple. Then came the tale of the Ecuadorian peon enslaved by the Baroness. When he rebelled, he was shot and killed. The tabloids loved to tell about the Baroness's cruelty to animals. They said she wounded animals so that she could have the pleasure of nursing them back to health.

People we met in Panama who had visited the islands recently told us more stories. They said the feud between the Baroness and the doctor-dentist Ritter was growing menacing. The Baroness told one of our friends about her first meal with the Ritters. Dr. Ritter had brought out white sugar to pass, but Frau Dore snatched the bowl out of his hands and substituted a shallow dish of brown sugar. The Baroness and her men spent their first night on the island on the Ritter's porch. The night was cold, but the Ritters did not offer blankets, nor would they allow the Baroness to kindle a fire anywhere on their premises. In the morning Frau Dore said, "Don't bother me. I do not want to be disturbed. I am writing." Frau Dore scolded the Baroness once for overloading her donkey, but the Baroness could see with her own eyes that the Ritters had inflicted multiple cruelties on their animals. The Ritters wouldn't even share seeds, as the Baroness had done with the Wittmers.

Once, the Baroness asked Ritter for sugar cane for planting. She'd seen the doctor feeding large pieces of cane to his donkey. He'd even offered a large piece to the Baroness's donkey, but he would give the Baroness only one small piece. When the Baroness asked for a little more, Ritter just took the small piece he'd given her and chopped it into ten smaller pieces and handed them back to her.

Captain Johnson, Exy, and the *Yankee* crew had visited the Baroness and Ritters about a week before we met at Tagus Cove. Johnson advised us to visit the Baroness before taking time to meet the Ritters. He reported that the Ritters were well-educated, but, like all fanatics, dull. He said their place was full of ingenious contrivances but thought the Baroness more engaging, though garrulous, a plain woman but with great personal charm. Johnson thought Philippson too quiet and Lorenz a cipher.

One of the best parts for me, studying these strange Germans, were the lessons I was learning about sex, a subject never discussed in our family. There was one time, however, when I was eight, when my mother took me alone into the front parlor, sat me down and said: "Now I am going to tell you about the 'facts of life.'" She then proceeded to read me a book about birds and bees. The bees were the end of the story. I didn't get the connection with humans and wasn't the least bit interested in birds or bees. I remember feeling flat disappointment in my mother. I knew she knew more and just wasn't telling. And why not, pray tell?

Up until now, I had not really understood much about the rules governing lovers, mistresses, and marriage, but I was learning fast. There had been that surprising bit when Mother cried because of Pa's lady friend in New York. Then Anthony Adverse provided insight through some of his interesting love affairs. And now I had Lorenz to puzzle over. As I got the gist of it, I figured Lorenz had been the favored lover at first, but the handsome Philippson gradually took over the top spot. By virtue of his manly physique and large size, Philippson became the Great Lover and claimed his Queen. One paper wrote of the ". . . daily duels of strength by the two knights for the favor of their queen who watched and urged them on . . ." as they fought with bare hands, clubs, and rocks. Poor Lorenz not only lost his place as a chosen knight, but was also reduced by Philippson to scullery maid, the Queen's slave, and her Consort. Ma and Pa never commented on these arrangements. As usual they were just letting me read and think for myself. I certainly was thinking hard.

The *Blue Dolphin* cast anchor in Post Office Bay on Charles Island on January 13, early in the morning. Grandmother, father, mother, and five children set out to be Yankees in Queen Eloise's Court. My thirteen-year-old brain, ready to absorb new data on love arrangements, wasn't much interested in the Wittmers—a regular ordinary everyday family, innocent bystanders, discounting the fact that no family I had ever known had lived in a pirate's cave, much less borne a child all alone without medical assistance in one. I was hot with the purple prose I had been reading that described the passion and barbaric love on this wild land.

We rowed to shore, getting soaked from the choppy sea, and pulled our dory up on the shining beach. Beyond the beach, the mood changed. We walked into a desolate ghost town, traces of mankind blowing away in the dry equatorial wind. A layer of brown dust lay on the buildings and covered the tall wispy grasses growing up in the well-marked paths. A crumbling wooden pier undulated out into the water, wavering into a final collapse into the sea, a caterpillar that would never know metamorphosis. A flagpole remained erect, bare, whitened, bony.

Ten-year-old Willy, in love with trains and hoping to become an engineer when he grew up, ran to a rusty railroad track and climbed into a battered car, consisting mostly of wheels. The car had come to its conclusion, stiffened in orange rust on the rails. Willy tried to breathe his love and animal energy into the car, but it was past caring and would not budge. Piles of rusted machinery lay about, stubbornly resisting their doom, twisted and useless, half-hidden by the silky, shimmering grasses. Pa poked at them disconsolately, grieving at the loss of so much valuable equipment.

"All this decay you see here," Pa was off on his morning history lesson, "is because some Ecuadorian played an old con game on a bunch of gullible Norwegians. He knew this group wanted to leave Norway, so he sent them maps and pictures of Post Office Bay taken just after the rainy season, which made the place look quite attractive. The Norwegians paid the Ecuadorian for the land and moved out here; but that Ecuadorian had a slight lapse and forgot to mention there was not much water, if any, in Post Office Bay. I'm amazed the Norwegians got this far in settling. These are their ruins we are looking at. Good stock, Norwegians. Very hard working. But come along. Let's get on to the post office up there on the path. That's certainly a more cheery sight."

Al, John, and I passed a house at the end of a path, high on concrete piers. We walked around it quietly, subdued by the ugly desolation around us, not anxious to stir up remnant ghosts. The bungalow was about forty by twenty feet, elaborately wired for electricity. A screened porch, looking out over the bay, was intact, but the tarpaper on the roof had blown off. The wind funneled into the house to rot it away. Mother, Nana, and Quita stood at the bottom of a beacon—three oil cans, one on top of the other, their white paint flaking off as rust blistered up under it. Like the house, it was wired for electricity; also like the house, it stood unfinished with no bulbs in the lamp, no hand to turn the switch, a fraudulent signal post signifying a sepulcher.

Pa broke the silence. We were grateful to have the space filled with his voice. "This island has one of the best harbors in the Galapagos, so it was a favorite stopping-off place for our whalers from Nantucket. We're coming to their post office now. They left their animals here, like Noah, two by two, to multiply, and then returned to eat them and used them to assist in heavy work. Now herds of diminutive wild horses, cattle, cats, dogs, goats, pigs, donkeys, and, I'm sorry to say, rats run wild over these arid plains. The whalers used to hunt here for the giant tortoises, too, and would carry off five or six hundred of them at a time for fresh meat and oil. That, obviously, is why these islands gradually acquired the name, Galapagos. That's Spanish for tortoise.

"And then there were the usual convicts. One of the fiercer ones, who arrived here in about 1850, was called the Pirate of Guayas. He'd been exiled here, and was he ever full of guile and ready to slaughter his enemies. He and seven others managed to escape, sailing to Ecuador where they were caught and hanged. A second major convict settlement here ended in a drunken orgy of murder and burning. Only one man survived. Then, in the 1890s a man named Antonio Gil tried settling here but moved to Albemarle where his group did themselves in with civil war, terror, hunger, and thirst. Say, I never made the connection before. I wonder if he was any relation of our new friend, Señor Gil of Villamiel?"

By this time we had circled the post office, a painted barrel on a tall pole. A small, hinged square door sliced out of the middle of the barrel was hooked shut. "In the old days," Pa continued, "the whalers tied a cask like this on to a tree for their post office. Letters stayed in the cask until a visiting whaler picked them up on its home-bound voyage." Faithful to tradition, we deposited our letters written the night before and set aside letters from the *Yankee*, ready for pick-up on our return from the Baroness.

Our friends had warned us that the walk up to the Baroness's was not easy, a six-mile hike over a steadily steepening incline of volcanic rock. They said that with steady walking we might be able to make it in two and a half hours. We were ready and began our march, single file, in high spirits. We were following a faint path that wandered along a flat plain through dried bushes. Then we began our ascent over lava streams toward a string of little volcanoes rising up beyond the plain.

Gradually I realized this walk was not going to get us to paradise by Pa's Unitarian way, onward and upward forever on a direct and pleasurable path. This would clearly be more in line with Milton, a torturous journey through purgatory before the final golden gates appeared. The same intense equatorial sun that beat down on Africa's steaming jungles scorched us. No Humboldt Current to cool us off on the singed sheet of hot lava. No trees, no leaves, no palms, no vines to crawl under to escape the brutal sun. The lava crumbled as we stepped on it and cut our sneakers. A smell like new varnish stung the linings of our nostrils. Slowly, slowly, the inside of our noses, mouths, and throats lost their moisture. I began to understand, for the first and, I hope, the last time in my life, what thirst really was.

We crawled over the rough lava rivers, cracked in the sun, broke through clearings that came after the low bushes, and went past a scattered growth of scraggly cotton and the whitened bones of a steer—dead,

I assumed, of thirst. After an hour of walking up the slope, we came to a full, discouraged stop and sat down.

John had a Boy Scout canteen tied to his belt. We each had a swig of lukewarm water and felt refreshed. After ten minutes of rest, we were encouraged enough to go on. So we slowly picked ourselves up and started off. Pa, Nana, Mother, and Quita fell behind. Willy trotted on ahead, leading Al and John, finding the notched trees that marked the way. The three of them were soon out of sight.

Walking alone through the serried ridges, I came to a pass between two high volcanic peaks and sat down. I took off my torn, hot sneakers and examined my growing blisters with a sigh. I ran a scratchy tongue over my dry palate and teeth. Putting my hand on the soil, I decided if I had a thermometer like Darwin, I would find the soil a lot hotter than his 137 degrees. Just as I was getting my sneakers back on, I heard a crackling in the undergrowth. A tusky wild boar, farmyard size but leaner, came trotting towards me. He took one look at the startled girl sitting in his domain, turned, and ran off, twitching his curling tail. I fled up the path to find the boys fleeing towards me. They had been frightened too. As they'd come around a cliff, they'd startled a grazing herd of wild horses into a stampede. Our courage renewed by the size of our band, we continued on our way, shrugging our shoulders, resigned to the knowledge that our only salvation would come from sticking to this singular path.

Emerging from a thicket, we stumbled onto a high plateau. The walking was easier and lasted for about an hour as we passed leafless skeletons of stubby trees. But after this trekking, we found each step growing harder, marked by a contradictory combination of futility and determination, which resulted in unsteady half-steps forward.

We spread out, and I was alone again. I was in a grove of stunted, twisted lemon trees. I sat down and took off my sneakers once more and blew on my blisters. Little finches in their drab, brown plumage hopped from branch to branch looking at me curiously. I had been thinking about a bit of our readings—tales of thirsty sailors taking cactus and sucking the liquid out of the stalks. But I hadn't seen any cactus anywhere. Now suddenly before me were lemons. Here, at last, was hope for release from the throbbing thirst. A weak run of saliva came into my mouth at the thought of the pungent juice. My mind drifted to frosted glasses and sprigs of mint. I stood up and plucked a lemon from the tree. I scrutinized the fruit for a moment, and then bit into it. The bitter oils of the rind burned the linings of my lips and mouths. There was no way to alleviate the pain—no water for rinsing, no food to chew on. I never did get to the juicy part. I spat out the fruit and shook my hand at the tree. The delicate little brown finches flew away. Three frigate birds, big buzzardy black creatures with red neck pouches and long, pointed, curving white beaks, flapped down and took their place on the lemon trees. Clapping my hand over my mouth, I fled in pain and dread up the path.

I came upon John sitting on a lava rock. I fell at his feet and begged first aid, a sip of water from the Boy Scout canteen. I swilled the water around and around my burning mouth and then noticed John's quizzical look.

"What's your problem?" I asked.

"Well, look," he answered. "We have to make a decision. Which way shall we go? Believe it or not, this rock marks a fork in the path. Who's going to risk taking the wrong path and having to retrace his steps? Not I, for one."

We waited until we had all gathered together and decided that John would go down one path and Pa the other. I dragged myself at a distance behind John. Soon I caught up with him. He was sitting triumphantly in the middle of the path, grinning a broad grin. Without a word, he raised his arm and pointed to the hills above. There rose the roof of a house. Shouting for the others to follow, John and I were quickly joined by Al, Will, and Pa, and we were soon striding through the entrance to the Hacienda Paradiso, the name the Baroness had given her territory, much to the anger of the Ritters, who had already claimed to be in Adam and Eve's paradise.

A half-finished barbed-wire fence enclosed the Baroness's paradise. Two tall hand-hewn poles supporting a crossbeam with the skull and horns of a steer nailed to it marked the entrance. We walked through the portals, passing four donkeys, two goats tied to bushes, a pen of black, white and brown rabbits, and strode into a clearing where we came upon a man chopping wood.

Tall and stripped to the waist, the man worked silently over his chore. He gave the impression of great physical strength as he moved his heavy, taut frame in a steady attack on the wood. Pa hailed him. The man stopped, dropping the axe to his shoulder, as he swerved towards us. For a moment, the expression on his Nordic face, under his damp mop of curling brown hair, resembled that of the wild boar that surprised me on the path. He was plainly stunned by the parade of children marching towards him. He collected himself quickly and ran to us, grasping our hands, introducing himself as Robert Philippson, and welcoming us to the Hacienda Paradiso. All the time he was talking, he was leading us toward the house.

"Eloise! Eloise!" called Philippson, "Look who's here!" The Baroness, responding quickly, ran down the path toward us. "Welcome! Welcome!" she shouted, holding out her arms with a look of compassion on her face. I suppressed a sob of relief as she bustled about making us comfortable, finding us chairs, bringing a basin of water to wash our faces and feet, and glasses of water to assuage our thirst, clucking all the while like a worried mother hen. An emaciated and bent figure moved silently out of the shadows of the house to assist his mistress—Lorenz. He helped his Baroness shyly, approaching us obliquely, not breaking out of his own world to acknowledge our presence. He would not look us in the eye.

After the flurry of introductions and first aid subsided, Pa explained that his wife, his mother-in-law, and another young daughter were still coming up the path. Philippson and the Baroness hastened to saddle a donkey. Filling jugs with water, they hurried off down the path with Pa to rescue the ladies.

Sitting in a comfortable cane chair, too exhausted to move or talk, I surveyed the scene. Lorenz did not speak English, and the boys weren't saying anything either. I watched Lorenz as he slipped back into the shadows. He stopped in the open doorway of the one-room house, and then turned to work over the cook stove that stood in the corner by the door. He busied himself beating up a sweet-smelling cake of eggs and cornmeal with sugar and cumin seed. I frowned. He surely did not fit any image I had of any kind of knight. He was more a scullery maid than a lover. In this, the papers had been right.

The boys and I were seated at a small, square table covered by a white cotton cloth with a flowered print border. Three orange trees shaded us from our enemy, the sun. Although the season for oranges was over, the trees had produced enough fruit to present a certain hazard. The oranges plopped unexpectedly on the ground next to us, or fell with a bang on the corrugated iron roof of the house beside us. The chairs and table were arranged on a hard-baked mud terrace, about fifteen feet long and twelve feet wide. Across the terrace from the house lay a pile of old casks and un-used poles, a makeshift barrier against the wilderness beyond. Before us lay the view of the slopes we had just conquered. A few yards behind us rose a fifty-foot cliff.

The house was a pleasant, simple, one-story, one-room shack about fifteen feet by twenty, built of wood, old kerosene cases and canvas. The roof lay loosely against the ridgepole. A long wooden window box with blooming flowers sat underneath two glass-paned windows with painted white mullions and white shutters. White curtains hung inside, jauntily offsetting the deficiencies of the house. A slab of corrugated iron lay against the side of the house, looking as if it might fit the empty door opening if it were put in. Straw mats on the dirt gave the sketchy effect of a floor. A spray of small logs, fanned out in a semicircle, decorated the gable. Three large dogs, descendants of those the whalers left to breed, skulked about the terrace, sniffing suspiciously at our bleeding feet and shaking off flies. Behind the house, I could see turkeys, chickens, ducks, and rabbits. Doves whirred in and out of the orange trees. A somnolent hum of bees came from nearby hives, white wood mounds banded by green stripes. With a surge of serenity that followed our physical ordeal, I could well believe we were in paradise.

Just then, Quita came through the gate and stumbled up the incline to the terrace, her feet swollen and badly blistered. Philippson followed, leading the donkey with Nana astride. Mother walked behind, and Pa and the Baroness, talking volubly, brought up the rear. We gathered around the table for Lorenz's lunch, slices of cold beef and tea. The Baroness passed us sugar, picking out ants as she handed the bowl around, remarking, "My grandmother always used to say that if you ate ants you would cure rheumatism. Look on these ants as a therapeutic part of your diet!" Lorenz's sweet cumin cake finished our first meal in this newfound paradise.

We children, sitting on the caked earth, having given up our chairs to the grownups, listened to their talk. The Baroness began by apologizing for the unmatched cups and saucers. Ma and Nana countered by cooing over the color of the beetlewear plates. I'd seen Lorenz run out to the garden and take glasses off the tender green shoots they were protecting, so we would have something to drink out of, but I didn't mention it. The silverware, however, was grand—heavy sterling with a baronial crest.

After we had run through the preliminary patter required by deportment, the Baroness began to speak of her ancestry in her slightly guttural accent, and mentioned she was the granddaughter of Richard Wagner. There seemed to be a question of legitimacy; at least Mother's left eyebrow shot up, and Pa laughed his curtain laugh that covered lapses and signaled an immediate redirection of conversation. The Baroness then went on to describe her life with her father in the deserts of Arabia. She said those childhood experiences had saved their lives on this arid island many times.

I watched her grow more and more animated as she talked on. She sure would disappoint tabloid reporters now, I decided. How could a woman in a modest square-necked, capped-sleeved, batiste blouse with a shabby white jumper over it, which fit her ungainly body too tightly, be thought seductive? I caught no hint of black lace. She was short, and in spite of her hard physical life, rather plump. She squinted behind thick-lensed glasses. She looked like an American Indian to me, not some elegant Parisian lady. She had an oval face with high cheekbones and long, sensuous lips. Her dark, unkempt hair was held back by a white ribbon, its broad bow at the top of her head. She wore no socks or stockings, just high white Keds. Her brown legs were scratched and scarred.

Lorenz slithered to and from the cookstove, waiting on our table, expressionless and silent. His long, yellow hair flopped over his high forehead. His trousers, cut off at the knees, looked, somehow, like tropical lederhosen. His heavy leather army boots and brown cotton socks, his tweed jacket, rumpled and too big for him (hand-me-down from King Philippson?) made Lorenz seem more Germanic than the other two. His face was gaunt, his neck long and thin, too frail, it seemed, to hold such a large head. His hands, too, were out of proportion to his body, big, working hands, reddened and leathery. He never smiled. His only conversation was in grunts, negative or affirmative, directed only to the Baroness. He was young but shrunken prematurely into the casing of an old, wasted man. He reminded me, somehow, of the flightless cormorant.

The Baroness explained in a whispered aside to Mother that poor Lorenz was not well. Got off to a bad start, she said. Starved when a growing boy in the Great World War. This had ruined his life. Now he had tuberculosis and was planning to go back to Germany for medical treatment.

Then the Baroness turned to talk to Pa with more animation. "I have come to this island to broaden and advance myself in the world, just as immigrants left Europe to move into the then wilds of the Dakotas in the 1860s. But I have an advantage over them in climate! The lack of water in the dry season is many times compensated for by the complete absence of subzero weather, tornadoes, and snow. I want to show that Europeans can live and prosper here. As we increase the means to support humans, we'll bring more shut-in-souls out here to enjoy the grand, free life."

"You sound like a female John Smith at a modern Jamestown," commented Pa. "You know, you have quite a reputation in America. They call you the 'Empress of Charles Island.'"

The Baroness threw back her head and laughed. "I can probably explain that. People come here shipwrecked, or just interested in our project. We take them in. But one or two of these people have refused to work for the common cause. They pretend to be too delicate and give weak excuses. I force these people to work for our mutual survival. If they continue to be lazy, I make them leave our small domain to shift for themselves. Once a man tried to attack me, but I frightened him away by shooting at him. My two neighbors, the Ritters and Wittmers, really may be kinder than I. They just tell strangers and shipwrecked people to go away. They never help the people I send away from here. I guess my mistake is to even attempt hospitality.

"The Ecuadorian governor did come out here to investigate me, you know. He didn't like hearing about this "queen" or "empress" setting herself up on his territory. We entertained him. He went away happy. I have letters from all over the world giving me advice on how to run this island, with offers to help. These people usually want to come out and set up a little kingdom of their own.

"All I want, really, Mr. Chandler, is a little home of my own with my own quiet privacy and my two men. Frankly, I am not too interested in Europe and America. I just want to make this little world here happy. I do not have time to write silly slop for monthly periodicals about idyllic life. I have lost patience with people who write that stuff. My aim is to establish a haven for hard-working, healthy people and, with luck, I will accomplish this. I wouldn't mind doing articles, serious articles in this vein. I have already contacted publishers I know in Europe. Do you have any contacts in America that could help me?"

Pa started, "Of course. Of course. Now there is my close friend . . ." but Mother hushed him. I don't think she was sure yet that we should be involved with these people. The conversation shifted when Pa mentioned the pearl-handled revolver and the photographs he had seen of her in the tabloids. Again the Baroness laughed and Philippson joined her. She ran into the house and brought out a fairly new, low-cut bathing suit.

"Once a big white yacht came into Post Office Bay," she said. "The owners invited us to come aboard for lunch. We had a happy time. Then they wanted to take my picture. I remembered those pictures in American papers, you know, actresses leaning on the ship's rail, pulling up their skirts."

"Cheesecake," Pa contributed helpfully.

"Yes, exactly, cheesecake." The Baroness went on. "So I borrowed a pistol and a bullwhip from one of the gentlemen on the big white yacht, and I posed for him against the rail. Good cheesecake, right? But like most cheese, apt to ripen in the sun. You know, I wish I did have a pearl-handled revolver. We are dangerously short of guns. All we have are a a .22 and a 12-gauge shotgun. I used to be a crack pistol shot when I lived in Paris. My husband and I did a lot of target practice together. But if you are shooting a moving bull for supper you desperately need something else again." Here she stopped and pulled up her white skirt and raised her lacerated right leg almost to the level of the table, right under Pa's eye. He drew back instinctively, on guard against this assault to decorum.

"Look at my poor legs!" she exclaimed. "I can thank hunting for this damage. I was out last week and shot a calf on the plateau, but I failed to make allowance for the mother cow. She charged me. I fled to the nearest tree and climbed in desperation, the mother cow hot on my heels. Unfortunately, the tree was a prickly pear. The thorns ripped my skin. To make matters worse, when I got to the top of the tree, it bent down under my weight and deposited me on the ground right in front of the angry cow. All I could do was rush to the next tree and clamber up and, of course, this tree was all thorns too!" Three kittens came rubbing their soft pelts against the Baroness's scarred legs, mewing for food. The Baroness fed them crumbs from the table.

"We hunt almost every day," continued the Baroness, "out on the plateau, but during the dry season, when food is scarce, we find the bulls come and stand in our path right next to the house, but we don't shoot those bulls, believe me. We are afraid of them and let them alone. But you know what happened three nights ago? It was dark. We'd gone to bed. There was a crashing noise in back of the house, then a terrible thud and a bellow. We ran out with our two guns and found a huge bull right back there. He had fallen off the cliff. We shot him and put him out of his misery. That's fine service, isn't it? A slaughterhouse in the back yard! You have just had part of that bull for lunch. Come, I shall show you where he fell."

We all rose, stretching stiffly, and limped after our hostess. "I found water here because I had a vision. We landed on this island seventeen months ago. We were stranded on the beach at Post Office Bay with all our equipment. We did not know where to go to find water, and we could not settle until we had found it. The island looked very large to start exploring inch by inch for water. On one of those first nights, I remembered a dream, a vivid dream, a vision I had had in Paris. I dreamed I was walking through barren hills and came to a green cliff covered with vines, and here I found water. We set out the next morning to look for the cliff. That afternoon we came to this great stone wall. But no water. Then I remembered my father's experience, out in the deserts of Arabia. The expression in Arabic for drilling a rock to get water from it can be literally translated as 'striking a rock with a stick.'"

"So you pulled a second Moses and all was well?" asked Pa.

"Exactly. In Arabia they find water in sandstone rocks. Sandstone holds water. I scratched at this rock and, sure enough, water began to drip out. We had found our water." We drew closer to the limestone rock and examined the intricate system of grooves and channels on its face, chipped out by the Baroness and her men. The grooves led down to a wide sheet of corrugated iron that funneled the water into a cask. Even in the longest dry spells, they had water. It was an amber color, but the taste was sweet and pure.

We continued on our tour, walking behind the house to the gardens. I felt as if I had been transported to a rugged hillside farm in Maine where such gardens had been wrested from difficult soil. The walls around the flower and vegetable patches were made of volcanic rocks that had been cleared from the plot. The vegetable garden was well-ordered and lush in its growth, with fat orange pumpkins, tall leaves of leeks, sprawling cucumbers and squash plants, beans, corn, and radishes. Tomatoes climbed up to the tropic sky, and banana fronds waved over the papayas. The flower garden ran to reds and oranges and yellows. At the end of the flower garden stood a tall cactus with a semicircle of painted white stones around it. The Baroness obviously needed aesthetic pleasure as well food production.

She led Nana, Mother, Quita, and me inside her house to take a siesta. A canvas curtain partitioned the one room. The front section had a double bed under the window—the Baroness's bed—and another double mattress on springs on the floor with the head of the mattress against the cloth partition. Behind the partition, boxes, crates, and casks stored supplies. I stifled my wish to wander back there and probe around for monogrammed lingerie. A high shelf, running along the wall by the Baroness's bed held a library of about fifty classics. We all curled up on the Baroness's bed. I looked for the famous bedpost with notches for captured lovers, just to check tabloid accuracy. There were no posts, however, much less a scoreboard.

The Baroness opened a chest at the foot of her bed and took out pieces of canvas and hanks of richly colored wool. She showed us the jewel-like petit point she was working on and samples of gros point in classic patterns of Egyptian leaves, tree of life, and vine borders. Quita was enchanted because she was still working on her cross-stitched pillow cover of the *Blue Dolphin*, the sea, and palm trees. The Baroness went over to the cook stove by the open door and took down a large needlepoint canvas she had done with a German culinary motto surrounded by designs of fruits and herbs. Then she took out her needle and gave Quita a lesson in needlepoint stitching, showing her how to make shadows, shade contours, talking as she worked, telling us about her singing lessons in Paris and the concerts she used to give. Through the open door came the rumble of men's voices as they conversed quietly in the shade of the orange trees. We were drifting through a bright world of cosmopolitan sophistication when Nana mentioned something about the little gray finches we had seen walking up from the Bay. The Baroness's face tightened. She sat up straight. Temporal realities rolled in like a thunderstorm.

"Those are the birds Frau Dore Ritter traps!"

"I beg your pardon," snapped Nana. "Traps?"

"Yes, traps! She has a well next to her house with a good deal of water. Frau Dore is a jealous woman—oh! so jealous!—she is even jealous of the birds. She does not want them to have what she has. So she has put an iron cover over her well and ingeniously rigged it so that when those little finches come to drink a tiny sip of her water, the iron lid falls on them and kills them. Then she feeds those poor little birds to her horrid, mangy cats!"

"Horrors!" shrieked Nana, recoiling. "The woman's a fiend!"

The Baroness warmed to her sympathetic audience and went on in a lowered voice. "The other day I was riding along the path from the bay on the pet donkey I caught and tamed myself. I was alone and minding my own business when, out of the blue, I was ambushed, shot at. The donkey dropped dead beneath me. Before I could collect myself, the killer fled. I know it was Frau Dore. She is after me. She thinks I have designs on her lover. What a lover! That dentist. Pfffgh!" The Baroness with great dignity spat on the floor. "That man!"

Quita and I sat bolt upright and grabbed our knees, hugging them, leaning against each other. Here was the war at last, and we were in the midst of it.

"Time to go home, kids," announced Pa, sticking his head in the door. "If we want to get back by dark, we'd better start now."

The effect of Pa's statement was almost as dramatic as if Frau Ritter had walked in with a gun.

"Don't make us walk that path again!" I wailed. "We'll die! Look at my bloody feet. I'm not rested at all!"

Quita was acting out of character, or perhaps acting with a character usually veiled. With firm steps she marched out to the hard-packed mud terrace, sat down with legs crossed, arms folded across her chest and burst into sobs. Between sobs, she cried, "I won't walk. I won't walk. Never! Never! Never!" Willy got the pitch right away and began moaning and limping as Pa pulled him along, readying him for the march.

Mother was taken aback. The Baroness hovered over Quita, putting her arm out to touch the seated weeping girl, acting like a nurse on a battlefield. Mother, probably with the Baroness's solid silverware and her clearly motherly attentions to Quita in mind, relented. She accepted the Baroness's invitation to Quita and me to spend the night. The Baroness would bring us down in the morning after a good night's rest, when she and her men would come to the *Blue Dolphin* for a visit. The others would go back to the ship.

The march down the awful terrain began. The Baroness and Philippson led the donkey carrying Nana to ensure that the troops took the right path at the various turns. Pa dragged a reluctant Willy. Al and John brought up the rear, waving as they went. They reached the exit from Paradise, where Will, also out of character, but learning fast, threw a temper tantrum. Pa let go. Ma sized up the situation and then ordered him to join his sisters. He stopped crying instantly and ran back to Quita and me on the terrace.

The three of us settled down to await the Baroness's return in silence. Quita and Willy, once more their amenable selves, wandered over to the penned rabbits, picked up the babies and held their soft, warm furry bodies close to their faces. Since I was slipping into the role of substitute mother for these poor waifs, I walked to the basin on the bench next to the stove and set to washing dishes, as any good mother-housewife would. I eyed Lorenz next to me muttering to himself over the cook stove, beating up another cake. I couldn't escape the notion that he was casting an evil spell over me. Once again I tried to imagine him as the great lover, but none of Scott's novels Pa had read to us had ever described a knight lover that was as scrawny as this. In my own limited experience of men, such a mute, wizened, specimen simply could not be classified, even remotely, as a lover. Again I marveled at the unreliability of newspaper reporters.

At dusk, the Baroness and Philippson came striding up the path, donkey in tow. Their faces were set, stern. I ran forward to greet them, anxious to talk again, to be reassured that all was well. They brushed by me into the house without even acknowledging my presence. A chill ran through my body and came back to stiffen the heart. Where was the warm, gracious hostess, the tender nurse of this afternoon? What were they expecting of us? The chill turned to horror as the Baroness and Philippson came out of the house, each carrying a gun. "Follow me," commanded Philippson rudely. With no further explanation he set off down the path, the Baroness right behind him, signaling us to keep up with them. Lorenz slunk silently back to his cookstove.

Quita and Willy walked before me as we hurried to keep up with the striding pair. Darkness magnified the noises of crackling grasses. Crickets scraped their legs against their bodies, their dry sound drumming up background noise. I tried to ask where we were going, forcing a nonchalant tone, but the Baroness swerved and hissed at me to be quiet. That did it. I knew, then, we were being kidnapped.

We were destined to be child slaves, beaten with the bullwhip. The tabloids had suddenly become the bible truth. Lurid and indelible memories of the Lindbergh kidnapping flooded me. I thought of the barred windows of so many of the children's bedrooms in Wilmington that would prevent just such an awful crime happening. I used to scorn those bars. Now I understood. I tried to look determined as I faced my destiny, although I was completely at a loss as to what to do about it. I stiffened my back, and holding my head high, clenching my teeth, and jutting out my lower jaw, I walked on. I was ready.

We came out onto a long plateau flooded in moonlight. Clumps of tall milky white grasses stood like ghosts in the cold light. We had come to another planet. We were in outer space; airless, timeless, breathless in its beauty. An owl sliced open the sheet of stillness with his plaintive cry. Philippson motioned us behind a black rock that stood high over our heads, a frozen form of a ghoulish giant, a fossilized hump of an extinct dinosaur. He strode over to another tall rock and stood motionless. The Baroness crouched beside me and hissed in my ear.

"He's waiting to shoot."

I nodded. I knew. I glanced lovingly, lastingly at my dear brother and sister. Poor innocents!

"Listen!" growled the Baroness. "You can hear them coming," I turned my gaze on her and frowned in confusion.

"Who's coming?"

"The herd." She whispered. "Food. Meat for tomorrow."

I collapsed weakly against the rock. My blood resumed its circulation again. Well, well! Hunting! I should have known. I blushed in the darkness.

A small, gray ass poked his head out from behind a nearby rock. He pricked his ears forward and finally dared to come out into the open stillness, but he timidly stayed by the great boulders edging the meadowland. I clutched Quita when a calf bleated close behind us. We stayed a long time thus, immobile, waiting, hardly breathing in the rarified atmosphere. Philippson came back to our huddle and whispered, "Let's go across the plateau and wait over there. I think the hunting will be better tonight on that side."

We followed him. I felt vulnerable to attack and cringed as I crossed the open plateau. Hunters could be hunted, and who could tell what eyes, which bizarre Galapagos character, was watching our single-file march through the dry, white moonlit pampas grass? Again we waited behind rocks, but still no game. Philippson finally shrugged his big shoulders and beckoned us back onto the plateau in the dim, shadowless light. We were going home.

Suddenly, though, Philippson drew up short and held out his hand to stop us. He pointed to the end of the plateau, to a ravine from which great boulders had long ago tumbled out onto the grasses. A herd of thirty wild cattle was slowly wandering down the plateau toward us, searching for good grazing. They came on slowly, snorting and shuffling, throwing up dust. In a wisp of air, they caught our scent and froze in fear.

The Baroness and Philippson walked steadily toward the bulls. Instinctively, I clung close to the guns and moved right in on the haunches of our guides. We walked to within two hundred feet of the bulls. Then the Baroness took aim and fired. The cattle stampeded. For an instant I thought they were coming right over us, but they swung around and galloped out the ravine, throwing up opaque, yellowing clouds of dust with their thumping hooves. The Baroness was off her shot that night. She cursed and beckoned us to follow her home.

We wove our way in and out of the walls of rocks. When we finally reached the woody path, we came upon the owl, still sending out his plaintive cry, sitting immobile on the long, bare branch of a low tree—a disembodied spirit, unblinking, swaying just a little. Philippson took a coiled rope from his belt, knotted a slipknot, and heaved the loop at the owl to lasso him. The line fell short. The bird stretched out his wings and glided off to another branch to take up his watchful haunting.

Lorenz had supper ready for us. We ate around the little table by the light of an oil lamp that cast an orange glow over the sliced cold beef and fresh warm cake. After supper, the Baroness brought out an old portable Victrola—the kind with a picture of a white dog listening to his master's voice—and cranked it up. I rubbed my aching leg muscles to the tune of "Good Night Sweetheart" and "Lazy Bones" and never felt the slightest twinge of homesickness. We must have been in bed by eight, all in the little room together.

The Baroness and Philippson slept in the bed by the windows and talked for a long time in the darkness, their voices rising in thick, curling Germanic sounds. Willy slept with Lorenz on the mattress on the floor. Mother knew before she set off that Willy would sleep with Lorenz. As she would never allow us to go to the circus for fear of picking up germs from the great unwashed, how she ever allowed Willy to sleep in a bed with a tubercular man, I'll never know. But there he was, in bed with Lorenz. We heard them complaining at each other. I could tell from Will's tone that he was scared. Will, when he relaxed into sleep, rolled down to the hollow of the mattress where he encountered the sprawled tubercular Lorenz. Lorenz was unhappy with the intrusion and growled at Willy. Will would quickly pull himself up to the edge, trying to keep a grip on the side of the mattress. Then he'd doze off again, lose his hold, and tumble back again into the ghastly hollow. In the end, of course, the reluctant bedmates snuggled together.

Quita and I were sleeping on a double mattress thrown down on the hard-packed mud. It covered most of the available floor space in the room. My side of the mattress blocked the doorless doorway. At first, we couldn't go to sleep because cats gamboled through the door over our bodies on their way to bed down on the casks in the back partition. Quita nudged me and whispered something that had clearly been bothering her.

"When I was r-r-esting on the path coming up here, I l-l-ooked out over the plain to the sea and I said to myself then, 'If I were in a b-boat at sea and was this thirsty, I KNOW I'd drink salt water. We've been told over and over n-n-n-never ever, even if shipwrecked, drink salt water, but I KNOW I would. I was so thirsty. Wouldn't you have drunk salt water? W-wouldn't you?"

I allowed as to how I probably would and urged her to sleep. It was behind us now, that terrible, terrible thirst. Once the cats had quieted down, Quita and I slept peacefully enough except for the howling of wild dogs, the braying of wild donkeys, the bellowing of wild bulls just outside our open doorway, and the frequent banging of oranges on the loose, iron roof.

We were up at 5:30 in the cold dawn. Having relieved ourselves in a primitive privy out behind the garden, we were ready to warm ourselves with morning chores. Lorenz was back prowling around the cook stove. Philippson chopped wood again with Willy at his side stacking the growing pile of lemon-wood logs. Quita and I followed the Baroness to the three casks of water under the green limestone cliff. She filled a basin with water and handed it to Quita and me to wash ourselves. Then she gave us a yellow crockery bowl full of eggshells, the residue of Lorenz's cakes of the night before.

"Mash them up fine, girls," she said, tying up her dark hair in the big white ribbon. "Get them as powdery as you can." Feeling like alchemists in a medieval apothecary, we precisely followed the Baroness's instructions. The simple delight of an easy chore passed, however, when I found, to my dismay, that we were making this mash for the poultry.

Apologetically, but firmly, I asked, "Baroness, don't you think it's a mistake to feed the chickens and ducks and turkeys their own egg shells? Gosh. I think they'd end up pecking their own eggs if they ever got too hungry. They'd kill their own babies. That's horrible!"

The Baroness brushed by me on her way to the garden. Over her shoulder, she said sarcastically, "Run around the corner, dearie, and pick up some proper mash at the local feed store if you're so finicky."

Blushing again, chagrined, I finished up and went on to the next chore with great energy. Why, I wondered, was it always so hard to know what was right? I knew in my bones that little offspring must be protected, yet who was right, the Baroness who kept them fed so they could survive, or me, who would save them from future cannibalism? Could we both be right? How was that possible? And if so, how could you ever come to a conclusion? Quita and I were marching up and down the rows of vegetables and flowers spraying them with two huge watering cans. The Baroness interrupted my soul-searching and talked warmly of her plans for the homestead.

"Girls! Girls!" she exclaimed, standing still in the middle of her bright zinnias, her hands on her hips, her legs apart. "You must come back and visit me again a few years from now. Then you shall see changes! First I am going to make these gardens bigger, much bigger. I shall fence them off with a pretty fence. Robert will cut me poles. And down there," she waved her hand in the direction of the bottom of the garden, "I am going to build a duck pond and border it with banana plants. And as for the house, it will be a mansion!"

Lorenz called us for breakfast, an offering of tea and cake. We tidied the house and prepared for our trip down to the bay, filling baskets with pumpkins, leeks, cucumbers, tomatoes, oranges, and lemons, tucking bright flowers wrapped in wet paper around them. "Boy, Charlie's not going to be too happy with this," I thought to myself. At nine o'clock, baskets strapped on the donkey, we were all set to leave, but the Baroness cried, "Wait!" and ran back into the house. She came out carrying a large piece of needlepoint canvas and colored wool. "These are for you, Quita," and tucked them into a basket.

We walked very fast for an hour and a half. The downhill grade was mild, and we were rested and ready for the trip. But when the sun regained its terrible intensity, the three of us children lagged behind. When we reached the beach, our feet were just as hot, tired, blistered, and swollen as they were after our trip up to paradise. Once back on board, Quita and I ran to the head and fought for turns in the tub, with Willy banging on the door telling us to hurry up and give him his turn. We bandaged our feet and rejoined the grownups for drinks before lunch.

The Baroness and her men were as gracious guests as they had been hosts. Lorenz was somber, but the rest of us laughed freely. Mother, Nana, and Pa interrupted each other describing their trip back to the ship.

"It was lucky Al and John had such energy," said Pa. "They'd gone ahead and had been out of sight for some time when darkness fell with its usual equatorial crash. They managed to get to the bay, where they found Captain and Sims smoking cigarettes and wondering how to proceed with our rescue."

"By this time," broke in Nana, "Carol and I had given up. We just could not see the path. We hardly knew which direction we should go. Trees and scrub seemed to block our way whichever way we thought might be right. So we finally sat down on a lava bed and made up our minds we would rest there until morning."

"Of course I could have had the ladies back safe in their own beds," Pa continued, offering up another jigger of corn liquor to his guests. "The moon came up and it would have been easy enough to work our way down. But the ladies were dog tired. They needed that rest. And just as we were getting used to all the animal noises rising up about us, along came Captain, Sims, and the boys with flashlights, calling to us through the scrub."

The boys joined us soon. They'd shot six ducks. Willy was providing too. After his tub soak, he'd gone to the bow to fish and soon was piling up his catch. The fish sparkled in the sun, their radiant, brightly colored scales reflecting light like jewels. He brought them to the stern and presented them to the Baroness for her supper.

When the visit came to its end, Pa gathered paint, rope, and other supplies for his offering to Paradise. Charlie came aft and gave the Baroness some potatoes for planting, but the Baroness held onto his hand and said, "Do you have any grapefruit? We do so want to try and grow that seed." Alas, we had eaten our last grapefruit just that morning for breakfast, and Charlie, only a half hour earlier, had thrown the rinds and seeds overboard. Philippson offered to take our whisky-water casks up to Paradise by donkey-back and fill them for us, to be returned the next day. Pa accepted eagerly. Our supply of water was running low. Quita and I hugged the Baroness. I wanted to hug the handsome Philippson, but he stiffly held out his rough hand for me to shake.

Just as she was about to climb down into the dory to go back to her home, the Baroness had turned, taken Pa by the arm and led him to the bow. They stood there, heads bowed in thoughtful conversation. "What did she say? What did she say?" I demanded as soon as the dory was out of earshot. Pa gathered us about, his happy mood dissipated.

"The Baroness says she is in mortal danger. She needs my help. She has asked me to take her jewels and a few of her precious possessions over to Señora Cobos, her friend at Chatham Island. She wants them there until this present danger is over. That was all. She didn't spell out the danger. Of course, I will help her."

On the afternoon following the Baroness's visit, we rested on deck, and avoided any footwork. The boys and I sat on the stern fishing. Quita lolled back in a deck chair, her blistered feet resting on a cushion. She was already sewing the Baroness's wools into a new needlepoint piece, following the Baroness's instructions on stitching. Mother sat cross-legged on the deckhouse, her brows pulled together in quiet concentration, drawing in pastels on her big rectangular pad, the box of soft-shade crayons at her side. Nana was below writing letters to mail at the post office on shore. Pa was muttering figures to himself as he studied navigation. A heavy peace hung over us, hushing us.

I was beginning to doze there in the shade of the awning, when a fourteen-foot shark caught my hook. It flashed by in a swerve and headed at top speed for Australia. By the time my reflexes worked up to my brain and a message came back to my hands saying it would be smart to let go of the line, the rope had singed the flesh off my palms and fingers. I was left, finally, holding nothing, standing in a state of shocked agony.

Mother jumped to my side. "Quick!" she commanded. "Disinfect the wound! Come below." She marched me to the little medicine cabinet over the basin in the head, opened the door, and found the shelves virtually empty. Apparently the crew had been using up medical supplies with no notice. Mother swore. She was endearing when she swore, I noted with a tinge of satisfaction, pain notwithstanding. She led me to her cabin, sat me down, and disappeared, to return with a basin of salt sea water. "Put your hands in this," she said. "It will purify your wounds." I did as I was told. As I remember it, my hair stood on end, heavy with salt as it was.

That night Pa read Dickens' *Tale of Two Cities* aloud to us in the saloon. This certainly was better than listening to a Scott novel, but I wasn't really listening. The pain in my hands demanded my full attention. I stared at George. Was he responsible for this horrible hex? How could he be after I had offered him such tender care? I looked at him harder. What must his suffering have been? Was he tortured before he was pickled? He seemed to wear an expression of hurt innocence. I shifted to the Ghost of Cocos, hidden in Ted's ditty bag. Perhaps he'd singled me out for this pain—from those tender, swollen lips, to this? Perhaps I was meeting the generalized wicked curse of the Encantatas. Or maybe a remnant ghost had got me. I remembered Pa's tale about the curse that came to treasure hunters. Had I become a wicked taker, forgetting Pa's command to be a giver, a true capitalist? I propped my elbows on my knees, keeping my palms up. Lowering my hands made them throb.

At six-thirty the next morning the crew, with the exception of Charlie, headed up the hills to the Baroness. Carrying empty jars for water, they set off noisily on their adventure. The family repeated the peaceful scene of the afternoon before: Quita sewing; Mother drawing; Nana now reading; Pa practicing navigation; and the boys plucking their ducks, pin feathers blowing through the rigging. But I sat all soul alone, on the middle of the deckhouse, suffering. If my hands made contact with anything, even eddies of air, I cringed. I gazed mournfully out to sea, waiting for the pain to subside.

At ten, Pa gathered us together for a swim. We set off in bathing suits for a sharkless cove the boys had found the day before. The others dipped and dove and swam and sunned. But I could only sit on a black rock on the edge of the dark water, brooding. It wasn't fair. I had outgrown my asthmatic invalidism and had not wheezed or sneezed for the whole trip. The sun had burned away my asthma, and I had fallen in love with my healthy new body and soul at Cocos. And here I was again, a dependent child unable to play and have adventures like the others. The feeling of power that came with a strong body and mind working together ended with my burned lips and now my painful hands. We had come to these weird islands, returning to primordial times, retracing our evolutionary path. Had I lost myself because I had gone back too far in time and history? Had I been too feeble and unsure to hold together? I thought about the silly flightless cormorant. Was I akin to that ambiguous creature, not one thing or the other, neither chick nor child, unevolved, unevolving?

Pa emerged from the water and came over. He patted me on the shoulder and reminded me of the virtue of patience. A fine thing, I thought. He can talk, but what does he know about pain and patience? He was bursting with health and vigor and bubbling off into new adventures all the time. Patience, indeed! I shrugged him off. John ran up and sat beside me a silent minute, then ran off again and belly-flopped into the sea.

Suffering began to bore me. I no longer saw or felt my immediate world. I was transported by a memory that eased me into hope. My memory was of my doctor, Margaret Handy. I was wondering what she would do to take away my pain. Dr. Handy had been our pediatrician since our move to Wilmington. She had graduated from Johns Hopkins Medical School, one of the early women doctors, and had come to Wilmington to practice. This had proved unusually difficult for her. Parents generally wanted and were used to kindly male figures as their pediatricians. Nana saved her, however, helping her financially and presenting her with a rotation of grandchildren needing care. Being the sickliest grandchild of the lot, I saw a great deal of Dr. Handy, and I loved her. And she was interested in me: She declared that I, along with another girl who shortly thereafter died, were the worst cases of asthma in the state.

Before the trip, I had often hoped I would grow up and be a member of Isadora Duncan's dance troupe, clothed in filmy gauze, posing by Grecian temples. Now I knew I would never be beautiful, never be graceful, and didn't want to pose anyway. I would be a doctor. This was not a wholly new idea for me. A member of Al's gang, the one I secretly loved and planned to marry, wanted to be a doctor like his uncle. During lulls in our gang's shooting wars, he would let me sit beside him on the warm stone dam of the pond and help him dissect tadpoles. After all, I was the nurse. You had to know how things worked inside, he said, if you wanted to be a doctor. I watched with awe as he stretched out the tadpole's intestines in a long line. Yes, I would be a doctor. That would take care of being a woman and doing interesting men's work at the same time. That would make me a giver, not a taker. Pa would be pleased. So would Nana. She was always extolling Dr. Handy's virtues and bravery. But Ma would not like it. She was not fond of doctors or interested in brave females. Women got married and had children. That was their calling. My swimming family came back into focus as my black spell lifted. I forced my new self to move into the future, where a fresh order stretched out into infinity. I would be a doctor. I would know how to stop pain and suffering. I would know how I worked inside.

That afternoon, under the awning, we listened to Pa read about the outrages of the French Revolution. This story was confirming my conviction, already established by the movies I'd seen, that heroes in love affairs should be English. But how was John in any way related to the English? Was I going to have to enlarge my lover category to include American Catholics? Seemed a big step.

Just then Al looked up and interrupted the reading. We turned and saw Smitty, all alone, pacing up and down the beach. Pa rowed in for him. We asked him why he had come down before the others. "That lady's too sociable for me," our quiet pirate answered with an expression of acute boredom on his face. "She talked too much. I didn't stay for the lunch party. I just filled my water bottles and came on home."

In the late afternoon, the rest of the men returned, popping out of the underbrush onto the beach with Philippson at the end of the line leading two donkeys carrying water casks. I noted with satisfaction that each man held his sneakers in his hands and each one had a marked limp. I went forward to talk to Ted about their visit. Unlike Smitty, he found the Baroness simply charming.

"I know she isn't pretty," he said defensively, "but she sure had 'it.' What did all those newspaper reporters mean writing all that junk about her lace panties? She was a sensible and determined woman. No nonsense. And say! Was she hospitable! She and I were walking around her garden, and we came to that great, big pumpkin, and I admired it as it should have been admired. Well, you know what she did? When I wasn't looking, she ran out and cut it and took it to Lorenz. He made it up into a delicious stew. And she sang to us. Did she sing for you?" I allowed she hadn't, but she had sewn for us.

"Well," Ted went on, rolling a toothpick back and forth over his tongue, "she could sing all right. She gave us some of her grandfather's operas. And say, what about this Philippson? He'd make a complacent lifeguard draw on a shirt for fear of being called unhealthy. Some coat of tan! His physical development would do credit to a professional athlete. But you know the part I liked best, Nina, was that phonograph player. She played a song to us over and over again, and I'll always associate it with her. I don't remember the title, something about 'we two together.' It seemed to symbolize their life together out there in the wilderness. It will be interesting to see what happens to them, don't you think?"

What happened to them was more than just interesting. It was bizarre and fitting for the Galapagos genre. Philippson, before he left, gave Pa the Baroness's box of jewels and papers. They'd had a drink together and shook hands.

"Strange," Pa said quietly, watching Philippson row back to shore, "this is a strange place."

Strange indeed! The story unfolded over several months. Stories, clues, threads of lifelines spread out before us. The Baroness and Philippson were said to have severely beaten Lorenz when he tried to revolt against his slavery. He had fled to the Wittmers, the quiet, unassuming family with the two children who lived close by, now out of their cave and in a house. And there he stayed until his strength returned and his wounds healed. He felt brave enough then to walk back to his domineering mistress. On March 28, 1934 (some reported the date as March 23; we'd walked into Paradise twelve weeks earlier), the Wittmers heard such terrible shouting and banging and furor coming from the Baroness's house that they went over to investigate. They found Lorenz standing alone, outside on the terrace, wild-eyed and shocked. He said he and the Baroness had had a terrible fight, and that the Baroness and Philippson had just walked off to leave the island on an American yacht that was waiting for them in the bay. Records show no ship in the islands at that time except our friends of the honey bear in Panama, the William Robinsons in the *Svaap*. The *Svaap* at that time was anchored at Chatham Island, where the Robinsons were visiting the Cobos family. A resident of the Galapagos wrote the following to Robinson:

I suppose you have read of the tragedies on the Galapagos Islands, only it seems to me that the American newspapers are of the opinion that the Baroness went away. We down here that know the conditions on the islands believe differently. First it would be almost impossible for a vessel to arrive there without anybody else seeing it, and besides if the Baroness had gone away she would have taken along her clothes and other personal belongings, and everything was left behind. Also Lorenz and Wittmer started pulling down her house a few days after her disappearance, something they would not have dared to do if they had not known for certain that she would never come back, as both the Wittmers and Lorenz were her bitter enemies. Everyone believes Lorenz guilty. But did he commit the crime alone? Nobody suspects Dr. and Mrs. Ritter. They were nice people even if they had queer ways. Dr. Ritter's sudden death is also a mystery. Mrs. Ritter went back to Germany, where she is to finish and publish a book of Dr. Ritter's. She is also writing one herself.

Why would the Baroness even want to leave the island, I wondered? I remembered her glowing description of her future garden and duck pond. How could Lorenz, that shadow of a man, single-handedly kill the big, brave Philippson and the ebullient Baroness? And who was the person the Baroness told Pa was threatening her life?

Lorenz could not be questioned. Two corpses had been found on Marchena Island, one hundred sixty miles north of Charles Island, one of them being positively identified as that of Lorenz. He had taken a small fishing boat out of Post Office Bay, the *Dinamita*, an unreliable craft owned by a Norwegian called Nuggerud, who was a resident of Academy Bay, Indefatigable Island. On November 17, 1934, ten months after our visit, the *Santa Amaro*, an American tuna fishing boat cruising around Marchena Island, sighted a pole on a beach with a tattered pennant fluttering at the top. The captain landed to investigate and found a skiff overturned with no oars or oarlocks. The legs of a corpse poked out from under the skiff. A few feet away lay another badly decomposed corpse, a white coat over his face, the head on a pile of clothes, his knees bent.

Beside the body lay a batch of unmailed letters from the Ritters and Wittmers (none from the Baroness or Philippson), a little French money, a bundle of baby clothes, and the half-eaten bodies of a seal and an iguana. On the corpse lying beside the skiff, in the pocket of the shirt, was the passport of Alfred Rudolph Lorenz.

The captain of the *Santo Amaro* reported that the Norwegian, Nuggerud, had picked Lorenz up at Post Office Bay on his hitchhike back to Ecuador. Nuggerud took him to Academy Bay on Indefatigable Island, where a small colony of Norwegians had settled. Lorenz stayed there briefly but grew impatient and begged Nuggerud to sail him over to Wreck Bay at Chatham Island where his chances of catching the island schooner for Ecuador were greater. They left Academy Bay with their mail and the gift of baby clothes that one of the Norwegian women was sending to another expectant Norwegian woman, Karin, wife of Señor Cobos at Wreck Bay. They sailed on the thirteenth of July but never reached Wreck Bay. Their motor probably broke down, or they ran out of fuel, or they hit a reef. In any case, the *Dinamita* must have eventually sunk. No trace of her was found. The men left the doomed mother ship in a little skiff. Strong currents swept them northward to the outer fringes of the archipelago, where they managed to row to the black beach of Marchena. Here they died of hunger and thirst.

Then came news of Dr. Ritter's death and/or murder, the return of Frau Dore to Germany, and the publication of her vitriolic book attacking the Baroness. We also learned that Ritter and Frau Dore had grown to hate each other, so it seemed logical that the wicked Frau Dore could have murdered him. Frau Dore said the doctor-dentist died of a stroke. One report, however, out of Charles, said Ritter had been murdered, having eaten a poisoned chicken. This caught our attention since Ritter was a vegetarian. The fanatic Frau Dore could easily have murdered the Baroness and Philippson, and probably her husband too, in fits of jealous rage. The consensus in the press, however, seemed to be that Lorenz murdered the Baroness and Philippson, perhaps while they slept, hiding their bodies in a pirate cave or enlarging the shallow grave the Baroness and Philippson were said to have already dug for Lorenz to keep him mindful of their authority. A small boat was missing from the island at the time. Maybe Lorenz put the bodies in it and pushed the boat off into the rushing currents.

I had no trouble figuring out these conflicting and confusing facts. It was simple. Frau Dore, that jealous, clever, little woman, had already been shooting at the Baroness and Philippson when we arrived. The Baroness had clearly told us Frau Dore was a villainess; and I liked the Baroness. Therefore, she was right and the villainess was guilty. I dismissed Lorenz as a murderer. He was too frail, too numb, I thought, for such passion.

When we landed on Charles Island, I had sensed I was about to take part in a war between the Empress of the Island and her opponents, Adam and Eve. Paradise versus the Garden of Eden. Paradise lost. The man Willy slept with might have been tubercular, but a murderer? Unthinkable. And that, quite simply, was that.

27

The End of the World

"THERE IS NO pier at Wreck Bay. A pipeline brings fresh water to the end of the pier." Thus read the *Pilot Book*, describing succinctly the ambiguities of the Galapagos in general and Chatham Island in particular. We sailed into this harbor on a light south-southeasterly wind, coming in slowly over a slight swell. We anchored at noon. The harbor at first glance looked desolate enough. A reef stuck its spiny back out of the water along the entrance to the harbor, waiting to ensnare visitors. It had already made off with one schooner whose two masts now shivered in its stony grasp and whose crow's nest was all that showed above the water. On shore two groups of seemingly deserted and disintegrating houses stood near a feeble facsimile of a lighthouse. A ladder leaned against a tall pole, which provided access to a platform that supported a large kerosene lantern. Whether this lantern was ever lit was questionable. No humans were visible anywhere in the bright searching sunlight.

Since this was the port of entry for these islands, we had our requisite papers from the Ecuadorian Consulate in Panama ready to present to the officials in the town of Progresso, four miles up in the hills. Pa, for our history lesson, was reading William Beebe's *Galapagos, World's End*. Pa and Beebe stressed over and over that the Galapagos were the outpost of civilization, the remote never-never land between prehistoric past and modern, mechanized society. And in a way, they were right. Here civilization was only beginning to invade and control. Its real impact would not hit the islands until after World War II—airport, scientific stations, tourist traps, and ecological controls. But, for now, we were on our own to explore what was still considered the end of the world; or, following Darwin, the beginning of the world.

This island, too, had a shadowed history. Manuel Cobos had ruled as tyrant here, working his huge sugar plantation with convicts as slaves. In the 1860s, Cobos had virtually separated himself from Ecuador, coining his own currency, keeping his own court. Cobos was casual about human life. He lashed slaves to death in the hot sun for minor misdemeanors. Occasionally he sent men off to a waterless, treeless island to die of hunger and thirst. In 1904, seventy-seven men and eight women rose in rage and murdered old man Cobos, burying him on the spot he used for lashing convicts. They found Cobos's hidden ship on the other side of the island and sailed away. Left behind was Camilo Casanova, who had been one of those chosen by Cobos to be planted in a distant cove to die of thirst. He was found three years later when an Ecuadorian gunboat, the *Cotopaxi*, came to the island to investigate Cobos's rule, following up on the tales told by the fleeing convicts. Casanova survived by eating raw turtles and iguanas, drinking their blood and chewing cactus pads. Twice, English ships had landed in his cove with their crews. And, in spite of the tears and supplications on the part of Casanova, the English would not remove him from his hell. After three years, this inhumanity was explained. Cobos, on leaving Casanova to die, had posted a sign on the other side of the island from Casanova's cove that read in English and Spanish as follows:

"Do not take this man away. He is twenty times a criminal."

We furled our sails, coiled the sheets, tidied up the ship, and waited for the reception committee. And we waited and waited. Pa grew impatient. Still mindful of danger, Pa made the ladies stay on board while he and the three boys went to the deserted shores to investigate. As I watched them row in, I hummed a tune that had been going through my head. I could not make it go away. I had learned it the year before when I hopped around in the chorus of a production of Gilbert and Sullivan's H.M.S. *Pinafore* at our school. I walked to the stern singing aloud.

Things are seldom what they seem,
Skim milk masquerades as cream;
High lows pass as patent leathers;
Jackdaws strut in peacocks' feathers
Very true, so they do.

I joined the ladies under the awning in a game of Rummy 500. We could see Pa and the boys approach the crumbling pier, land, walk to the beach, and disappear around the house at the end of the pier. Pa told us on his return that to the mutual surprise of both parties, they had come upon a small, dark man dressed only in a long, black beard and a pair of BVDs. He was working on the bottom of an overturned boat.

Pa spoke to him in Spanish. "We have just arrived at this delightful island on a schooner. We seek the proper authority to ask permission to visit here."

"I am he whom you seek, *mi amigo*," said the little dark man. "I am the major in command here, and the governor and the captain of the port and the keeper of the light."

Pa bowed. They shook hands.

"On ship board," continued Pa, "I have the proper papers from your government permitting us to land." The small dark major, confronted with the huge frame of my father, stretched as tall as he could and replied,

"Such, of course, is the manner of a true gentleman. You and all your party are a thousand times welcome to our poor island. But excuse me, please, just a moment. I shall retire and clothe myself, and then we shall make arrangements for your proper entertainment."

"*Muchos gracias,*" said Pa as he watched the major scuttle off in his BVDs to a nearby whitewashed house, from which he emerged in a few minutes, resplendent in a stiffly starched, gold-braided, bemedaled khaki uniform with epaulettes and wearing a highly polished pair of shoes. As he walked back to Pa and the boys, another uniformed man came galloping down from the hills on a small horse with a beautifully tooled leather saddle. The major, nodding to the new arrival, went through the introduction to Pa again as if he and Pa never met before and then came out to scrutinize the ship's papers.

With formalities concluded, the Major asked Mother to give him a list of supplies we might need. He said he would be only too glad to try and meet her requests. Mother asked if they could do laundry. The Major suggested that it might not be wise to send in laundry, since chicken-pox was raging through the town and germs might be in the water system. Nana nodded her head in avid agreement, liking the little bristling uniformed major much better for his grasp of germ circulation. The major suggested Pa come up to Progresso and meet Señor Cobos, the direct descendent of the murdered tyrant, since he was in charge of the ranch and plantations. The Major explained that the plantation had fallen on evil days. Most of it had been sold to the Ecuadorian Government, but Cobos still retained a small part. Pa, of course, accepted the invitation immediately.

After supper, Willy rowed Nana, Mother, Quita, and me to the pier to await Pa's return from the hills. Pa and the major soon came galloping down the dusty road. Before we said our formal goodnights, however, the major excused himself and ran to his house, bringing back a black land tortoise about a foot long, which he presented to the wide-eyed Quita. Quita was delighted and smiled her shy smile, saying hesitatingly, "I shall call him 'Galap.'"

Once on board, Pa sank back in the creaky leather armchair in the saloon under George, put his palms across his paunch, twirled his thumbs, smiled his superior smile, and began his tale before his faithful waiting audience.

"End of the world! That's a laugh! End of the world, indeed! I rode up to Progresso and the first thing I saw was a Glasgow-built sugar mill, built in 1904." He paused and ruminated, "Wasn't that the year Cobos was murdered? I wonder what, if any, are the connections? Well, anyway, these people down here at the end of the world manage to mine their own coal and supply visiting steamers. The town consists of about four hundred people, five white men, one white woman, and the rest Ecuadorian Indians. They run a large sugar plantation and actually get two crops of sugar a year. You realize, children, that this is considered impossible in Cuba or Puerto Rico? And they have fruit orchards. Coffee is becoming a permanent crop. Guava grows like a weed. Added to all this, you might think you were in Texas when you hear these men talking about their herds of cattle and see the cowboys galloping into town on their handsome ponies. They seem to have plenty of water piped down from a lake behind the town. I believe Mr. Cobos has a spring of his own. I was still trying to consider myself far from the madding crowd, deep into the world's end, when I was walked to a white stone building that housed the radio station. Mr. Cobos introduced me to the radio operator and this man kindly said he'd send any messages I wanted to the States, but when I found it would cost me $1.35 a word, I decided Mother wouldn't approve. So I left my greetings unsent. Just jokingly, I asked if I could get today's New York Stock Market closing prices.

"'Señor Chandler,' said the radio operator, 'we are in the habit of tuning in on a certain broadcast that gives us that information each evening. Just write down the ones you want me to note and by six this evening, you can have them. I can also get any orders you want sent your broker before the opening tomorrow.' It appears that the local boys are in the habit of betting on market trends. Hence the interest in closing prices. Every Tuesday evening the whole village gathers in a large stone building to listen to a Spanish broadcast from Schenectady. I find this particular end of the world mighty close to the Hudson. O.K., kids, off to bed! I have arranged a big day for us. Eight horses are being brought down in the morning, and we'll ride up in style to call on the Coboses in Progresso."

By nine the next morning, lined up on the pier, we looked at Pa with that "Oh, yeah?" look of scorn. The place was deserted, no horses in sight. Nana took charge. "Come on, boys, come!" she commanded. "It's a lovely day for walking." We set off on the red dirt road to Progresso. It was fairly smooth, a definite improvement over the crumbling, searing path to the Baroness's. Green trees with yellow blossoms shaded us, but Quita, still limping from her blisters, trailed behind. Mother, Willy, and I walked ahead, watching little lizards with bright red bellies scuttle off their warm stones in the middle of the road to run to the cactus and century plants lining the banks. Mockingbirds watched us from wild cotton bushes. We had gone about a mile when, suddenly, from around a bend came twelve small horses at full gallop, throwing up dust, running tightly together, their manes and tails flying.

Three men rode the lead horses. Mindful of bandits, we ran up onto the cactus-covered banks and awaited our fate. Once abreast of us, the leaders reined in their horses and all twelve animals came to an abrupt halt, rearing up on their hind legs and snorting in the dusty air. The leading gaucho leaped to the ground. With a sweep of his arm and a low bow, he presented the horses to Mother, declaring they were for her and her family to use for the duration of our visit.

With no hesitation at getting off our overtaxed feet, we jumped into our saddles. Once the horses' heads were turned toward home, they broke into a full gallop. John, Willy, and I took the lead, and we made no attempt to rein in our steeds. They were fleet and sure-footed and knew exactly where they were going. I couldn't have pulled my horse in if I wanted to—my raw, bandaged hands could barely hold the stiff leather reins. We galloped along the uphill road, breaking through the hot air, rounding a small green hill through a double row of ciruela trees. The land grew more cultivated. Galloping through an open gate, we entered an area fenced by barbed wire that marked the outskirts of the town. Chickens fluttered, squawked, and flew up into the air as we rushed by. Donkeys in dooryards pricked up their floppy ears. Thin pigs rose up and squealed before they settled back into their wallows.

Racing into the town of Progresso at full gallop, I thought for a moment that I was on a Hollywood set in a Wild West film, charging down the main street, ready to jump off and hitch my mount to the rail outside the saloon. I was prepared to swagger in through swinging doors to chat with the sheriff about the outlaws I was pursuing. But when I focused, I saw a different scene. False fronts of wooden shacks gave way to mud huts with thatched roofs. On their own accord, our horses slowed to a trot on the mud street. We passed the Glasgow Mill and ended at the house of Señor Cobos, an impressive building compared to the mud huts. It stood two stories high, but seemed three stories because it was built high off the ground on stilts. The unfortunate Norwegians, whose ghostly settlement we had visited on our way up to the Baroness, had bought wood from the fourteen houses on Charles to build this house. John poked me and whispered as we climbed up the steep stairs to the elevated first floor.

"This is the house where Señor Cobos was murdered. Watch for blood!"

Señora Karen Cobos greeted us in her sparsely furnished room. The daughter of one of the Norwegian families, and the only Anglo-Saxon among the Spanish and Indians on Chatham, she was locally famous for her beauty, her generosity, and her hospitality. Our new friends, the major and his lieutenant, were also to have dinner with us. While we waited for the return of Señor Cobos from the range, Señora Cobos introduced us to her two toddlers, born on the island without benefit of doctor or midwife. After introductions, the children were sent off with their nursemaid, a brown-eyed child of seven.

When Señor Cobos came in, we sat down to a hot and peppery meal of six courses: a stew of chicken, potatoes and yucca root, roast chicken with stuffing, French-fried potatoes with a casserole of rice and sausage, followed by a puffy omelet and finishing with sweet cake and essence of homegrown, freshly ground coffee. The women and children concentrated on eating quietly while the men, in Latin style, carried on the conversation. Señor Cobos, staring sadly at the green hills beyond, where wild horses grazed by a crater, recounted his seven years of schooling in Paris.

"This island must be a contrast to that life," commented Pa.

"This is my punishment. *Ce n'est pas gai.*"

I stared at him. Why punishment? What had he done? Another Galapagos mystery to solve. Galapagos and mystery were becoming synonymous.

We had an hour's siesta. As we rested we sucked on fuzzy guava seeds that tasted like sweetened cotton. Then the little lieutenant led the children off to see the sights. In spite of Pa's enthusiastic description of the night before, I could not view the scene with the roseate glow he'd provided. We were a thousand feet above sea level, and the air was bracing, but it could not dispel the muddy smell of the town. The hovels were roofed with thatch, and split sugar cane braced the mud walls. The rutted streets were crowded with animals. The mill had been out of commission for a year for lack of business, and the train was broken down on its short track. The town's one automobile was wrecked, and no one knew how to fix it. Each little hut had four or five children playing in the mud around it. In front of one hut, a bathtub stood bereft of pipes. A little naked boy stood in it screaming in gasping spurts as his placid mother scrubbed his soapy body and poured water on him from a tall, tin pitcher.

The lieutenant took us to his baked mud backyard where he kept an assortment of Galapagos animals. When his tour of duty was over, he was planning to take them with him to Quito to start a zoo. Dwarfing all the other animals, the little turtles, the iguanas, and lizards was an ancient Galapagos land tortoise—a monster weighing about four hundred pounds. He was nearly four feet long and probably two hundred years old. Will crawled up his mountainous, scalloped-edged back and sat astride. In the momentary stillness of our awe, the ancient turtle jutted out his bony skeleton head, startling us. Willy caught the fierce intensity of the black eye of the beast and slid abruptly back to earth.

The lieutenant took us on to the white stone, Spanish-style radio station. John spotted a boy holding a small land tortoise and began bargaining. He had to give up his shirt to gain the tortoise. Christening the reptile "Gus," John carried him back to the ship to join Quita's "Galap." (Both of them, Galap and Gus, sailed home with us and are now achieving their great old age in the New York Aquarium.)

On our way back to the harbor, John, Quita, Willy, and I galloped out ahead of the others, playing bandits and posse. By the time we arrived at the port and charged up a dead-end street of the deserted village, our horses were lathered and foaming at their bits. We careened around a house and almost ran down our bearded jovial Sims. He had been exploring, awaiting our return with his blue trousers rolled up to the knees. "Whoa, Nellie!" Sims called, as he grabbed my reins, catching me just as my saddle's girth broke—saving both the saddle and me from a hard fall.

Nana arrived a few minutes later, flushed with rage and heat. Two men on horseback had been assigned to chaperone her down to the sea.

One beat her pony with a large stick, the other galloped after the racing pony to seize the reins and jerk him to a stop. Not speaking English, they had no idea what Nana was shouting all the way down as the pony alternated between balking and bolting. Once on board, we scrubbed, brushed, and tidied up, for in keeping with Mother's urgent sense of social obligation, we were "paying back" the Coboses. They arrived at dusk for dinner, Señor and Señora Cobos with their three-year-old boy, and the major, the lieutenant, and the radio operator. Señora Cobos looked elegant in a black silk dress, the major magisterial in his pressed uniform with its rows of medals and draped gold braid. The others were clean and conservative in their dark suits.

At dinner, Pa and Señor Cobos again held the conversational floor.

"Señor," said Pa, "your reputation in the States is of a wild and dangerous man. This is certainly false. Can you explain how such tales grew up about you and this island?"

"It may be partly our fault," laughed Cobos. "We like to please our guests, and if they'd be satisfied upon finding that this was a wild, outlandish place, we try to put on a show. Now here's an example. Not so long ago, a lone Frenchman sailed into our harbor and came ashore heavily armed. It was plain he really wanted trouble. So the local people consulted together. Our lieutenant is always careful of ammunition since he has so little here, but, thinking it our duty to provide our guest with what he wanted, we decided we could shoot off a few rounds. Fortunately, Señora Cobos has a collection of antique sabers and pistols that we could use to arm our men. We dressed them all as bandits and sent them down the road to hide behind rocks.

"As dusk approached, the lieutenant and I offered our guest a drink. We sipped our drinks and told stories of the fierce convicts who lived on the island. By six, we had him in the proper mental state for the ride down. There was one risk, however. He might have hurt someone if he was really frightened, so the lieutenant and I rode close on each side of him, for better protection, we said.

"Such a fine act our men put on at the ambush site! Shooting and shouting and waving their swords, they rushed upon us. The lieutenant and I each grabbed a rein of the Frenchman's horse and galloped off with him down the road so fast that he had no time to shoot. He needed both hands on the saddle to stay on his horse. As soon as our bandits saw there was no danger of being shot at, they pursued most lustily, firing into the bushes near us and shouting at the top of their voices. We two escorts nearly fell off our horses from restraining our laughter. We added to the din by shouting to the Frenchman to dig in his spurs, yelling, 'Faster! Faster!' Oh, what a two-mile gallop that was!"

After dinner the sad-eyed Karen played for a while on Charlie's accordion, the melancholy chords warming us for a moment and shielding us from the harshness of these stark islands. Pa presented Señora Cobos with the box of jewels and papers from the Baroness. The lieutenant realized the significance of the occasion and drew up a formal receipt for Pa. Cobos leaned back in his chair and said, "Charles Island is as big as Manhattan, but it's too small for those three families."

Mother asked Señora Cobos about the chicken pox said to be raging through the town. Had her children been affected? Mother's and Señora Cobos's Spanish didn't seem to jibe, so Mother pulled down her Spanish-American dictionary from the shelf behind her. Together they looked up the word used by the Major to describe the illness. Mother slammed the book shut and both her eyebrows shot up. The word Señora Cobos pointed out was not chicken pox but smallpox. This stopped all conversation.

In the silence we heard a strange noise, a watery slurping sound, unlike any sea noise we had ever heard before. Willy and I ran on deck to investigate and found children leaning against the rail. They were sucking ice in a state of rapture. While we had been dining below, villagers rowed out two boatloads of supplies—pineapples, potatoes, and strange fruits—and the children had hitchhiked out to peek at the visitors. Charlie and Ted gave each child a piece of cake and a handful of ice, but no one spoke. I think they were even too preoccupied to notice that we'd come on deck. When Al and John joined us, a young man named Garcia, a friend of the lieutenant's, walked down from the bow where he had been waiting for the boys. He presented them with two lovely sealskins, a purely spontaneous act of generosity. John's was long enough to cover the whole length of Nana's cabin.

The party began breaking up. The men were on deck exchanging farewells. "More mistakes and errors!" Pa was saying. "We were told we should stock our ship with extra essentials such as sugar and flour to give to you poor starving islanders. Instead we have been offered more stores here than we could ever possibly have given you. Now we are supplied most bounteously with fresh eggs and vegetables. You grind your own flour and make sugar for export. So I am delighted we have at least one thing to give . . . the humble ice cube! But tell me, there must be some special article in demand here but hard for you to get. When I return to 'civilization,' I will arrange to send it to you."

A long thoughtful silence followed, broken finally by the lieutenant.

"Yes, there is one thing we would all deeply appreciate. Would you, on your return, forward a dozen good footballs? The schedule for the coming season's soccer games is long, and our present supply of balls is short. The balls we have are old and worn."

Pa burst into his genial laugh at the surprise and seriousness of the request. He pumped the young man's hand up and down, assuring him that his wish would be granted, and we said goodbye with the gravity befitting the occasion. Our guests descended into the waiting launch manned by Sims and Smitty. We could hear the little Cobos boy screaming in terror as they crossed the dark water. I decided he had recognized our crew as the pirates they surely must be. Once they reached the pier, Sims and Smitty held the bow and stern as close to the stones as they could so the Señora could be helped out onto the pier. Her men readied themselves to follow her. The major, in his burnished brass and smart pleats, was the last to ascend but lost his balance and his grip and fell into the sea with a phosphorescent splash. Sims and Smitty pulled him out, quietly watching the poor man's morale, press, and glitter run out over the bottom of the boat. As Mother went off to bed we heard her muttering, "That Sims and Smitty; they did it on purpose."

28

Turtles, Seals,
and Sharks

B Y AFTERNOON WE were coasting the shores of Indefatigable, as barren
and bleak an island as we had yet seen. Wanting to land, we drew in
by the shore; and finding a cove, begged Captain to anchor. He tacked
back and forth for a while studying the cove but glumly and emphatically
decided the spot was too dangerous. He would not risk landing there, not
with ladies on board. The five children, disgruntled, turned to fishing.

About sunset we found another cove, this one uncharted. We diplo-
matically christened it Boutilier Cove in honor of Captain, who dropped
anchor in seven fathoms of water on a sand bottom. The cove was unprotected from the growing seas mounting upon us. The wind had come up
to such force that the captain ordered an anchor watch. Al, John, and Pa
stood the early watch, four hours of careful attention to wind, sea, and the
safety of the ship. They didn't seem to be much concerned about their responsibilities, I thought, for Al and John came along when Pa led us below
to read *Tale of Two Cities* until very late. Pa and the boys, did, however, take
up their watch after the reading and paced the deck until midnight.

Sims had the next watch. At two in the morning, he came below and
shook Pa awake. "Say, Mr. Chandler," he whispered. "Don't know if you're
interested, but there's a volcano erupting off to starboard. The sky is all
glowing red." Pa thought a moment and answered, "Thanks, Sims, but I

think the children need their sleep." When Pa told us at breakfast, though, I was furious. What an opportunity missed! Was Pa just lazy and protecting his own sleep, or did he think we would be scared, remembering Benjamin Morrell?

After breakfast we studied our new cove. Round, black boulders guarded the entrance. The tumbling rocks closed in on each other, leaving a small stretch of white sand beach. Tucked behind the boulders on the port side was another strip of white beach, inaccessible from the sea. We were dressed now in our perfected Galapagos expeditionary costumes—white gob hats with air holes sliced in them, bathing suits with long pants over them, and leather L.L. Bean boots.

Sims and Smitty rowed us in. A colony of sea lions slept on the inaccessible sand spit. On the beach ahead of us, five giant sea turtles basked in the early morning sun. We came in through the long, rolling surf and ran to catch the turtles before they could escape into the sea. Silent Smitty, for once, joined us happily in the race. He smiled broadly, his slanting eyes mere slits. He could run faster than any of us, so to keep things equal, he just jiggled along in a mincing pace, always ahead of us. We needn't have hurried. We forgot that sea turtles are deaf. They did not hear or see us but remained motionless on the beach. Smitty's smile disappeared, however, when he reached out to grab the biggest turtle and the turtle jutted out his big head and hissed fiercely at him. Smitty jumped back in genuine alarm, and the next time, he approached from the rear.

The turtles began lumbering their way back to the sea. Before the men and boys turned four of the huge antediluvian beasts over on their backs, we took rides. But an encrusted yellow and brown shell, slimy with the residue of hundreds of years of sea growths, makes an uncomfortable saddle. Quita and I were appalled by the reaction of the great, antediluvian beasts to the humiliation of being overturned and helpless. They paddled their flippers against the unresisting air and sobbed. Real tears rolled down their tough old bony skulls. Their sighs and moans tore at our hearts. We knelt beside an ancient creature and patted his hoary shell. We spoke softly into his deaf ear to sooth him. Quita and I exchanged glances, aware of our hypocrisy, knowing full well that the animal was as good as slaughtered. Undone by the unrelenting sobs, Quita and I implored mercy from the executioners. They begrudged us two turtles, righting them and letting them go, but they were adamant about keeping two for food. These were the days before such turtles were in danger of extinction. We were just following ancient Nantucket whaler tradition, ensuring ourselves of fresh food for a long sea haul ahead. One turtle was to be butchered then and there, the other to go on board for future processing.

Rather than witness this murder and kidnapping, Quita and I hastily organized an expedition into the interior. We wanted to reach the sand spit with the colony of sea lions that lay behind the boulders. The sand soon turned to the familiar crumbling clinkers of desiccated lava reflecting the glare of the equatorial sun, and the smell of burning furnace came again to dry out our nostrils. Willy ran ahead, scrambling up a slipping incline held in place by cactus. At the top, he stopped, screamed, and tumbled to our feet. He had surprised a large herd of wild goats—and the herd had apparently surprised him. We crawled cautiously to the top of the incline to find the big goats still there. A few patriarchs with long, straggly beards stood at the head of the herd, frozen, staring at us for a few seconds. Then they humped their rears around and jogged off across the fields of swirling lava.

We hadn't gone more than a few yards through a cactus forest when Willy called again. He was standing before a giant land iguana, the kind that Byron, on his visit to the Galapagos with the king and queen of the Sandwich Islands, called an "imp of darkness." Beebe, defining the "world's end," had warned that these iguanas were vicious. Indeed, this giant lizard seemed malignant, a demon standing there, ready to hex us. His four-foot-long spiky back and tail stretched along the lava ridges. He was indistinguishable from the background except for his bizarre head—orange, with lewd yellow lips and a reddish eye encircled with a white band, a painted clown caricature of a dragon. He walked on five-toed taloned claw-feet. Flaps of overlapping leathery scales covered his neck like a coat of mail. A distinct sulfurous smell seemed to rise from his distending nostrils.

"I believe," said Pa, standing a safe distance from the evil-looking iguana, "that we stand on the edge of hell. That animal couldn't guard anything else. But be brave, children. Be like Virgil descending into Hades. He learned a lot down there."

We skirted the immobile devil dragon and walked on for a mile or so in the direction of the sand spit. When we arrived, the sea lions were still asleep. Yet, as we walked down onto their strip of white sand, they woke up. A fat old bull moved out to the black boulders and settled down to scratch his hind parts with his foreflipper. His wives would not sit still but waddled nervously from boulder to boulder, eyeing us suspiciously and edging away. They were clearly worried about their nursery of pups, four shiny, sleek creatures diving and swimming in a tidal pool, their ears back flat against their heads, twitching their whiskers back and forth when they picked up our scent. Willy stripped to his bathing trunks and slid into the pool. He sat still, waist deep, his brown body the color of the pups. At first the pups paid no attention, but then they grew more curious, coming up to sniff him, dive under his legs and nuzzle his outstretched hand. If he moved too abruptly, the pups dove off to the opposite side of the pool and waited for him to quiet down. When Willy finally stood up, his sudden change in size really frightened them, and they hurried off to join their barking mothers.

We walked back to the turtle beach, this time hugging the rocky coast. A high thicket of dense dry bushes kept us close to the water. We jumped from boulder to boulder across the swirling sea. Will tried to find a shortcut through the undergrowth, startling a male sea lion and his soft, furry mate, who were sleeping under an overhanging mat of bushes. They snorted, disgruntled at him, and waddled off down to the water. I found two baby seals alone in a hidden pool and patted them gently. They nodded to me as I went on.

Back at the turtle beach, we found the remains of the butchered turtle. A line of steaks lay along a driftwood plank. The heart was lying discarded, drying on the hot sand, still pounding. Melville said turtles encompassed the condemned souls of wicked sea officers, especially commodores and captains. I crouched, spellbound, watching the undaunted rhythmic contraction of that heart. I turned to the bloody-handed Smitty.

"See what you've done. You killed the turtle, but you can't kill the ghost that lived in the turtle. He'll haunt you forever. Serves you right for killing the helpless beast."

Smitty wrinkled his nose, squinted at me, and said nothing.

We stripped to our bathing suits and cooled off in the delicious water. Quita and I were content floating on our backs and spouting like whales. A pile of turtle eggs, some with leathery shells, some just jelled yolks, lay in a heap on the beach and inspired the boys. War! They grabbed armfuls of eggs, ran into the water, and began heaving them at Quita and me. The eggs splattered and squashed on our faces and hair. We shrieked and thrashed, much to the boys' satisfaction. At that moment, Mother swam hurriedly out to us. She had been unable to penetrate our noise to warn us. Once near us, getting her quota of misfired egg yolks, she yelled,

"Stop! Stop! The eggs are attracting sharks. Wash off your heads and get out of the water RIGHT AWAY!"

We didn't bother with a second rinse.

29

Dig Ten Feet Under

S AILING AWAY FROM Indefatigable early in the morning, heading toward James Island, we passed Daphne Major and Daphne Minor, a
pair of symmetrical volcanoes rising abruptly out of the sea. Quita and I,
disconsolate, stood a rotating watch over our new pet, the sea turtle, who
was lashed amidships, slobbering, sobbing, and rolling its eyes in homesick sorrow. We took turns dumping buckets of water over it and brushing away tears.

By two-thirty we had closed in on the coast of James, looking for a
place to land. James, a serried line of dark, dried-up, old, and light-brown
new volcanoes, was uninhabited. We spotted a steeple of triangular volcanic rock, sixty feet high, jutting up beside a small bay and decided to
land there. This bay, Captain told us, was called Sullivan, a safe harbor.

Two sea lions escorted our launch to the beach. We hopped out quietly and hauled the dory out on the sand. Wet from the chop, we were
soon powdered with sand that had been covered with ash that had not yet
blown away. We became gray ghosts.

Sleeping seals lay on shallow ledges of the triangular peak. The more
lively seals darted and fished around the bay. They were watching us, interrupting their chase to raise pointed noses out of the water, flicking
their ears and sniffing at us curiously, only to suddenly sense a school of

fish nearby and dive in pursuit. The dominant sea lion, a leathery old bull, barked at us in warning. A twelve-foot shark was slicing his black fin through the water. He came right to our feet when we landed and bumped his nose on the shore, feeding on several small rays that were trying to flick away from him.

We walked quietly down the beach toward the sleeping seals. One female woke up, alerting the others, and they all slid down to the water— all but one, a small furry baby left asleep on his back, his round soft stomach warming in the sun. Even when we stood around him in a circle, peering down at him, the baby slept on. John leaned down and pulled his flipper.

"Hey, time to get up, boy, time to get up." The baby seal grunted but did not move.

"Maybe he's s-sick," said Quita, frowning.

Willy pulled a flipper. "Hurry up, you'll be late for school."

The soft brown ball of fur rolled over, his eyes still shut tight. Then dark-bearded Sims, in a peaked painter's cap with black visor, knelt beside the little animal and tickled his stomach. The baby seal stretched his flippers contentedly and slowly opened his eyes. His expression changed from bliss to horror as he lay eye to eye with Sims. After a second of silent shock, the baby seal rose perpendicularly from the ledge as if prodded by a hot electrical wire and streaked down to the water to his nervous waiting mother. His sudden movement sent us into panic. We fled as if a herd of elephants were stampeding us, never mind a tiny seal. I tripped over John and skinned my knee. And Willy never stopped running until he reached the dory.

Our next diversion was catching rays. Sims used an oar to flip one up on the beach. It had been badly bitten by the shark but even in his death throes on the beach he was capable of swinging his daggerlike tail to deeply slice Sims's hand. Ma bandaged him with a handkerchief while I begged to use his knife to try out my new role as a prospective medical student doing dissection. My first startling medical discovery was that rays have green blood. Sims stood over me, nursing his wound. "No wonder sailors call it a devil fish," he said with feeling. I knew the iguana stood guard at the gate of Hell, but surely if Hell is under water, a ray guards the gate.

We wandered off into the hinterland, crawling over the ashy remains of a recent burning. We were puzzled. No volcano was near. We had not gone far when Pa shouted, "Say, look here, kids!" He stood by a charred cactus about six feet tall, black and spiny. Ashes and burned bushes lay about its base.

"Now look at this. This is most unusual," he said as he circled his find. The spines had been scraped off the north side of this cactus, leaving the green insides of the plant oozing out, shiny and smooth. Down the scraped area ran a vertical line of Japanese characters.

"Most interesting. Most significant. Now what are the Japanese doing here, I wonder? Maybe some fishing boat came in, but why would they build this shrine or whatever it is? Very curious," he muttered. "Very curious." He reached down and picked up a charred twig to copy the characters onto the cuff of his shirt. And that small act determined my future life.

Of course, Ma sent the shirt to the laundry when we reached Panama, and Pa had forgotten to copy the characters. He thought he remembered them, however, and when he met with his brother, our Uncle Charlie, he redrew the Japanese figures as best he could. Uncle Charlie had been a spy in Naval Intelligence in World War I and spoke seven languages fluently, including Japanese. He studied Pa's reconstruction and announced with booming conviction that the characters read, "Dig ten feet under." Pa wrote Captain Johnson to alert him to this finding so he could explore it further when the *Yankee* went around the world again. And then we all forgot about the cactus.

Five years later, in the early fall of my freshman year at Smith, due to an alphabetical seating plan for a French class, I found myself next to a young woman who liked to discuss men with me as we awaited the arrival of our perenially tardy professor. She was trying to persuade me that her brothers would interest me, but when I heard they had graduated from college, I rejected them as boring. "But one of them is really interesting," she said. "He has just returned from sailing around the world on the *Yankee*."

I sat up straight and stared at her. "What," I demanded, "was under the cactus?"

She didn't know, of course, but arranged a meeting with her brother. Yes, he indeed remembered the cactus. The *Yankee* had sailed into Sullivan Bay, and an expedition left the ship with shovels and a wooden rectangular contraption about five feet long—a primitive metal detector. They found the cactus just as we had left it, the area around it still clear from the burning. They cut the cactus down and put the metal detector over the spot. Faint signals emanated from the machine, leading the boys to attack their job with fervor. By this time, however, it was noon, and the equatorial sun blazed down on the treasure seekers chopping away at nearly impenetrable lava. A photograph records the event. The future movie star, Sterling Hayden, all six-feet-five of him, is trying to slam his pick ax into the lava. The suffocating heat, alas, forced the *Yankee* crew to give up their quest with only three feet dug.

A few weeks after my friend's brother—the *Yankee* crew member—and I met to discuss the cactus, we, having been stricken with love at first sight, were engaged. Immediately after my graduation from Smith we were married.

I have often brooded on the curse that hangs over treasure seekers. Pa had warned us about it as we approached Cocos, and I thought of it again when, after ten years of marriage and four children, our rich and treasured life dissolved in divorce, a romance ending in deception and tragedy just as the curse would have predicted.

30

Ornithology Dismissed

T HAT NIGHT WE sailed to Tower Island on the northwest fringe of the archipelago, ghosting along in a southeasterly wind over a glassy sea. By morning we were still moving slowly through light airs toward a field trip in ornithology. Mother and I read French in her cabin. The boys worked on geometry in the saloon. Nana continued reading *A Child's History of the World* to Quita and Willy in her light-filled after-cabin.

By two o'clock we were tacking off Tower, a circle of cliffs rising straight up from the ocean, its walls an old crater. Hundreds of years before, portions of the outer wall of the crater had crumbled and the sea had rushed in, creating a bottomless bay a mile in diameter. Captain jogged the ship back and forth as we set forth in the dory. Six sharks glided beside us as we poked along. This island was a natural bird sanctuary, a barren waterless waste. The sides of the volcanic cliffs were covered with man-o'-war birds and blue-footed boobies. No humans had ever tried to live here.

Not talking, trying to masquerade as visiting birds, we rowed to a sandy stretch of beach to disembark. Just when we were ready to jump ashore, we realized that what we had seen as rocks from a distance turned out to be cold-eyed sharks. Though they swam off when we prodded them with oars, we hesitated, loathe to jump onto the beach. The sharks came right back, their wicked noses bumping against the dry sand, waiting and watching their prey, formerly birds, now us. Finally, jettisoning our avian masquerade, shouting courageous remarks to each other, we jumped to the beach and walked up to a level, treeless plateau, through flocks of tame birds. We were awed and silenced by their shrieks and squawks, their piercing calls to one another.

Many types of bird seemed to congregate here. Covering the lava ledges, sitting in the low bushes, weighing down the branches, were man-o'-war and frigate birds with bright crimson bags ballooning out from their necks—cousins, I presumed, of my Charles Island lemon-tree ghouls. Boobies with red or pale blue feet stood stupidly with their wings stretched out in drooping arches, immobile, statuary in a sanctuary. Black gulls stood next to white gulls making patterns of stripes along the ledges. Nana was excited when she discovered four egrets and made us stand still looking at their majestic elegant white plumes. We listened to her tirade against the Victorian fashions she had grown up with that had made these regal birds almost extinct.

We passed a pair of small mouse-gray gulls with a mockingbird on one side and a bright yellow warbler on the other. A pair of doves, sitting on a ridge, cooed their lament as we approached. Out by the water's edge a solitary blue heron stalked his evening meal. Bright red crabs clicked along the dry rock, scuttling before our feet. The small tidal pools were filled with fish, little bass in one, yellowtail in another.

In a cavity behind the ledges we came upon clouds of petrels, thousands and thousands of them, circling and swooping over our heads, screaming in their graceful flight. We stumbled on two parent boobies guarding their huge ball of helpless white down. We tried to approach the chick who stood as tall as his parents, but the parents attacked us like geese in a barnyard, hissing and charging at us, beating their wings, forcing our retreat.

Nana reviewed Darwin with us as we explored, telling us again how tame he found the birds, how he walked right up to them and caught them with a cap or hat. Earlier visitors than Darwin wrote in their logs of the tame birds alighting on their heads and arms. Nana had a few piquant words to say about man's cruelty to birds, remarking that introducing a new bird or beast of prey into an established colony, as the Nantucket whalers had done here, caused havoc in the indigenous population. They would live and evolve only by fighting for survival. "It takes a long while to adapt to a stranger's craft and power," she concluded.

Craft and power. There it was again, the ominous, the evil. It seemed to ooze from the rocks. I was glad when Pa said we should get back to our ship. The smell of guano, the noise of the birds, the number of sick, dying, or dead birds lying around us made this island repellent. My interest in ornithology, never very great, was waning fast.

That night, after supper, Charlie came up on deck to cool off and leaned against the taut jib in his usual white undershirt, white apron, and white duck pants, looking absently out over the sea, standing motionless. Two white gulls circled the bow. One, enticed, perhaps, by Charlie's whiteness, fluttered down, and in the manner of tame Galapagos birds, stood on the deck directly before the watchful cook. Charlie flashed out an arm and grabbed the gull gently by the neck, calling us in triumph to come see his trophy. As we gathered around him, Charlie let the bird go. But the gull was either too stunned to fly or perhaps injured. He stood still there, looking at us one by one. Al said, "Let's call him 'Henry.'" We all chatted with Henry, cajoling him to stick around and then went to bed. Henry flew off, however, during the dark watches of the night. And I was sorry, thinking we had accepted each other as pets. That was it for me with birds.

31

Heading Home

A T TWO O'CLOCK ON the afternoon of January 20 we set all sails and swung the bow of the *Blue Dolphin* northeast toward Panama. This hour, this turn, marked the end of the trip for me. We still had a thousand miles to sail across the Pacific before we reached Panama. Beyond that, we had the whole Caribbean to cross, checking out new ports in South America, new islands, then on to the Gulf of Mexico, into the Atlantic, and up the southeast coast of the United States to our triumphant end in our homeport of Georgetown, South Carolina. Not until then would our trip be truly over. But facing toward both Sophie and home made the voyage different. Venturing forth and heading home are two different kinds of travel.

The horse on Chatham Island came to mind, his exuberance as he turned toward home, galloping along the road to Progresso. This reminded me of my Sunday rides with Pa in Delaware—shivering chilled, riding over frozen fields, my toes numb in pointed jodhpur boots. Pa would say, "Isn't this glorious!" And I'd whimper about the cold. He'd admit that it was about time to get back for Sunday dinner, so we would turn the horses' heads towards our barn. Horses seem to know immediately when they are going home. My little black horse, Gypsy, would crowd up on the rump of Pa's huge hunter, Fox Horn, in danger of a swift kick. He would prick his ears forward and close his teeth on the bit making my efforts to slow him fruitless. He stopped shying, as he did on the way out, each time we crossed a fox path. He pushed and pulled to beat Fox Horn home for a stiff rubdown, a warm stall, and dry hay. Absently, I put my hand out and patted the deck of the *Blue Dolphin*.

"Go!" I whispered. "Go!"

The next few days also marked a change in my journal. I was having a hard time recording the day's events. In the beginning of the trip, I put down all the details I could remember. I wrote about what I saw, what went by, what happened. My sentences were connected by ". . . and then . . . and then . . . and then." I had only been a spectator. Now I was a part of a new adventure, caught in a novel kind of unsolvable algebra problem, sensing strange meanings for old symbols, balancing each across the equal sign. The simple, dichotomous "a" and "b" had given way to parentheses enclosing new letters, representing new quantities and qualities. I would have to solve these equations, rearrange the parts. Nothing was coming out equal any more. If I were to write a life story, I would have to construct the plot. I did not know how. My pencil made squiggles on the sides of the page, but the center remained empty. My new reality, my new world, was beyond my grasp. I could no longer "see it," and I was far from explaining it.

I gave up, closed my journal, and went up on deck to stand my watch with Quita. After that, and finishing our homework, Quita and I began the next dramatic episode that our hand-carved wooden puppets were playing out. My puppet was called Madame Angela deBois. Quita had made a bright scarlet vest for her sticklike young lady, Señorita Vestido Rujo. This spontaneous playacting was a lot easier than keeping up with my journal. We were in the midst of the drama of Madame deBois, who was instructing Señorita Rujo on the wicked ways of the evil world, warning her of that Fate-Worse-Than-Death. Mother and Nana, listening to us, began showing signs of discomfort. My florid interpretation of the evil forces in the world and their Melvillian consequences made Ma scowl. She wanted to be sure we understood that babies were the happy natural outcome of all ladylike adventures. Wanting to define what a ladylike adventure was, she quickly carved a new puppet, a baby, and Nana wrapped it in a baby blanket. They asked to be part of our drama, and we let them join us, but I thought they complicated the plot unnecessarily. It grew boring.

We ate steaks cut from the turtle killed on the beach. They tasted like tender veal. Ted figured our turtle had steaks enough for fifty people. Charlie tried to cook the eggs, boiling them for over an hour, but they never did harden. They were like ping-pong balls, only soft and mealy. We used them on deck as playthings, bouncing them into a bucket and throwing them back and forth at each other.

Quita and I were still nursing the sobbing, broken-hearted surviving turtle. We made a secret pact with Ted—he would drop the beast overboard at Tower Island while we were off studying birds. But Ted lost his courage, and when we returned we were dismayed to find the slobbering turtle still lashed amidships. At night in my upper bunk, I heard his nails scratching and scratching the wooden deck above us as he vainly went on and on pushing against his captivity. Finally Quita and I won permission to undo the lashings, sure he would stop crying if he had a little freedom. Alas, we had to tie him up again, because he sobbed harder than ever, rolling his eyes back, and jamming himself in the crew's companionway, blocking access to the deck. Ted told us the turtle's lament was driving them all crazy up in the fo'c's'le. Twice, he said, he and Sims and Smitty had snuck up on the turtle at night to throw him overboard but backed away at the thought of Ma's anger at the loss of fresh meat. Unfortunately for the grieving turtle, we had tasted turtle meat and that sealed his fate. Galap and Gus, being land tortoises, didn't seem to be as histrionic as their cousin up forward. They munched yucca root and basked in the sun on the after deck, lazily content.

"Women and children first!" Ted shouted as he ran down the corridor past our cabin. No familiar Houseman reveille, and no "Rise and shine!" this morning. As I stepped into the corridor, pulling on my white duck pants, I was horrified to find water rising up over the floor, making a swishing sound as it ran from side to side with the ship's roll. I could hear Sims and Smitty running on deck and shouting to each other. Captain was in Nana's cabin calling crossly to Chief who shouted replies from the engine room. An unfamiliar thudding noise made the ship vibrate: the pumps at work.

By the time we were all fully dressed and standing quietly in the stern awaiting Captain's orders, the crisis was over and we were safe. Nana and Pa immediately fell into an altercation. Nana, awakened by the strange sound of masses of water rolling just under her floorboards, had called Pa and Captain. They pulled up the floorboards and their flashlights showed a full bilge. Chief had forgotten to turn off one of the sea cocks while he was cooling the motor, and the ocean had been flowing in all night long.

"That man is stupid!" announced Nana. If she'd been at home in Dalhousie, she would have fired the miscreant with imperious rage. But here, a thousand miles from Panama, where would the hangdog Chief go once fired? Pa was just as mad, mad at the break in normal routine, mad at Nana for being mad, mad that his beloved fellow man had failed in any way.

"Oh, Mother," he bleated, nervously twirling his big bloodstone ring around and around his finger. "The man is not incompetent. He's just a man of ordinary caliber. If you had ever attempted to run a factory as I have, you would know it is the exceptional man who can be counted on to turn on the right cocks at the right time. And stop and think. Maybe it's not his fault at all. Usually a check valve in the line would have automatically closed it to prevent the sea from coming in. Maybe some waste caught in the pipe and jammed the valve in the open position. I'll admit, for safety's sake, Chief should have closed the sea cock by hand, but how do you know he wasn't called by one of us to do some odd job just at that moment, or that Willy had taken his bill-nosed pliers again, or what about just plain forgetting?"

"Hmmph!" snorted Nana and stalked below.

Poor Chief was in for more trouble. In all the excitement, he miscalculated the oil intake into the motor, and oil overflowed before he noticed the problem, spilling out and seeping under the partition between the saloon and the engine room. The new heat we were experiencing, now that we were out of the cold Humboldt Current, made the smell sickening. Fortunately a willy-wally blew up late in the afternoon, hitting us with frenzied force. The wind came from every direction, making it impossible to steer the ship. The main sail slapped back and forth, more of a hazard than a help. Captain ordered it down. Battling the elements restored equanimity and a memorable sunset bought serenity to the end of the day. Over the blue sea horizon, the sky turned saffron yellow merging into a cold, pale green. Roseate clouds drifted over the sweeping bands of fading light as bright pricks of stars came out in a sudden debut, dancing in their southern constellations.

The next morning, Sims and Smitty came up on deck with new but recognizable faces. They had shaved off their beards. Sim's was smiling: he'd won the crew's kitty for having the longest beard for the longest time.

Serenity never lasts too long. This was one of the philosophical generalizations I had recognized early in childhood, pain being the usual intervening factor. Whether he had been cooped up too long in the cramped quarters of the fo'c's'le, or whether Mr. Doyle irritated him beyond caring, I could not guess, but one afternoon Smitty mutinied. He could no longer contain his long-standing dislike of Mr. Doyle. In his usual silent, determined manner he began his afternoon watch polishing the brass binnacle before the wheel. Captain told him he could lay off now, but Smitty didn't stop. Without a word, staring at the compass, he rubbed on and on, around and around the binnacle. Captain, with the change of watch, went below to write in the log. Mr. Doyle took over the wheel. He spoke harshly to Smitty. "You heard Cap'n. You quit that!" But Smitty went on and on, around and around. Ted hustled to the bow and whispered to Charlie, who was leaning against the foremast. Charlie came ambling back, shuffling along in his blue carpet slippers. He hooked Mr. Doyle by the arm and moved him to the bow and told him to lay off lording it over Smitty, as only Charlie could, being a fellow Gloucester fisherman. Meanwhile Ted took over the wheel and quietly picked up a conversation with Smitty. Gradually the frozen face on the angered sailor melted down to movable creases again. Mr. Doyle's only action was to record the mutinous deed in the daily log, inking in a permanent mark against his nemesis.

I watched all of this holding my breath. I was puzzled and pleased. It was not authority, command, or the rule of the sea that saved the day, but the sensitivity of the lowest-ranking man aboard—Ted, who respected his fellow crew men and understood how to deal with them. For me, the rules of the sea, the hierarchy of command, had been, up until now, the ultimate authority. I'd learned this during the awful storm our first days out. We did what Captain ordered and no talking back. Now I knew that even life at sea could be too complicated for such a simplistic approach. And it wasn't just physical pain that ended serenity. Hurt feelings could do this too, but sensitive negotiations could restore serenity. I was intrigued. A novel equation was popping up.

On the sixth day of our voyage home, we sighted the gray mountains of Panama. Cape Mala light was visible after nightfall. We rejoiced.

"This is fine," declared Mother. "We shall be in Panama in time to get the mail and go to the bank before they close on Saturday noon. We might even do some shopping for the weekend. We really must get some shopping done. We are running short. The Klim is all gone."

"Yea!" shouted Willy, hating that dreaded powdery milk.

"And the sugar, flour, and potatoes are almost gone," continued Mother, paying no attention to Willy's glee.

Like Ulysses returning to Penelope, we had to undergo unexpected adventures before we made it home. To begin with, we would not follow a straight line to Panama. The winds came up suddenly, and the seas climbed higher and higher in uneven, choppy cliffs. We drifted backward. Finally we conceded defeat. We hove to in a gale.

Ted, serving breakfast the next morning, said, "I've lost track of how many times I've been washed out of my bunk. We've got to get air up there, so we leave the hatch open just enough to ventilate the place and just enough to let every wave drop down on me. I gave up last night, came back here and slept with the boys."

"I was out on deck before breakfast," John added, "and I would judge from the amount of floating trees and bushes around us that either Panama has sunk under the sea or the Caribbean has washed over the isthmus. You wait and see! It's terrific!"

After breakfast, with the storm raging above decks, Mother and Ted sat at the swaying table discussing supplies and making shopping lists for Panama. Ted knocked out his pipe and salvaged unburned tobacco with a toothpick to be used for the next smoke. He turned to me and said, "It's a wonder I'm not getting a Scotch accent."

As he was picking up the last particle of tobacco, we were hit by a rogue wave. It smacked us broadsides, dropping a heavy mass of green water over the whole ship. The *Blue Dolphin* shuddered, shook itself like a wet dog, and rose again on the next wave. The scuppers were still backed up with swirling water when Mother and Ted popped their heads up the companionway to view the wreckage. Smitty, at the wheel, had been swept down against the rail. Sims was leaning over, giving him a hand up. The rest of the crew were checking for damage. The family gathered by the wheel.

"Where's Willy?" Mother gasped. "Ralf? Wasn't he up here with you?"

"Oh my God!" roared Pa. "Where's he gone?" Pa charged below by the after companionway. In a few seconds he came up again, grinning. "You should see him! I guess he must have been lying in his bunk reading when the wave came. It filled our cabin halfway up the bunk with water. Did he panic? Did he flee? Not our Willy! He's taken out that fleet of model boats he's been carving and is sitting cross-legged on my bunk right now chugging them around the swirling lake over the floor of our stateroom. He's totally unaware of any difficulty. He has no idea he's been missed."

The storm drove us a hundred thirty-five miles back off course. It finally subsided enough to let us get in the lee of the Perlas Islands, where we could proceed in spite of the gale. Later, in Panama, we heard that three big ships were put out of commission by the same storm. One lost its propeller and had to send out an SOS to be rescued by tugs. The surging seas broke a propeller blade of another ship and bent the plates on still another, forcing both ships back to port. These stories made me feel smug. We'd sustained no damage. Lucky those big boats hadn't been in the first Atlantic storm we'd experienced. They would have sunk, all three of them.

Mother was growing desperate about the supplies we needed for our diminishing larder. She burrowed down into the storage spaces behind the bookshelves. Close to the bilge, along the hull of the ship, she came on a row of rotted, exploded condensed milk cans. "Phew! Stinks like a charnel house. Get down that narrow space, children, you'll fit down there easily, and bring those awful cans up here." We did what we were told, tasting vomit in our mouths as we picked up the cans, but hurried up on deck to let the wind blow the stench out of our nostrils. Then Al and John made Quita, Willy, and me throw Poland Spring Water bottles tied to string up into the air to arc over the sea so they could take pot shots at them with their guns.

A parade of ships began to go by, a Grace liner, a Japanese passenger ship, and four freighters. Four submarines came within hailing distance and their crew waved to us. Finally a Navy reconnaissance plane flew out and buzzed us. "Splendid! Splendid!" said Pa. "Just about the only good thing Little Rosie has done is beef up our Navy. We must have our Navy to keep the trade routes open. With commerce moving easily and safely, prosperity can come to all nations. Then we can forget about wars."

Pa's historical back-up discussion on this subject, which would have been prolonged, was cut short by the arrival of the pilot boat that would guide us into Panama. When the pilot jumped on board our ship, Nana greeted him, hands on hips, with "This is a wonderfully run Panama Canal, I must say! An hour and a half we've been waiting for you. Heavens! May I ask how you expect to handle the United States Fleet when it comes in?"

Undaunted by such a reception, the pilot introduced himself with a Southern drawl. On investigating the source of the drawl, Nana found out that he was from Charleston, South Carolina, and the two of them immediately found they had mutual acquaintances. Nana shifted back to her pleasant demure self, the delay forgotten.

Once we'd tied up in Balboa, mail sacks were delivered to us. We grabbed them with cheers and ran to Nana's cabin to read. Nana started by opening a fat letter from Aunt Mary Morris and began to read it aloud. But the first sentence announced bad news, and Nana skimmed silently ahead. She lifted her head, scrutinized us individually, and must have judged us old enough to learn about pain and suffering. She read to us that her daughter, Mother's thirty-eight-year-old younger sister, had attempted suicide by drowning, swimming off in the current of Winyah Bay towards the sea, wearing only her underwear. She had washed ashore on a little island, where she had been found. Sharing the news with the group seemed to lessen the shock on Nana, but I struggled to understand. Ivan Kreuger, the match king whom I read about in the newspapers at home—his suicide I could understand. He was evil and deserved to go, but our own aunt, a regular housewife and mother, why would she do such a thing? And how did it fit into Pa's engineering schemes of the continuous improvement of us all? She could easily have been a Scott heroine. She was dark and beautiful, yet here she was, acting like a Melville character, consumed by some devouring passion. But one thing really bothered me: How could she try to commit suicide in her underwear? Cotton. She must have been wearing cotton. It was mandatory in our family after all. Not appropriate, I decided. If I had to go, I'd go in silk.

That night, walking home after our first meal ashore (five courses and loaves and loaves of fresh French bread smeared with sweet butter piled on each slice), Nana, Mother, and I walked together down the dark wharf with linked arms. We moved from puddle to puddle of yellow light cast by bulbs strung on a drooping wire. Nana talked quietly, calmly.

"I shudder at the thought of that poor child trying to drown herself, slipping away on that black swift tide. How did she ever have the strength or luck to land on Bird Bank Island? To think she lay there all the next day, no food nor drink. Poor, poor child. I think," said Nana, stepping into a bright puddle of light, "I think you can never run away, or even try to escape your troubles, without hurting the people you love the most. We are too closely knit not to unravel a long way when one stitch is dropped. Carol, I must go home. I am needed at home. And once I get home, I'm never going to go away again." Mother and I silently shook our heads in agreement. Nana went on. "She is too young to be going through womanly changes, but maybe that time is coming to her early. It's so common for a woman of changing age to do queer things. I remember my time, how terrible I felt. I longed to be out of things, out of this world. I have the strongest sympathy for her if that's what's happened. But I also know that when she is mentally and physically better she will have an entirely different point of view."

This was a blow. I had grown used to "the curse," but now what was in store for me? "Women of changing age?" What age? Was I fated to have a "mental and physical crisis?" Every time I grew confident in being a woman, I was either physically battered out of shape by sun or shark, or invited into womanly mysteries that seemed ominous. I held Nana tighter. She thought I was comforting her and squeezed my hand. Really, I only needed her support.

Once aboard the *Blue Dolphin*, Nana, Mother, and Pa talked about alternate ways of getting Nana home. Pa explained that money was running out anyway, so we might as well skip our long-planned itinerary and go directly to the plantation in South Carolina. Nana, assured we would sail home without delay, decided to stay with the ship, accepting the fact that the ship had to be hauled and cleansed before we sailed.

The next morning at breakfast, somewhat silenced still by my respect for Nana's sorrow, I was amazed to have her walk into the saloon looking not the least bit unraveled but holding up her hands in open delight, laughing again.

"Sorry I'm late, boys," she began, "but I've been held up by the most delicious drama. A huge cockroach has been running around my stateroom since dawn. He crawled up into my porthole. I could hardly tear myself away. Willy, that tractor you made out of the wooden spool—you left it in my porthole. Well, this ambitious cockroach came up and examined your tractor from all sides. He heaved himself up on his hind legs and leaned his forefeet against the tractor and danced and pushed! You could practically hear him grunt! He was determined to get that good piece of machinery home, but he'd start it up the circular rim and then it would roll back on him, knocking him over. He persisted and tried again and again, but he finally gave up. Somewhat squashed, he went home to his wife and children empty-handed. By the way, have I ever told you about Sisyphus?"

We skipped Sisyphus and breakfast, however. Sims leaned down the companionway and alerted us to action topsides. The biggest yacht in the world, three hundred forty-four feet long and forty-three feet wide, John Pierpont Morgan's *Corsair,* was docking directly behind us. Her stern moved in and hung high above our lowly decks. She looked like a seagoing skyscraper, rising in black tiers over us. She was three times as long as we were, and her beam was half the length of our ship. A group lounged in deck chairs on the afterdeck. By and by, the noise and confusion of a large family doing morning chores attracted their attention. Several well-dressed people leaned over the canvas rail and watched us. They called down, finally, and Al, John, and I engaged them in conversation. Just then Mr. Jack Morgan, the son of senior J. P. Morgan of the big nose, came and looked down at us. Mustachioed and beaming, he called out jovially,

"Our curiosity is overcoming us. How about joining us for a visit at 10:30? You can tell us what you're up to down there!" Shortly afterwards, a neatly uniformed sailor arrived with a written invitation.

Mother ordered us to get dressed up. I was thrilled because Mary Morris had sent me a glorious new dress, white linen with a heavy Irish lace collar. Much to my surprise, though, Nana went into one of her sulks. "I refuse to dress up for that man," she snorted. She was in her green seersucker dress with the collar turned under to keep it clean. Pa began to argue that Mr. Morgan was a respectable man. Nana loudly proclaimed he was not. She had read the testimony in the endless Congressional hearings about his doings. She remembered the revelations, the confessions, his manipulation of the market, the pools, his selling short, pegging prices, not to mention the lady dwarf on his lap. Not respectable, not in the least. Not the kind of man she would go out of her way to visit.

This was too much for Pa. "Morgan is a different breed than the ruthless earlier financiers of bad taste and upbringing like Diamond Jim Brady. Morgan is well-educated and cultured and has acted beneficently towards this country. He's been trying to ensure its economic stability. He's like one of our Federalist princes who set up our Republic. You simply have no idea, Mother, what the stock market is all about. Yes, it is a repository for your beloved husband's DuPont stocks. It's great that you are so loyal to your Will Ramsay that you will not sell even one of those stocks he left you, but you are not grasping what it means for America to have this exchange, to allow money to circulate to businesses that are the base of our economy. Morgan did his best to keep that market stable during the crash. When he failed, all Americans were hurt by the collapse. Lord! Look at me! Wall Street does not fluctuate because of one man and his friends. Stocks and bonds find their own level of equilibrium. They get rocking and oscillating, but they always return, unconsciously, to their 'natural levels.' They are self-correcting."

No one was paying attention to Pa, certainly not Nana. We were busy following Mother's directions. She had us lined up and ready. "Come on, Ralf, it's time to go." Pa shut up and slipped into his blue blazer, grabbing his yachting cap with the Nantucket Yacht Club insignia. Nana fell into line at last. She had not changed her dress but she did turn her collar out.

At 10:30 sharp, we marched single file up the canvas-sided gangplank behind Pa, our leader, with furrowed-browed Nana bringing up the rear. Mr. Morgan himself met us as we stepped off onto the deck. He led us to the stern where his party had gathered. Pa found himself happily greeting Junius Morgan, Jr. and his wife. Pa and Junius had been classmates at Harvard. Another classmate and his wife were in the party too, Mr. and Mrs. Louis Curtis. A pleasant-looking, frail, gray-haired lady rose from her deck chair. She was tall and thin, a long scarf of pink chiffon around her neck. Mr. Morgan introduced her. "Mrs. Ramsay, may I introduce you to Mrs. John Davis."

"Not the widow of John W. Davis, the one-time Democratic Presidential candidate?" asked Pa, *sotto voce,* of Junius Morgan.

"The same, and he was my father's lawyer," replied the junior Morgan.

Mrs. Davis crossed the deck towards Nana with outstretched hands. Nana stood with dignity in her simple frock at the edge of our group, her hands clasped together at her waist. She looked deeply tanned in contrast to the wraith woman approaching her. "I didn't quite get your name," said Mrs. Davis.

"I'm Mrs. William Ramsay from Wilmington, Delaware."

"Not Mrs. William Gouverneur Ramsay?"

"Yes," replied Nana, tilting her head questioningly.

"Do you know who I am?"

"No, I'm afraid I do not."

"I'm Nellie Basil. You are Lena Canby."

The two women ran together and grasped each other, shouting exclamations of surprise and joy. Nana turned to us. "She almost got my husband!"

"*La rencontre de les deux belles esprits*," said the elder J. P. Morgan.

Tears were in Nana's eyes. Nana turned to the group and said, "Nellie Basil! When Major Ramsay and I were secretly engaged, he was sent out to do some engineering work for the Baltimore and Ohio Railroad in West Virginia. He met this lovely girl out there. 'His Nellie,' he called her. They were very taken with each other. I, at home, sensed this and hurriedly wrote him a 'holding letter,' and he came back to me and we eloped. I did get my man!" She smiled sweetly at Mrs. Davis.

The senior Morgan, seeing the grownups preoccupied with their reunions, turned to the young and said, "Come with me, children! Enough of these old people. I want to show you my ship." Taking Willy by the hand, he began the tour. He led us stem to stern and from bilge to bridge. We were immensely impressed, of course. The uniformed crew stood at attention as we passed. The size, the style, the fittings were far beyond anything we had ever conceived of as nautical. Mr. Morgan delighted in explaining every detail to us. We almost lost Willy in the engine room, but I grabbed him and dragged him along to follow the others. Mr. Morgan ordered tall glasses of lemonade for us when we rejoined the grownups. He kept Willy by his side, impressed with his questions about the ship and how it ran. Then he brought the conversation around to our trip. He wanted to know where we had been, where we were going.

When we told him about Cocos and George Cooknell, he threw back his head and laughed. They had just returned from Cocos. Mr. Morgan said George was still digging in his hole but had not mentioned the cave and the treasure. Mr. Morgan also said he had offered George a ride back to Panama, but George refused. When Pa told Mr. Morgan I was keeping a journal of our trip, Mr. Morgan asked me to send him a copy when I was finished. A copy was dutifully sent and now resides in the Morgan Library in New York. Mr. Morgan had met us at the gangplank and led us there when the time came for us to return to our humble little ship. He took Pa by the arm and said, "You are doing the finest thing possible for your children."

Pa was gloating as we settled down in the saloon to swap impressions. Nana had clearly changed her mind about Mr. Morgan and lamented her seersucker dress. "How silly I was!" she said. I said I loved Mr. Morgan because he reminded me of my uncle, Bill Phelps, now Sophie's substitute father, my highest compliment for any man. Al asked Nana about Mr. Davis and his relation to Al Smith. Pa, of course, had floated off on old Harvard memories. As the talk rushed on, I reflected on Nana. I was proud of her, the little, simple lady winning out with Will Ramsay over that tall, sophisticated woman.

Mother stopped our chatter. She had gone up the companionway and turned squealing in horror. "Oh my goodness! This is awful! The *Corsair* is sailing away and we haven't paid them back!"

We went in to dry dock the next day, wedged in between a freighter and a United States Navy submarine. We started off as if in a huge swimming pool, the size of a Canal lock. Then workers pumped out all the water, and we sank to the bottom. Being the littlest ship, the *Blue Dolphin* was still afloat when the others hit bottom, resting on their keels. I sat on deck holding my knees tight against my chest, watching the huge cranes towering over our heads, dropping giant staging and ladders around us, listening to the men bawling at each other, seeing the water drain out, marking our descent. Our ship seemed to shrink to the size of a model, and the larger ships with their deep hulls grew bigger and bigger. Now the workers were ready to scrape all the slime, the weed growth, barnacles, and rust off our hulls, readying us for the fresh paint job of Baltimore bronze that we so badly needed.

We children spent a good deal of time on our neighboring submarine, making friends with the sailors and shuddering in the claustrophobic closeness of its crowded space. There was also a giddy round of children's parties, with movies and fudge feasts, at friends of Ma's and Pa's in Balboa. These friends took us to inspect a new dam and to visit more forts. Mother, Nana, and Pa went to cocktail parties and even attended a Navy dress ball. Everyone was celebrating the repeal of Prohibition. Once again I was pleased to hear my father approve of Roosevelt. At last, he said, Roosevelt understands that individuals are responsible for their own habits, and that the government certainly is not.

Ted came to the saloon one evening to give us children an extra snack before we went to bed. He took out his pipe and started to relate his adventures in town. "First stop for me was the barber shop," he said, between puffs, "that poor barber winced when he saw the condition of my hair, and he took so long cutting it that I went to sleep. I only woke up after he shaved me, and I shot right out of that chair. Look what he did! The glorious mustache I've spent so much time raising. Why, he's cut it right down to Charlie Chaplin size! For a minute there I was tempted to start a new revolution, declare myself president of the Republic, and lead an army against that particular barber shop, but I decided against it after I'd fumed a minute, and went out and consoled myself with some German beers."

Mother was soon preoccupied with how to pay back our charming hosts and ended by asking them all, with their children, to motor with us through the Panama Canal to the Atlantic side. This required extra-duty peace-making work on the part of Ted in the perpetual war of Mother versus Charlie. Charlie wanted to prepare sandwiches in advance of the party so he could get a look at the sights himself. Mother insisted on mountains of spaghetti with tomato sauce, hot dogs, deviled eggs, and freshly cut ripe pineapples. Ted made several trips from stern to bow and back again with written demands and counter demands. Mother won, of course. Charlie stayed below and cooked.

Just before our guests came aboard at Balboa, Ted was leaning against the anchor, having his morning chat with us, telling us more about his adventures ashore.

"You've seen all the sailors around, haven't you, kids? They're off all those Canadian destroyers anchored over there in the harbor. They sure give the town a festive air, those boys. Everything is wide open. I just don't know what the devil got into us boys. Dan, Sims, Smitty, Chief, and I stopped in at this café, and we got to thinking we didn't much care for the entertainment being provided. So we just got up and put on a floor-show of our own. We gave them some close harmony, a few ballads, and then a dance or two. They didn't hire us for further appearances, but at least they didn't throw us out." He stopped to knock out his pipe, staring at the pickled head of George. "Oh say," he suddenly started again. "You know, for years, Charlie's been looking for a parrot to take home to his daughter. A couple of nights ago, I was riding around in one of those sea-going hacks, a Victoria? I saw this cute little beggar . . ."

"Was it a b-boy or a girl?" asked Quita tentatively.

"No, no, Quita, not a child, a parrot, a pretty, green parrot. I told Charlie about it, and we went back the next day and hired a coach and brought the parrot back to the ship. Charlie paid a dollar for her. Her name is Laura. By the way, kids, don't say anything about this to the old folks, because your mother once told us boys that she wanted no pets on board. I'm not quite sure how she would feel about Laura. Step to, there, Willy, here come your guests."

We had a two-day stay in Cristobal, on the Caribbean side of the canal, taking on oil and water. On our second afternoon there, Ted quietly gathered the five children in the engine room.

"Remember I told you about the parrot?" he asked. "Look what Mr. Doyle just brought in—there—sitting on the rocker arm. Isn't that the mangiest, most outsized, disagreeable bird? It's stupid, too. He can't talk at all, not like our Laura. Well, that's Mr. Danny Doyle's idea of a parrot. I call him "The Crow." I've been telling Mr. Doyle there's been a scandal back in "The Crow's" family somewhere. Well, that's not all. Altogether we now have five parrots on board. And just this morning Chief brought home a little monkey. Come on, we'll go around the engine and call on him. But remember, for heaven's sakes, don't tell your mother!"

32

More Vicissitudes,
But Home at Last

THE SEA HELD us back as we tried to sail north across the Caribbean. Once more winds blew high waves over our desired path, obliterating our progress. We had to tack, close-hauled, heeling way over, battered, soaked, and driving through the waves. Mother, Quita, and I were seasick. This was a humiliation I kept from the boys as best I could. Quita and I lay perilously on our humped-up mattresses, pulled up against the edge of the bunk to keep us in our berths. We pretended we were reading, emerging on deck only to view one phenomenon, the sharply drawn line between the muddy waters of the river Atrato flowing into the Caribbean and the blue, blue waters of the sea. We looked longingly at the mere suggestion of earth. Since even Nana was beginning to grow black circles under her eyes from lack of sleep, Pa ordered the *Blue Dolphin* into Cartagena, Columbia, for a respite.

Pa loved Cartagena, an ancient city enclosed with crenellated walls. He was reading *Henri of Navarre* in the evenings. "Look!" he proclaimed as we drove along the twisting streets in old horse-drawn coaches. "This place was a thriving community when Henri of Navarre was a little boy in 1500!" He regaled us with a succession of naval battles that had been fought here, but I didn't take in much of the lesson. My imagination was working up a novel that began with the hero (John) helping the heroine

(me) open the trap door in the floor of the cathedral and run through a secret tunnel to the fort at the top of the hill a mile away . . .

We were still waiting for the winds to calm down when Mother returned from a shore trip. She carried two parakeets—brilliant green with
occasional gold feathers. They kept uttering quizzical peeps inside their
red lacquer cage.

"Pets?" we exclaimed together.

"Yes, pets. I want to take one back to Sophie. And Nina, the other
one is yours. You must take care of them both . . . and carefully. Here."

We eyed each other and sensed the time had come to let her in on our
secret of the menagerie in the fo'c's'le. She made no comment after our
tactful revelation, consenting to come in and watch the parrots and the
monkey swinging around their newfound jungle, the many branched engine. The men stood sheepishly, congratulating her on her beautiful parakeets, welcoming them to the bird playground. An air of conspiracy hung
over the engine room. Ma, at last, was one of our gang. I was elated with
her new maturity.

We thought the wind had abated and set sail again, northward, but
we did not sail far. The headwinds buffeted us again. For four days we
made our way through overcast, heavy weather. Even Mr. Doyle, the experienced Gloucester fisherman, noted in the log that we sailed a "mad
sea."

Almost within reach of Jamaica, Willy woke up one morning with a
high fever, his knee swollen and black. Ma started questioning him, and
he told her that in Cartagena he was really bothered by a scab left by a
mosquito bite, so he had picked it off with his knife. Mother looked at the
knife, encrusted with rust, and sighed. The abscess on his knee grew as
the poisoned blood circulated around his system. It was clear to us all that
a major crisis was upon us. Mother set to work, dressing the sore with hot
compresses. She moved Willy into her cabin. That night Nana stayed up
all night sitting on the stiff bench beside the berth cooling his hot forehead with a cold washcloth soaked in our corn liquor-flavored water. Pa
paced the narrow corridor outside the cabin, while Mother tried to catch
some sleep back in Nana's berth.

The next day Willy was delirious. Mother went in and out of the room silently. Nana couldn't bear watching any longer and retired to her cabin. Even the crew lowered their voices, subdued, as they worried over Willy and tried to think up ways to make the ship go faster towards port. Willy had long since been the undisputed favorite on board. They always loved watching him slithering up and down the hatches from dawn's light to dark night like a seal after fish. With no transmitting radio, and in adverse winds, we could not get help.

That night, Quita and I crouched in the corridor outside the closed door and sang, "Jesus, tender Shepherd, hear me," part of the very small repertoire of hymns we'd picked up somewhere. We sang the hymn over and over, supplicating any god who would listen. It was all we could think of to do.

The next morning the abscess broke and drained. The fever went down and Willy weakly sipped a cup of rich broth brewed especially for him by Charlie. He began to take an interest in his pet cockroaches again. That night we sighted the lights of Kingston, Jamaica.

The next afternoon, Willy was wrapped in blankets and carried out on deck by Ted and placed gently on pillows. Mother was sure exposing the knee to sunlight would help. Ted signaled to John and me to follow him down to the saloon.

"Bad news, kids. Chief's monkey died last night. Chief buried him at sea early this morning."

My eye caught a flicker of light from the shrunken head of savage George, as a sunbeam crossed his glassy eye. Ah, I wondered, has there been a hex? Had the disease been transferred? What had George been up to? Had he seen to it that the monkey took on Willy's death-dealing poison to save him? I stood up and stretched and walked casually over to George and patted his cheek. Just in case.

Dr. MacLean, the port doctor, boarded us in Kingston, Jamaica, a nice Scot with a burr. He put a large antiphlogistine poultice on Will's knee and said Will was well enough to make the rest of the trip to the States. Pa was so pleased he sat Dr. MacLean down, and we all had rum swizzles, even the children. None of us was interested in visiting Kingston, beautiful as it looked. We had done enough sightseeing. We wanted to go home and we headed off for Miami immediately.

Before long, we began to get faint sounds out of our radio, which had been silent since leaving our homeport of Georgetown, South Carolina. We caught the southern accent of a radio announcer telling us with strained urgency of the latest Depression horror stories. We laughed. We couldn't match his stories to any current affairs we'd been learning about, say naval warfare in the West Indies or pirate operations in the Pacific; but we were up to date, it seemed, on all those mistakes Roosevelt kept making.

Alone in the saloon after supper, we children listened to music on the radio and began dancing. We danced to "Tea for Two" and "Night and Day," not graceful dancing, since we wore sneakers, the heavy carpet held us back and the waves shook us off balance. But we danced, and what's more, we rejoiced. Willy was well. Miami tomorrow. Georgetown within a week. And I was dancing with John. In no time, we verged on hysteria. We jumped on the brown leather couches. We waved at the fluttering parakeets. We tweaked George's blue-black ear lobes. We had duels and wrestling matches until finally Pa's huge frame filled the doorway and he roared, "Children! For heaven's sake, BE QUIET!"

During our brief stay in Miami, we learned it was not only the children who had been changed by travel. Ma was definitely different. She knew that the port authorities would not look favorably on our importing all those parrots. So, before we raised the yellow flag to signify we were ready for boarding, Mother, *our mother,* organized the crew in a clever way: She had us all find hiding places for the seven birds, including Charlie's Laura, directing us to put them in dark places, hoping they would think it nighttime and would not start chattering.

Mother, her eyes wide and innocent, her smile demure, led the two officials who had boarded our ship, speaking pleasantries as they went from cabin to cabin, waving to dutiable imports, explaining health problems, never once glancing at the lockers that hid the evidence, never once exchanging glances with the fellow culprit crew. She kept the officials so occupied with the horrors of Willy's knee that they never bothered to search the ship. As they left in their launch, Mother stood by Pa holding his hand. She turned and smiled at Charlie. She winked. My! She was one of us at last.

The doctor followed port authorities. He looked at Willy's knee and decided to lance it. Mother was horrified. Only a specialist would cut into her precious child. And besides, that nice Dr. MacLean, who had been so reassuring and attentive, and who had applied only a poultice, had said Willy would make it all right to Georgetown, hadn't he? Pa shushed her and told the port doctor to do what he thought best. At last we could sail away. We brought out the bird cages from their dark hiding places, looked disparagingly at the glistening white skyscrapers, the lines of white motor yachts, all so foreign and unattractive to us, and, out on the ocean, breathed comfortably again.

Three days later, on February 25, 1934, at four in the morning, we dropped anchor in Winyah Bay in six fathoms of water in a light northerly wind, exactly where we had started our voyage so many months ago. When the sun came up, all of us were on deck, craning to see again our own Cat Island, lying there so still under her great, green live oaks hung with gray Spanish moss.

The lighthouse keeper spotted us and telephoned Uncle Bill Phelps and Aunt Mary Morris, Sophie's temporary guardians. They woke Sophie and drove her down to meet us. Pa, Quita, and Willy went in to the pier in the long boat to fetch the three out. Pa was dressed for the occasion in his admiral's get-up, just the way he was when we left—blue blazer, white shirt and tie, Nantucket Yacht Club insignia on coat and cap. Willy sported a beret, and there was Sophie, beaming, taller, thinner than we remembered, wearing her tweed coat and hat, climbing up the ladder to throw herself into Mother's arms, and to be hugged and kissed by us all. Quita and Sophie both shed a few tears of relief when they threw their arms around each other. With shouts of happiness, we were together again. We were home.

Pa ordered his five children and John to be on the first boatload ashore. But before I lined up with the rest, I ran below, just for a quick last-minute goodbye to George. I leaned down and kissed the wizened forehead of the blue-black, open-pored savage and whispered, "Thank you. I'll remember you always," and ran back up the companionway. There Pa and Ma stood close to each other, arm in arm beside the crew who had lined up to say goodbye. We shook hands with each one in a heartfelt farewell. We never saw them again, except for Ted who remained a stalwart friend until the end of his life, living close to me in Cambridge, where we often exchanged visits and pleasured ourselves with memories of the trip. Pa now stood at the top of the ladder, his arm around Mother's waist, and shouted down to his children as the longboat pulled away from the mother ship,

"Remember John Locke: 'A man's intelligence is limited by his experience.' At least I've increased your experience a bit." And then, as we waved back in accord, he gave his old familiar shout, "God made this world for us to enjoy. Don't let the Old Man down!"

We didn't. After such schooling, how could we?

Epilogue: Ashore

W HAT STARTED OFF as a rainy day diversion by Pa to keep his unruly children in line turned rapidly into our unforgettable adventure. Once underway, Pa rationalized his novel project as a way to ensure his children had a classical education, one that he would provide. By the end of the trip, however, with no one realizing it, we had been in a school that encompassed several philosophies of education—not only classical (learn through disciplined teaching), but also progressive (learn by doing). We had, in fact, been attending the sort of school that was best defined by the original Greek meaning of the word: a place in which leisure is employed, with discussion and philosophy, to provide a school setting. This comprehensive seagoing curriculum led us to the most important and lasting consequence of the trip—the awakening of our curiosity, as we tried to understand the novel situations that kept bombarding us. This curiosity never left the young mariners (now ancient) and still constantly goads them on in a world ripe for discovery.

As we sailed along, in addition to our daily school lessons, we began understanding stars, wind, and weather; and how to sail a ship over vast tracts of ocean; how to live in harmony in a very restricted space with those of different upbringings; and how to honor other people's rules and faiths. Even Mother and Charlie, at the end, were smiling at each other and working together. Mother taught us dynamic symmetry and the art of always being slightly off balance. Pa and Nana, reading aloud, spread other worlds before us. Nana led us into *Moby Dick* and kept prying open our minds. And I had *Anthony Adverse* to clarify matters of lust and love. Through it all, the awe I had for that magnificence, the sea, only increased as I probed the sources of its power.

Upon our return, Pa took no time to make up his mind as to what kind of a school we would attend. We'd had enough learning by doing, he said, both in our old schooling and our recent voyaging, so we would not go back to the progressive school we had been attending. I cried all of one night when he informed me of this. I wanted so much to be with my old friends, and I liked learning math in the Pooh Store and reading novels that taught me secrets. But as I have struggled with life's constant dilemmas, I have been so grateful that he had the wisdom to make sure his children learned how to think in a disciplined manner.

The warm-hearted worriers—those school folk, doctors, and friends so concerned about our voyage for various reasons—need not have fretted. Most notably, we had no problems with school. None of us had to repeat a grade, although Al and I did get some high-powered tutoring for a few weeks to fit us for the demanding preparatory school curricula of Exeter and Baldwin (even with that, I never did get comfortable with algebra). After boarding school, I went to Smith, followed by Quita and Sophie; Al and Willy went to Harvard. Still alive to Pa's excitement as he introduced each port to us with a stirring account of its past, we all majored in history, except Willy, our persistent fixer and inventor. He majored in physics. Even now, history remains exciting for us. It lets us go exploring again, from one new port in our lives to the next, looking always for the treasure buried somewhere out there.

The worriers had also predicted we would lose out in sports, would not keep up with the demands of teams. Well, maybe so. We all did try out for team sports, and did reasonably well, but where we truly excelled was in sailboat racing. We had a regular fleet of boats at Nantucket and consistently brought home pennants and prizes. Al was our authority on tactics and racing rules. Will tuned the boats before every race, adjusting main stays and choosing the weight of sails to fit the velocity of the wind. Kingman Brewster, who used to race against us in interclub regattas, when president of Yale, told a friend, "the most competitive sailors I have ever raced against were the Chandler sisters."

The worriers had warned, too, that our friends would slip away from us, that we would be excluded. I was disappointed to find that no one was particularly interested in hearing me tell of our adventures. They were polite, listening with interest at first, but then wanted to get right back to the doings of their cliques. So, in a way, I was back where I was before I left—the outsider—but with an important difference. I had my new self, found on the paradisiacal Cocos, tender and tiny, to be sure, but there. It's still pretty tender, but tiny? No.

Romanticism, implanted in me by Pa's reading of Scott's novels, held me in thrall for a goodly portion of my life. I even went so far as to marry an Episcopal priest and become a believer. When I told my father that I was going to marry a minister, I braced myself for his scorn. I was astonished, though, when he fell into an armchair, exploding with loud laughter, and then throwing back his head and exclaiming, "I *knew* God would get back at me some time!"

In my early thirties, facing divorce and the necessity of providing for children, something I knew nothing about, I left romanticism behind. I turned to Melville, whose ironic, grim masterpieces—especially *Pierre*— gave me comfort. I resonated with his prose and his love of ambiguities. At this time, I was beginning to immerse myself, too, in science, concentrating on neuro-cognitive development and the functions of the brain. This soon made me a non-believer in religious doctrine, just like Pa, but certainly for different reasons. Politics was another Pa-inspired passion. All that arguing I did with him about Little Rosie convinced me that I was a Democrat, and a Democrat I have remained all my life.

Al, during his career as a professor of economic history at MIT, Johns Hopkins, and Harvard, has won many prizes, including the Bancroft prize in history, a Pulitzer Prize, an honorary degree from Harvard, and, so far, nine other honorary degrees, here and abroad. I'm sure some of his articulate and engaging teaching and writing can be traced, in part, to his practiced ability in telling spellbinding Wrinklebelly stories. So unforgettable were these characters that when I was raising my five children, I remembered the series and invented more Wrinklebelly chapters of my own—material guaranteed to keep children quiet on any long-distance drive, or anywhere else where calm was necessary. My daughter, Caroline, even tells Wrinklebelly stories to the disturbed children she teaches. Hyperactive, loud, and unmanageable boys don't even fidget when she starts a Wrinklebelly chapter.

I never managed to get a medical degree to fulfill my Galapagos dream of dissecting bodies to learn what was going on inside, but after my fifth child entered kindergarten, I began a seven-year stint to achieve my doctorate in school psychology. At least I was learning what went on inside the minds of growing children, and I could fit my working days around my own children's school vacations. Before I even finished my doctoral program, however, I left the field of school psychology and moved to straight clinical work. I ran Boston University's Diagnostic and Referral Clinic for children at risk and joined the Boston University faculty, dutifully climbing the academic ladder, learning about and teaching normal and abnormal cognitive development of children. As a climax to my career in providing services to children through public and private institutions, I was appointed lecturer at Harvard Medical School and to the clinical staff of Harvard's teaching hospital, Massachusetts Mental Health Center (how these Harvard appointments would have pleased Pa!). There I helped set up a clinic for post traumatic stress disorders, was part of a major research project studying Cambodian genocide survivors in a refugee camp in Thailand, and worked in experimental clinics set up in inner-city schools to help traumatized and disturbed children.

Quita followed Mother into the world of art, and with her husband, raised children and animals on her great farm in Virginia. It is to Quita that the family turns whenever one of their children is having difficulties. She takes these children in and nurtures them and makes them work hard. Willy, long before most people were even familiar with the word, experimented in building computers and went on inventing programs for them. He still has his beloved bill-nosed pliers that he used to keep under his pillow on the *Blue Dolphin*. Now they rest in a drawer in his desk, and he uses them to tweeze out pills from bottles to keep his Parkinson's symptoms under control. Sophie, as if to flaunt her independence, and perhaps as a reprisal for our leaving her, left us. After Smith, she took a master's degree at Cambridge University in England, married an Italian sculptor and went off to live in Rome. When the marriage dissolved, she returned to the States with her four children and worked as an executive in various arts organizations, only to return to Rome again. The experience of dealing with her loneliness and drunken caretakers while we were all off cavorting in tropical seas probably helped her to be a canny operator when faced with the politics of becoming the first woman director and then president of the American Academy in Rome, but that experience also left her prone to a cynicism that never quite abandons her.

John—what happened to John? Pa's plan to start a business with John's father didn't work out, so we began losing track of him. The last I heard from him was in 1942 when he sent me a congratulatory telegram on the occasion of my marriage; but then, alas, he disappeared from our lives. Each of us kids, including John, took off at such speed on our return that it was hard to keep track of each other. And John was so far away—all the way off in distant Connecticut—he just became remote. When I think of how much he taught me by being so sympathetic, so kind, polite, and gentle, letting me discover so much about the beginning spirals of love, a truly great friend, I yearn to thank him. Where are you, John?

Ma and Pa went on squabbling, but they had a new set of memories to hold them together, supplementing their earlier memories of their successful life in South America. On that unusual, nay wild, project of sailing off into the world with their young children, they were forced to hold to each other with increasing strength, fighting to survive the trip. Pa lived to ninety, Ma to ninety-five. Toward the end of their time together, with senility setting in, they enjoyed summers in their Nantucket house overlooking the entrance to the harbor. Often, Pa, out on the porch, would call to Ma, shouting down an imaginary companionway, "Come on up on deck, dearest, and see this lovely schooner coming in. She'll probably anchor next to us." Ma would oblige and come out on the porch, often taking his hand, staring with him out at the sea. She, too, was easily moved back into that almost mythic realm of the *Blue Dolphin*.

Except for Willy, who tends the two-hundred-year-old family homestead in Maine, all of us, including Sophie, are in Nantucket in the summer. We have our separate houses on the island, but we swim together in the surf and gather on my porch on rainy days, all ages, children and grandchildren. A few years ago, when we were a bit more spry, we had a series of sailboat races among the five of us. We had never raced against each other. Willy won. I came in last. Much to our surprise, we all were speaking to each other at the end of the series.

In my retirement, I have chosen to live year-round in Nantucket. Nantucket had always seemed to be my real home, and now it is. I built a small, one-room apartment over a garage adjoining Ma and Pa's old house on the cliff, which I inherited. Looking over the entrance to the harbor, I, too, in my doddering years, can go out on deck and see the ships coming in, retreating in memory to past harbors. And in the winter, alone in my cabinlike space, I look out to see great sheets of ice, carried by the surf underneath them, crash against the jetties, sending shards over the seals wintering on the rocks. I am glad then, as gales blow and jar the house, and horizontal snows fly by, that my father with his typically creative, extravagant imagination, took his children out to sea to learn how to live.

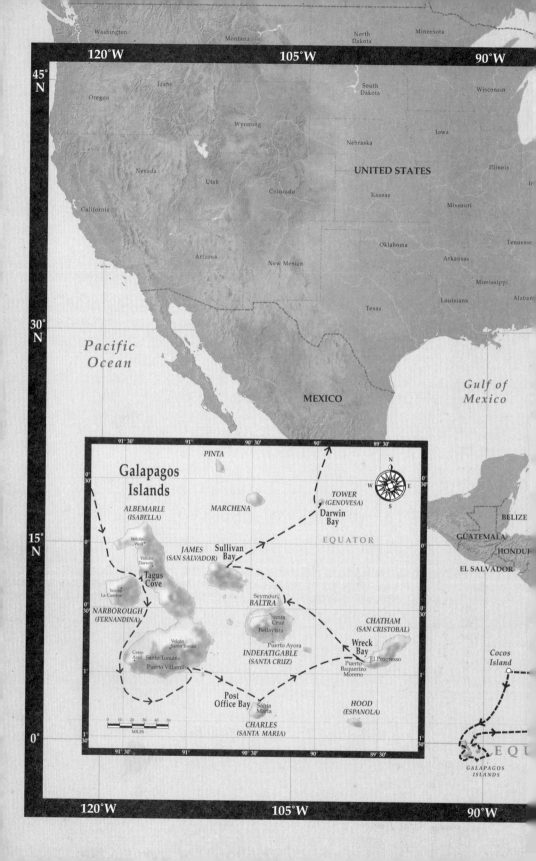